GOOD TIME PARTY GIRL

Good Time Party Girl: The Notorious Life of Dirty Helen Cromwell, 1886–1969
by Helen Cromwell with Robert Dougherty

Originally published as *Dirty Helen: A Zany, Wonderful, Unconventional Ex-Madam and Tavern-Keeper Tells of Her Adventures, the Fascinating People She Has Known and the Exploits That Make Her a Living Legend*, Sherbourne Press, 1966

Images on pages 289 and 304 courtesy of the Milwaukee Journal Sentinel
Image on page 296 courtesy of the Milwaukee County Historical Society /
Photo by Lyle Oberwise

ISBN: 9781627310789

Feral House
1240 W. Sims Way Suite 124
Port Townsend, WA 98368
www.FeralHouse.com

Printed in the United States of America
Design by Lissi Erwin/SplendidCorp.

GOOD TIME PARTY GIRL

The Notorious Life of
Dirty Helen Cromwell
1886–1969

by **Helen Cromwell**
with **Robert Dougherty**

Afterword by Christina Ward

FERAL HOUSE

Prologue

THE FRIDAY AFTERNOON HAPPY HOUR at the Naval Officers Club was at its peak. Peals of laughter mingled with the tinkling of ice in tall glasses. The club, at Naval Air Station, Glenview, Illinois, had never been so filled with gold-emblazoned blue uniforms and bright cocktail dresses. It was 1952, a high point of the Korean War era, and the air station was abuzz with the drone of overhead planes, alive with thousands of officers and enlisted men being schooled in special skills prior to leaving for the Far East. The big time of the week for everyone was the Friday cocktail hour.

Six of us—three couples—were finishing our first martini and plotting our course for a night on the big town; the Chicago Loop was only about twenty-five miles away. Should we go to the Blackhawk and dance to the music of Ray Anthony? What about dinner at the Empire Room of the Palmer House? Didn't someone say the show was terrific at the Chez Paree?

A lovely red-haired model, my BOQ roommate's date, leaned across the small cocktail table and cried, "I've got it! Let's drive up to Milwaukee and have dinner at one of those good German restaurants and then go to that wild, nutty bar called Dirty Helen's!" Delightful suggestion. I was excited over the prospects of the evening because I had long heard of Dirty Helen. She was a legend in her own time. How many college conversations had used Dirty Helen as a pivot point? What were all those tales I heard about her while on duty in the Mediterranean and in Japan? Fabulous stories and salty as hell.

< Helen, behind the bar at the Sun Flower Inn c. 1940s.

It was almost eleven p.m. when we finished dinner and nosed the car up the dark, hilly St. Paul Avenue, past industrial plants, foundries, factories, and assorted dingy-looking buildings to a little two-story, white frame house with orange-colored lights on either side of the door and a brass plaque that said The Sun Flower Inn. Parking was a problem because the street was lined with cars of all descriptions, including Cadillac limousines and one Rolls-Royce. We finally found a parking spot and tromped up the short flight of stairs to the doorway. The din and racket coming from inside The Sun Flower Inn was unbelievable.

When the front door opened I couldn't believe my eyes! How could that many people jam into one room? We entered a lower-level vestibule, our feet sinking into a thick-pile carpet, then up a couple of steps into the main level. Smoke hung in the air like a fog bank. The squealing babble of voices was underscored by the high-key strains of an electric organ. And, to my amazement, there was practically no furniture in the place; people were flopped all over the floor, some stretched over resting their heads on their arms, some sitting up prim and proper, some leaning against the walls. There were no conventional tables and chairs to be seen anyplace.

I knew her immediately, before she even opened her mouth to scream her dirty words. The raven-haired woman behind the bar, which was to our right as we entered, was Dirty Helen. When she saw us standing there she screamed to her organist—a scream, I might add, that silenced the place completely—"Hey, Martin, play 'Anchors Aweigh'! Goddamit, the fleet's in!" As the room filled with the booming of 'Anchors Aweigh,' Helen waved an arm out toward her on-the-floor customers and commanded "You people! Move your fat asses over and give some carpet to these sailors and their cute little bitches!" As we gingerly stepped around and over the sprawled-out patrons I got a glimpse of the lush, dark carpeting that ran from wall to wall; and, when we found a small vacant patch and plopped down, we found it wasn't half uncomfortable, only unusual. Imagine, a barroom without tables and chairs!

My roommate and his red-haired date had been to Helen's before and sometime during the evening, without my hearing them, had told the others in our group what to expect. I had been elected to be the patsy and was sent to the bar with the drink order: three scotch and waters, two bourbon and waters, and one brandy and soda. 'Anchors Aweigh' had blended into 'Ah, Sweet Mystery of Life' (Helen's favorite song!) as I endeavored to get to the bar without stepping on too many mink coats and sable stoles which were sprinkled around the floor like so much soiled laundry. People were crushed around the bar three deep, laughing, talking, hollering. Underscoring all the din was the blaring organ giving forth with 'Ah, Sweet Mystery of Life.' This is madness, I thought. Sheer madness. Finally, by pushing and shoving, I snaked my way through the throng and wedged myself into a position in the middle of the bar, a heavy wooden affair, battered and deeply carved with thousands of initials.

A male bartender rushed about frantically filling drink orders as Helen shouted commands to him, helped in mixing drinks, and kept her eye on the door so she could greet all new arrivals as they poured in. While waiting to get the attention of either Helen or the bartender I took stock of the place: behind the bar, strung along the wall, was a sixteen-foot-long mirror in a gold-leaf frame. The mirror was in four sections and each section was made up of beveled squares. Reflected in the great mirror from the opposite wall was an enormous painting of a nude woman, lolling on cushions and reading a book. I turned my back to the bar to view the painting and was immediately poked in the shoulder blades and asked, "So you like my portrait, huh, Lieutenant?" I whirled around to stare into the deep black eyes of Dirty Helen. The hub-bub around the bar died down; everyone wanted to hear my response to her question.

"It's very interesting," I replied. "Is it an antique?"

"Antique? You're goddamed fucking-a right it's an antique. It's a portrait of me when I was hustling the Yukon!" Everyone at the bar screamed with glee. "See that book I'm reading? You know what that is?" Without waiting for a response she answered her own question, "It's a goddamed Sears and Roebuck catalog!" Again her patrons screamed with glee. "Hey, Martin," she shouted to the organist, "Let's have a little hustling music!"

And 'Ah, Sweet Mystery of Life' melded into 'Blue Moon.' "Okay, good-looking, what's your desire?" Once again, before I had a chance to respond, she answered her own question with, "A good lay, probably, but you can't get it here anymore! I've gotten rid of the girls."

"Three scotch and waters, two bourbon and waters and one brandy and soda," I said.

"What was that last bit?" she asked.

"A brandy and soda," I replied.

"Hey, folks," Helen shouted above the noise of the room, "Guess what this Navy lieutenant wants?" Suddenly all laughing and talking ceased; there was a tomb-like silence. "He wants a brandy and soda! What about that shit?" She looked me right in the eye and asked, "What in the hell is a brandy and soda? Goose piss? Ah, shit, come on now!" Instantaneously the whole place was in an uproar of laughter. I had been the patsy for the big joke, but all I could muster up for a show of good sportness was a weak smile. 'Blue Moon' started up again and the various loud conversations continued. I knew then why the place was called Dirty Helen's.

"All I serve is bourbon and scotch," said Helen with a twinkle in her eyes, "Old Fitzgerald or House of Lords. Take your pick." I stuttered out the drink order, thinking that the red-haired model could drink Old Fitz or be damned.

As Helen mixed the drinks I studied her. She was of medium height, dressed in a deep blue faille outfit which picked up the blue highlights of her black-dyed hair. Her plunging neckline revealed an ample cleavage, punctuated at the "V" with a large baroque pearl pin. Her make-up was beautifully applied: black arched eyebrows, carefully outlined lips of dark crimson. But most outstanding were her hands, expertly manicured and tipped with shaped red-lacquered nails—the hands of a young woman. How old was this living legend? Fifty? Fifty-five? Sixty? (As it turns out, she was seventy-one at that time!) She moved with the swiftness of a tigress, dropping cubes of ice in glasses, pouring in whiskey, splashing in water, and talking all the while to her customers.

Plunking the drinks down on the bar in front of me she gave me a great big smile and said, "You're a hell of a good sport. The drinks are on the house."

"Why, thank you," I said.

"Obviously, you've never been here. Are you stationed at Great Lakes?"

"No, I'm at Glenview. And I want to tell you I've heard of this place for years but didn't know about your treatment of new customers!"

Helen threw back her head and laughed her famous, melodious laugh and said, "Now you know! It won't be long until you'll hear it pulled again on somebody else. I really turn on when they ask for martinis!"

"Well, thanks again for the drinks," I said.

"You're welcome. Weekends around here are like the lunatic asylum so I won't have a chance to talk to you. So come up some evening during the week and I'll fry a chicken and we'll have supper in the back room. I'm sure we have a lot of friends in common, I'm practically a plank owner of the Navy!" With that she shouted to the organist, "Come on, Martin, 'Anchors Aweigh' one more time!"

Getting back to my group, amid applause from the other customers, I sloshed Old Fitz and House of Lords all over the piles of furs and people but I really didn't care. I wasn't even mad at the red-haired model who was still rolling around on the carpet literally grabbing her sides with laughter. Because, after all, I was at the place called Dirty Helen's and I had met the woman known as Dirty Helen and like everyone else who had ever been there I was having one hell of a good time and was fully determined to accept Helen's invitation.

During the following weeks and months I saw Helen many times; as we sat in the kitchen of her place, nibbling fried chicken, she told me episodes and anecdotes about her life that were not public knowledge, that had never been mentioned in the innumerable press stories about her. I was enthralled with her as a warm human being and she had, indeed, become a friend of mine. After my transfer to an aircraft carrier in the Pacific Fleet we continued our friendship by mail: short notes from her letting me know how things were going at The Sun Flower Inn; picture postcards to her mailed from Hong Kong, Tokyo, Pusan.

Release from the service, the establishing of a civilian career, marriage, a family, all brought new places to live, new responsibilities. The correspondence between Helen and me slackened but there were always birthday cards and greetings during the holiday season. Then I found myself back in the Midwest, as managing editor of the book division of *Better Homes & Gardens* and later as editor of *Popular Home* magazine. During this period I would always visit Helen's bar whenever I was in Milwaukee, and our personal friendship was rekindled as if there had not been an elapse of so many years.

I was pleased and touched when I heard the familiar voice on my Chicago office phone that blustery February day in 1961. 'Do you know what day this is, Bob?" asked Helen.

"I do. In fact, I just had some flowers wired to you. Happy Birthday, Helen."

"There's going to be a big party tonight for me and I want you to come up, can you make it?"

"Sure I can make it. I'll come up on the Electroliner. By the way, how old are you?"

"None of your fucking-a business!"

"I thought you said once that you and I wouldn't keep secrets," I said.

"All right, all right! I'm eighty. But let me tell you something, Sonny, I'll be around to roast the goose that pisses on your grave."

"Dirty old woman," I laughed.

"That's what they tell me," she said wryly. "I'll meet you in the bar at the Plankinton House Hotel at six." With that she hung up the telephone.

At exactly six o'clock I jumped from a cab and pushed open the corner door to the cocktail lounge of the Plankinton House. The bar was humming with excitement and faint giggles were punctured with the clicking of cocktail shakers; it was warm and cozy and all the tables were filled with good-looking people. I took a seat at the far end of the long shiny bar and as my eyes became accustomed to the low lights I looked around the room, recognizing the types who were there: well-dressed sales executives with wives, sweethearts, or newly found companions; smart young advertising people in tweedy business clothes; a lone woman in black with pearls and a slicked-back blonde chignon, elegant but lonely-looking; a pair of over-dressed hustlers, eyes darting here and there at the unattached males; a few distinguished-looking gentlemen, maybe presidents of banks or corporations. That was the kind of place it was.

Suddenly there was a burst of cold air from the same door I had entered. It cut through the room like a sabre. The room became quite hushed, then in a flash it became all babble, babble. Rippling across the room came the comments, "It's Dirty Helen! It's Dirty Helen!"

The door closed behind her but Helen just stood there surveying the scene. I arose from the bar stool and started to go toward her, then I realized that this was a grand entrance, a "happening," and I wasn't going to botch it up. I sat back down, and leaned across the bar to get a better view. Never had Helen looked so dramatic; draped around her shoulders was a vast cocktail coat of lavender satin cuffed in great mounds of white fox ("Dior, darling"), around her throat was a glittering choker ("Don't tell anyone they are rhinestones"), but most memorable of all was the hat—a mountain of cerise feathers, layer upon layer, sprinkled with brilliants ("Last hat Laddie Northridge[1] made—he only did three—a white one for Grace Kelly, a black one for Hedda Hopper, and this cerise one for me").

Then like catapults people were rushing toward the place where Helen stood. There was a flurry of handshaking, hugging, kissing, people exclaiming "Dear, darling, how are you? Where have you been?" and stuff like that. When the commotion settled, Helen yelled across the room to the bartender, "How the hell are you, Benny? Is Bob here?" Then she saw me and started coming, slowly, to her reserved bar stool.

She stopped all along the line talking and laughing with people

---

1 Laddie Northridge was a famous New York City milliner. The Laddie Northridge label was available from the 1930s through the 1950s.

at the tables, at the bar. As she got closer to me I could hear her comments and those made to her. She stopped beside the two hustlers and asked one of them, "How are the tricks, Rosie?"

"Slow, Helen, slow," answered Rosie.

Helen laughed a soft, musical laugh and said, "You just don't know how to do it, Honey. I'll find you some business tonight!" One of the distinguished-looking corporation-types slid off his bar stool and went over and kissed Helen on the cheek. She looked up at him and cried, "Jimmy, you're still the best-looking bastard in Milwaukee. How's the Fox Point set?"

"Everybody's fine, Helen. Gertie was asking me last night if I had seen you around. When are you coming out for dinner with us?"

"Soon, Jimmy, soon."

I jumped off the bar stool and stood facing her. "Happy Birthday, Helen."

"Thanks, you getting any these days?"

She looked just past me at the man seated on my left and cried, "Jesus God! You're Larry! From New York! Why you son of a bitch! Still rum-running?" She let out a laugh that was echoed by everyone else in the place. Larry was the conservative type; he took her hand in his and said quietly, with a twinkle in his eye, "I don't have to 'run' anymore, Helen, I own the distillery. And the reason I'm in Milwaukee is to buy myself a brewery. I was hoping you'd still be around."

"Where in the hell did you think I'd be. I'll always be around!" Then she turned to me and said, "Isn't that right, Sonny? Order me an Old Fitz, will ya?"

The birthday party was fantastic. It was held at a restaurant taken over for the evening and hosted by a group of Helen's good friends. The place was loaded with roast beef, Old Fitzgerald, and the various beers that made Milwaukee famous, plus blue business suits, blue jeans, dinner jackets, and enough minks and diamonds to make any woman in the United States wish she lived in Milwaukee. There was a band and a birthday cake that was bigger and more multi-tiered than any wedding cake I've ever seen. And the presents were generous; lots of good jewelry and the type of gift Helen liked best—little green things with Presidents' pictures on them. It was a swinger.

At 2:30 a.m. the last guest had departed and Helen and I walked over to a coffee shop. I had something important I wanted to ask her and I had not been able to get her alone. A plan had been fermenting in my mind for nine years.

"Helen," I said, "I know you've been approached by other writers and this subject has been suggested to you before and you've always said no, but I think the time has come for you to do a book about your life's story."

"How in the hell could I do my life's story? Jesus God, my life's not over, it is really just beginning! I'm only eighty, you know."

I smiled as I said, "You can always follow up with a sequel. You've got a damned amazing story to tell, you know."

She grinned and said, "Are you suggesting that I tell all? I don't want to get bumped off!"

I could see that she was thinking that maybe my idea wasn't too bad and that maybe the time had come. There was a moment of silence, then she threw back her head and laughed. "Okay," she said, "I'll do the telling if you'll do the writing, but a lot of people are going to get goddamed nervous and pissed off when they hear about it!" Again she laughed and said, "Oh, well, fuck 'em! I'll do it."

At that precise moment we were interrupted by a gray-haired man who headed up one of Milwaukee's largest corporations and who was known to both of us. He nodded in greeting and whispered something in Helen's ear and she let out her famous laugh; then she reached into her voluminous handbag, pulled out a little black book, jotted down a phone number on a paper napkin and handed it to him saying, "Don't forget to tell Rosie I sent you."

He waved goodbye and I asked, "Still in business, huh, Helen?"

"You're fucking-a right, Sonny. Always. Now let's get down to this book. Let's get started."

"You mean now, at three a.m.?" I couldn't believe my ears. "Of course. Why not?"

"How can we? We need a tape recorder. I don't have paper, pencils, anything. We need a place to sit and talk."

"We'll sit on the mezzanine of the Plankinton House. No one

ever sits up there. We can't use my place because there would be too many interruptions," she said with a wink. "And don't you worry about paper, pencils, or tape recorders. I'll talk and you listen."

I thought it was idiotic but before I knew it we were in the elevator of the Plankinton House. We got off at the mezzanine and found a secluded spot. It became my home away from home for many months and countless weekends.

In the small hours of the morning Helen talked and talked and talked...

HELEN CROMWELL

Chapter 1

THE QUESTION took me by surprise and I really didn't know how to answer him. Jesus God, I thought, let me think of some bright, witty reply. Quickly I ran my fingers up the big, white plume and adjusted the headache band—anything to delay my answering for a few moments. "What did you say, Al?" I inquired, knowing full well what Al Capone had asked.

"I said I've had you checked and why does a girl of your background like this sort of life?" He extended his hand, holding the black cigar, and waved it at the room of throbbing dancers weaving back and forth to the mournful, moody music of King Oliver's[2] Storyville band. Then he turned his face toward mine and stared at me with his big, piercing brown eyes. The scar on his cheek stood out vividly in the low lighting and his wide mouth curled. I reached under the table and gently pushed Johnny Torrio's[3] leg away from mine. No good answer could come.

"Because I'm different, Al," I finally said. It was a piss-poor

---

2. King Oliver (Joseph Nathan Oliver) (December 19, 1885 – April 10, 1938) better known as King Oliver or Joe Oliver, was an American jazz cornet player and bandleader. He was particularly recognized for his playing style and his pioneering use of mutes in jazz. He was the mentor and teacher of Louis Armstrong. His influence was such that Armstrong claimed, "if it had not been for Joe Oliver, Jazz would not be what it is today."

3 Johnny Torrio (born Donato Torrio, January 20, 1882 – April 16, 1957) was an Italian-born American mobster who helped to build a criminal organization, the Chicago Outfit, in the 1920s; it was later inherited by his protégé, Al Capone. He also put forth the idea of the National Crime Syndicate in the 1930s and later became an unofficial adviser to the Genovese crime family.

He gained several nicknames but was mostly known as "The Fox" for his cunning and finesse. Widely considered one of the most influential personalities in American organized crime, Torrio impressed authorities and chroniclers for his business acumen and diplomatic skills.

< Helen's business card.

answer that night in 1927 at the Lincoln Gardens in Chicago, and it's a piss-poor reason today when I'm trying to describe the way I was raised. But it's the truth.

I'm different—and probably unfashionable—when compared with all the other whores and madams who attempt to make a story out of their past shenanigans. I'm different for three reasons: I've never been poor; I had a good education; I've enjoyed my profession to the hilt; and … you know what I mean!

I was born into a prosperous middle-class family in Cicero, Indiana. My Pa, J.C. Worley, was the town's telegraph operator at the depot, which may not sound too high-flown but was a damn good job in those days. Besides, and this could only be possible in a small town, he was also president of the bank. He had inherited a large farm and we had thirty head of Holstein cattle, three hundred registered Poland China hogs, a flock of about three hundred Rhode Island Red chickens, and five pedigreed horses. If you've ever had any hayseed in your hair, you know that a bundle like that isn't to be sniffed at. And my mother's family, the Josephs of Noblesville, owned the area's biggest brewery. All of this is to say we weren't exactly considered poor white trash.

Something I've never been able to figure out is why Mama married Pa. You see, Pa had his nice job and his farm and all but he was a sort of plain man. He wasn't good-looking and he walked with a limp. Mama, on the other hand, was very pretty and very rich and had social connections with the prominent set of Indianapolis. Everybody thought and expected that the lovely Emma Joseph would marry Harry Levinson, of the Levinson's Men's Hat Company. The Levinsons were very big in Indianapolis. But Mama surprised everybody in Hamilton County by up and marrying my Pa and becoming a Presbyterian.

When I think of my first home, I think of Grandma and Grandpa Joseph's large gray-brick house in Noblesville, not far from their brewery. Since my Pa was then being trained in telegraphic work, he and Mama were transferred from town to town, so I stayed a great deal with my mother's parents. My father's parents I can barely remember. They died when I was very small.

I adored Grandpa Joseph and the warm big house and the

stories he would tell me. As I perched on his lap before the fireplace in the back parlor, Grandpa Joseph would recall how he and Grandma had been persecuted by the Prussians and how they had escaped to America. He would hold me close, and as the story would unfold in Grandpa's German-accented English, I would shiver under my long flannel nightgown and push my face into the heavy gold chain that was suspended across his vest.

The Josephs fled from Europe on a tramp steamer and landed in New Orleans in 1839. They managed to bring a considerable amount of money with them, and from New Orleans they progressed by river boats up the Mississippi and Ohio Rivers to Louisville, Kentucky. They were engulfed in a strange country with strange customs and a strange tongue. But Grandpa knew a trade that had universal demand—the making of beer—so it wasn't long before he established his own brewery in Louisville.

Life in Louisville was pleasant and prosperous for the Joseph family until the Civil War started in 1861. The city was torn between the North and the South, and social and political pressures were brought to bear on Grandpa to declare on which side his sympathies lay. Grandpa had seen too much persecution of humanity in Prussia to be pro-Confederacy, so he disposed of his property and decided to move his family North to Noblesville where beliefs were more in line with his own conscience.

As the shadows of the snapping fire danced on the walls of the back parlor, I could visualize the surging mobs of people leaving Louisville to take sides either with the Union North or the Confederate South. I couldn't understand the reasoning behind this portion of the story, of course, but I knew that it was of vast importance to Grandpa by the way his voice would break and his breathing quicken. I would shiver and whisper, "Grandpa, tell me about the Dempseys. Tell me again." My breath would almost stop with excitement as my favorite part of the story would unfold.

Prior to leaving Louisville, Grandpa Joseph fought his nausea and went to the slave market. Grandpa went there to do something that was important to him: to free two human beings before leaving the South. The market was on the verge of closing; slaves were rioting because they realized they were only a river's width away from Northern freedom; everything was in a turmoil. Northern people who owned slaves had brought them to Louisville to be sold, trying to get any amount of money they could, rather than free them for nothing; slaves were being starved, beaten, and tortured. For one hundred dollars Grandpa bought a married couple declared by the auctioneer to be the "Dempsey niggers." The Dempsey woman was about twenty-five years of age, thin beyond belief, and only five feet tall; the Dempsey man was thirty years old, lean, tall, and obviously had a touch of white blood in him. The couple had tried a fruitless escape, been caught and beaten mercilessly with a horsewhip. Both of their backs were ribbed with whip whelps creviced with oozing, open wounds. Only one other market patron bid against Grandpa; nobody wanted the Dempseys after their naked, streaked chests and backs were exposed for the customers' inspection.

It was a sickening experience for Grandpa Joseph. Everything within him revolted at the sights, smells, and inhumanity of the slave market. Yet if he wanted to do this good thing, it was necessary to endure the gesture of actually purchasing human flesh.

After payment was made and papers signed, the Dempseys were delivered, shackled, to Grandpa's wagon. He often said he would never forget the hate, the indignation, that glared in their eyes when they first saw their new master. Before leaving the marketplace, before even starting up the horse, Grandpa Joseph told the Dempseys about his own persecution, as a Jew, at the hands of the Prussians. He explained that he had bought them for only one reason—to free them. The Dempsey woman burst into tears that turned to hysterics; her husband soothed her with a low monologue that was inaudible to Grandpa. When she was quiet again, Grandpa told them that he was moving his family to the North and if the Dempseys wanted to come, too, as free individuals, as hired servants, they were welcome to accompany the Josephs. He told them they would be respected as human beings, that he would pay them a regular salary, and that they would be well fed and housed.

If Grandpa's tale was completely factual, he bought the last negro couple ever offered on the Louisville slave block. Officially the market was closed after his purchase, and the remaining slaves were taken to other markets in the deeper South. The Dempseys couldn't believe their good fortune. They kissed Grandpa's hands and became the most loyal and devoted servants in the world. They were a vital part of my childhood days in Noblesville. I have always loved them dearly, and as soon as I could speak my first words, they became Grandma and Grandpa Dempsey. Grandpa Dempsey would let me visit in the carriage house, and Grandma Dempsey was always fussing with my hair. She would brush it, arrange it, and then rub in a homemade concoction she called Morning Glory Oil. I believe that my life-long insistence on stylish coiffure stemmed from Grandma Dempsey's constant fussing with my hair. It was in Noblesville, also, that a visit from the Levinsons made a deep impact on my imagination and my dreams of how an elegant lady should look.

Even though Mama hadn't married the Levinsons' son Harry, there was a tight bond between the two families. Years before, soon after Grandpa had settled in Louisville, he had financed the Levinsons' departure from Hamburg, Germany where anti-semitism, even in those days, ran strong. The Levinsons had stayed with Grandma and Grandpa Joseph in Louisville for several months before settling in Noblesville. To be near the Levinsons was the main reason the Josephs had chosen to move there during the Civil War. Though some years later the Levinsons moved to Indianapolis where they developed their famous hat business, the close link was never broken. The Levinsons became one of the city's wealthiest families. They often took trips to Noblesville, and I'll never forget a visit they once paid to the Josephs. It left a permanent mark on me, and even though I was to become known as Dirty Helen, the epithet was to apply to my tongue only and never to my chic appearance. I was probably the most stylish whore in the country.

I remember to this day the excitement of preparation in my grandparents' home. Fresh flowers were placed in the guest rooms. The finest silver and linens were brought out. Grandma Joseph, who usually left all the cooking up to Grandma Dempsey, had spent several days preparing special dishes for the impending visit. Although Grandma herself was not Jewish, she knew all about Jewish cooking. I sniffed with interest as Grandma busied herself with all kinds of spices. Then, when the great day arrived, Grandpa let me accompany him to the dark cellar where he selected vintage wines for his guests.

I remember standing in front of the house beside Grandma Dempsey as the Levinsons' carriage pulled up. The Empress of Austria-Hungary couldn't have held a candle to Mrs. Levinson. She was perfection. As she placed her gloved hand in Mr. Levinson's, she swung her magnificent bustled skirt to the ground. I remember that the dress was a sapphire-blue trimmed in silver fox; her hat was a mass of blue veiling above which fanned a mountain of white plumes. I gasped; I had never viewed such grandeur.

Harry followed his mother out of the carriage. When I saw that dark-complexioned face with its gleam of white teeth, that jet-black hair with eyes to match, I knew what woman was placed on this earth for. I wanted to grow up, grow up, grow up so I could marry Harry Levinson. Of course, I didn't marry Harry Levinson. But it was he who started me on my life-long love of expensive millinery. During that visit "Uncle Harry" took me to the town's best store and bought me a hat. It cost him fourteen dollars, which was a whale of a price for a little girl's hat in those days. It was a navy blue sailor with a long white ribbon streaming down the back. I preened proudly in front of the mirror, and Uncle Harry smiled at me with great affection. I had heard it whispered that he was still in love with my mother.

"Helen," he said, "never forget that a hat is the most beautiful thing a lady can wear. When you grow up, always wear a hat, and make it a good one. There's no such thing as a beautiful cheap hat." I've never forgotten Harry's advice. I love hats. There have been times when I've had over a dozen at once, but I've never had a cheap one on my head. I wear hats constantly, except to bed, where they might cause a degree of annoyance to my tricks.

Chapter 2

I WAS SIX years old when Pa was assigned as the dispatcher at the Lake Erie and Western Railroad Depot in Cicero. It meant that he and Mama would no longer have to travel around and I could come home and be with them all the time. Besides, it was time for me to start school. Mama was afraid that it was going to be hard to adjust to living in Cicero after my six years with Grandma and Grandpa Joseph, but it wasn't hard at all. I missed Noblesville, but it was wonderful to live in our own large house about a mile from town and go to school and play with other children of my own age.

When a childhood is pleasant, weeks pass rapidly, months pass rapidly, and years pass rapidly. When you reflect back, particularly on small-town life, you wonder where in the hell time went—it was all so goddamed dull: school, music lessons, and hanging out with my special friends and my steady boyfriend Roy Dale at his father's confectionery store. You know what I mean? Everything so fucking-a peaceful. I kept wishing something exciting would happen, and in my sixteenth year, it did. Cicero's peaceful bubble exploded with the discovery of a great source of natural gas. Gas wells sprang up everywhere, and our farm was riddled with them. Pa, being a good businessman, interested a glass company into moving in and manufacturing beer bottles for the Anheuser-Busch Company of St. Louis. You see, you need lots of gas for the glass furnaces, and Jesus God, we had it up the ass. Although I didn't know it at the time, it was to change the whole pattern of my life.

Construction started almost immediately on the large factory which was about a mile from the center of town. Cicero was booming! People began pouring into the town from all over the country. The furnaces at the glass factory were lighted on September 1, 1897. It seemed that most of the glass blowers were Portuguese and Italians and almost all were Catholics. A Catholic church was constructed in a period of weeks. Everywhere new houses were being built. Pa financed and built twelve of them himself. Main Street, which was only nine or ten blocks long, was the setting for twenty-four new saloons, plus at least that many restaurants. New stores, new shops, strangers wandering the streets, new children to crowd into the small schoolhouse, new dogs and new cats—all this was mingled into a gala celebration on September 6, 1897. That was the day Cicero declared itself a city of five thousand inhabitants and not seven hundred as it had been before the discovery of gas.

It was also the year which brought Philip Cappel to town.

"I sold the eight-room brick house today, Emma," Pa said one night as he sat down at the supper table.

Mama wasn't keen on the boom. In fact, every now and then she'd mention to me that she wished things were back as they used to be.

"Whom did you sell it to?" she asked, not really caring.

"A real nice lady from Cincinnati, a widow lady with six children."

Mama became more interested. "A widow lady, surely she couldn't be a glass blower?"

"No, of course not. Her sons are going to work here. She has five boys and a girl."

"J.C., don't tell me they're going to start using child labor at that factory! That would be just too much."

"The two oldest boys are adults, Emma. They both look to be over twenty," said Pa.

Mama was examining a dark spot on one of her silver spoons. "Foreigners, I presume."

"No, they aren't. You'd like Mrs. Cappel. She's a very refined lady, different from most of the crowd that's been piling in here. Mrs. Cappel paid me five thousand cash for the house. That was the best house I've built, and I'm glad somebody nice got it."

Mama was taking much more interest in the news. "Maybe Mrs. Cappel would enjoy my church circle." Mama was an active Presbyterian; her Jewish blood was an unmentioned subject in our home.

"No, she's Catholic."

Mama sighed. "Aren't they all. Well, it's a good thing that church was built."

"Yes, it is. It is very important to Mrs. Cappel that this town has a Catholic church. I doubt if she'd have moved here if there wasn't one."

"Are the two oldest boys going to work at the factory?" asked Mama.

"No, the oldest boy, Henry, wants to start a newsstand. I told him that this town could use one now that we have grown so. The next oldest, Philip, I believe his name is, isn't sure what he'll do yet."

"Probably start another saloon," snapped Mama. "If they don't work at the factory, they start saloons."

"I don't know, Emma," Pa said. "But Henry and Philip sure are nice boys."

I was to recall that conversation many times. It wasn't long after that that Pa lost his enthusiasm for Philip and I lost the thing Pa was afraid I would lose.

I was on the way to Dale's Confectionery Store with my best friend, Leona Neal, when I glanced into the plate-glass window of Johnny Plain's Saloon and saw him for the first time. Jesus God! I'd never seen anyone so handsome.

"Look, Leona, I wonder who he is?"

Leona turned to me with a funny expression on her face. She flushed and whispered: "His name is Philip Cappel. Haven't you heard the latest? He and Katie Heinz are supposed to be 'doing things,' you know."

"I don't care," I said. "I'm going to get him for myself, and the hell with that bitch Katie."

Leona gasped. "How will you do that, Helen?"

"Just watch me," I said. "I'll find a way."

The next nine days were spent flirting with Philip Cappel, and throughout that entire time not one word passed between us. I made it a point to wander slowly past Johnny Plain's Saloon at three o'clock every afternoon. He would be close to the window and our eyes would meet through the glass. Then, in about thirty minutes, he would come into Dale's for a dish of ice cream, and again we would carry on our mute flirtation. Leona was shocked, but she also found it exciting to be part of such a romantic sequence. I told her I would further my campaign by making friends with Henry Cappel whose newsstand at the depot was proving very successful.

Henry was shy. Unlike Philip, be wasn't handsome. He was slender to the point of being thin, and very pale. He was a kind person and already had established many loyal customers. I would see him often when I'd drop by the depot to visit Pa. Whenever I talked to him, just the knowledge that he was Philip's brother made me kind of tingly.

One day after Henry had picked up his papers from the Indianapolis train and had taken them to his stand, Pa said, "Henry is a fine young man and a real asset to this town. It's a shame that his brother Philip is so different. Henry told me that Philip had several good job offers but preferred being with the crowd that hangs out at Johnny Plain's. Have you ever met him, Helen?"

I didn't have to lie. "No, I've never met him, Pa. But I've seen him."

Pa looked up quickly.

"He's a fine-looking man. Maybe too fine-looking."

I didn't say anything.

"I thought you might have met him. Henry says he's running around with Katie Heinz. He doesn't think Katie is a nice girl. Is she?" Pa was after information.

"I really have no idea, Pa. As you know, I've never been close to Katie. In fact, I've never really liked her."

"I know," said Pa. Then, as I kissed him goodbye, he added,

"Be a good girl, Helen."

That slut Katie. So Philip Cappel was really doing it with her. There seemed no doubt of it now. Walking to Dale's, I remembered a slumber party at a friend's house. Katie had opened her bag and pulled out a small bottle of whiskey she had swiped from her father. None of us, aside from Katie, had ever tasted liquor before, but we all drank some and got a bit high. In the conversation that followed, Katie boasted that she was no longer a virgin. She said she had had "it" several times. This, in itself, was fascinating to us, and with little prodding she described the love process and got us all sexed up. We wanted to know who the boys were but the bitch wouldn't tell us whom she'd fucked.

I was still fuming at the thought of Philip Cappel messing around with the cheap slut as I entered Dale's Confectionery. The young people in the place were all a-twitter talking about the Mid-Summer Benefit Dance which was going to be held that night in the town hall. This dance was particularly important to my group of friends because it would be, more or less, our farewell gathering. We had just graduated from high school that spring and several of us were planning to go away to college. Pa had already signed me up at DePauw University in Greencastle.

My date for the dance was to be Roy Dale. He was cute, but he really didn't do very much for me, except give me brooches. He was absolutely crazy about giving me brooches; he had given me seven or eight of them. I felt he was swiping money from the confectionery till to buy them, but, what the hell, it gave him a kick—the same kick that many guys got from giving me jewelry later on.

Roy was sweet, and before Philip Cappel came to town I had resigned myself to the fact that I would eventually marry him. It wasn't an exciting prospect, even though I loved Roy dearly, as a friend. As I was leaving Dale's, Roy came up to me, smiled, and said with a toothy grin, "See you tonight, Helen." Then he pressed something into my hand.

Jesus God, I thought, another brooch—this time with a red setting.

I stepped out of the confectionery into the street. It was hot and humid as only an Indiana summer day can be. I dragged myself home, went up to my bedroom, removed my blouse and long skirt, and stretched out across the bed. Some time later I heard my door open and felt Mama running her cool hand over my forehead, sweeping the strands of hair off my face.

"Are you awake, Helen?"

I pulled myself up and looked into Mama's smiling dark eyes. Everything was right with the world again. I yawned. "Yes, Mama. It is so hot and the walk home really finished me."

"I sent Andy for you. Didn't you see him? I told him to meet you at Dale's."

Andy was the hired colored man who served as our driver. I told Mama I had missed him.

From a small tray on the bedside table, Mama handed me a frosted glass of lemonade, then she sat down on the edge of the bed. She again ran her hand over my forehead. She smiled. "I want you to look beautiful tonight, Helen."

From four o'clock until dinner time Mama and I stood before the long, walnut-framed mirror in her bedroom and worked on getting me ready for the dance. She had had her favorite dressmaker in Noblesville make my dress. It was white, sheer organdy, with a high neck and elbow-length sleeves. The hemline of the skirt was just above the ankles. My small waist was encircled with a wide band of black velvet caught with a large pink-red artificial rose. With this I wore my black calf high-heeled shoes and short white silk gloves.

As I stood looking in the mirror, while Mama was on her knees with needle and thread attending to some necessary detail, I decided that I had the most beautiful dress in the world and that I, too, was almost beautiful. And it came as a pleasant surprise. Nothing in this world does more for a woman than to know that her dress is perfect in every detail. I struck what I considered a femme fatale pose.

"Pretty is as pretty does," snapped Mama astutely. "Now stand up straight and stop posing or you'll have a wavy hemline." She smiled and walked over to her dresser. "Helen, I have a little surprise for you." She dug beneath her handkerchiefs and brought out a small leather box. As she opened the box I caught a glint of gold. It was the lovely cameo bracelet that Grandma Joseph had long ago received from her father in Hamburg, Germany. She had given it to Mama when she married Pa.

I threw my arms around Mama and we both cried and laughed at the same time. Mama clasped the bracelet around my left wrist, and to this day it has never been removed.

The stairwell boomed with Pa's voice. "Aren't we going to have any supper around here?"

Mama patted her eyes with her fingers as she went into the hall and called downstairs. "J.C., I want you to see what you helped to create. Helen, come show your father how you look."

I stole a glance at one final provocative pose, pinned on Roy's latest brooch with the red setting, then walked primly out into the hall and slowly descended the steps. Pa was standing there in his shirtsleeves holding a newspaper. His glasses were pushed up on his forehead. He looked up, then pulled his glasses down and focused his eyes. He smiled. I've never seen such pride, such joy, such love. Not one word was spoken. He opened his arms and I flew into them.

It was the last time I was ever to see that look on my father's face.

Roy and I had arranged to meet at the dance. Andy drove me in the phaeton. He was a grizzled old man given to very few words. He gave me an odd, wise look as he helped me out.

"Now I'll meet you at midnight, Miz Helen Now you mind your folks and don't keep Andy waitin'. You hear?" I nodded, smoothed my dress, and made my entrance.

The Mid-Summer Benefit Committee had chosen pink as their main decorating color for the dance. Streamers and garlands of pink paper flowers were hung everywhere. As the flickering light from the recently installed gas jets filtered through the pink streamers, a rosy glow was cast over the big room. On white tablecloths stood large vases of pink sweet peas and three empty voluminous glass bowls to be filled at intermission with fruit punch.

Young adults and a few of the high school set were dancing the two-step. I edged around them to my own crowd, and when Roy Dale saw me his eyes became as big as balloons. He looked proudly at the red glass brooch. "Gee. Helen, gosh, you look wonderful." He held out his hand and led me onto the dance floor. Roy had only recently learned to dance and he kept looking down at our feet, completely amazed that we were in step. I found myself looking down, too, so was completely surprised when Roy stopped still. A hand had touched him on the shoulder; then a low masculine voice said, "May I cut in?"

I snapped my head up and stared into the blue, blue eyes of Philip Cappel. In a flash I saw everything about him as though for the first time: crispy curly blond hair, a square strong chin, cleanly shaven, and gleaming white teeth. It was a face I was never to forget.

Roy didn't know what to do. He watched in stunned silence as Philip Cappel and I spun away from him. I don't know what happened to Roy after that. All I could remember about the rest of the evening was Phil. We danced every number. I have never danced so well. We sure did fit together right! Time had no meaning for me until I heard my name called. It was Leona.

"Helen! Andy's been waiting for twenty minutes to take you home. He's out front. Hurry!"

Phil pressed my hand and whispered, "Please don't go, I'll walk you home." I smiled, and together we walked outside to where Andy was waiting in the phaeton.

"You go on back, Andy," I said. "Mr. Cappel is going to walk me home."

"Yo' Ma and Pa gwine get mad, Miz Helen. You better come with Andy."

"Now do as you're told, Andy!" I said sharply.

"Al' right, Miz Helen, but you' Ma and Pa gwine get mad at Andy and you".

"You leave them to me, Andy. Now take the phaeton and go." He addressed his words to me, but his eyes were on Phil. "They're gwine be powerful mad," mumbled Andy as he made to drive away.

That proved to be quite an understatement.

The dance had been over for two hours—the most wonderful

two hours of my life. I walked beside him, holding his hand, listening to him laugh his deep man's laugh. He told me many things: about himself and his family, about his mother and how she had struggled to keep everyone together after the death of his father. He talked excitedly of Cincinnati. He loved it there. He called it the Queen City. With the moonlight shining on his face he said, "I'd love to take you there, Helen, and show you the sights." I pressed his hand. There was nothing in the world I would have liked more.

We had walked to the creek and were sitting on the big rock under the covered bridge. The rippling of the water and the crackle of the katydids punctured the stillness. I was encircled by his powerful arms. Our lips held together as though no force in the world could separate us. I felt sensations I didn't know existed in human beings and I was suddenly aware of what might happen. I pushed him away gently. The rays of the moon shone directly into his eyes and I could see the longing, the desire.

"I'm in love with you, Helen," he whispered. "I've loved you since the first time I saw you. I want you, Helen."

"Oh, Phil, I want you too. I love you. But it can't be now. Not here, not this way."

The spell was broken. He looked at his gold pocket watch. "It's two-thirty, Helen. I'd better get you home."

Phil's foot had evidently been on the hem of my long white party dress. As I jumped up I heard the ripping of fabric. I looked down and saw that about eleven inches of my skirt had been torn away from the waist line.

"Damn it! I've torn your beautiful dress!" exclaimed Phil.

"Don't worry about that, Phil. It can be fixed easily. My problem at the moment isn't the dress, it's what to do with Pa when I get home. I had no idea it was so late."

We walked hurriedly. As we turned into the lane leading to the house, Phil put his arm around my shoulder and held me tight all the way to the front porch. Then we saw Pa silhouetted against the hallway light. Phil quickly dropped his arm.

The light fell on me and Pa stared in disbelief at my torn dress. Then his eyes moved to Phil. Very deliberately and slowly he said,

"If I ever see you here again I'll kill you."

"But I love Helen, Mr. Worley. I want to marry her."

Pa started down the steps toward him with his arm raised in anger. "Never to a son-of-a-bitch like you," he shouted. "Now get off my property!"

Phil walked slowly down the main road as I turned to face Pa's cold fury. The gala night of the Mid-Summer Benefit Dance had come to an end.

The following weeks were webs of lies to Mama and Pa. I met Phil, furtively, any place I could. It was necessary to bring Leona into the intrigue in order to use her as an excuse.

One Friday night, when I was supposed to be with Leona, Phil and I met at our rock under the covered bridge. His voice, his lips, his hands were searching, pleading, coaxing. I trembled with excitement.

"Did you mean it when you told Pa you wanted to marry me, Phil?"

"I did, Helen. I do. Just as soon as I've saved enough money." In the bright moonlight his hair looked brilliantly golden. I ran my hand through it and kissed him passionately.

"I know the waiting has been hard on you, Phil. But it can't be here. It's too dangerous. Pa might catch us."

"I want you, Helen. I can't wait any longer."

"I know, darling. I have a plan. My parents are going to Noblesville for an all-day wedding anniversary picnic on Sunday. We can meet on the train Sunday morning and go to Indianapolis together."

Mama and Pa left for Noblesville soon after Sunday breakfast. They thought I would spend the day with Leona. My hands shook as I put on the only heavily veiled hat I owned and left the house to meet Phil. I had Andy drive me to Leona's house, and as soon as he turned back I walked the few blocks to the railroad station. As the thundering train stopped, I climbed in on the side shielded from the dispatcher's view. Pa's partner at the depot didn't see me.

I was nervous and weak and practically collapsed in a rear seat of the train. There was no one on board I recognized; even the conductor was a stranger. I stared out the window, then I turned as I felt a movement beside me and looked into the blue, blue eyes of my man.

"Phil."

"Yes, Helen."

"I love you better than anything in the world."

Without a word he reached into his coat pocket and handed me a tiny object wrapped in tissue paper. I removed the paper, and the late morning sun, streaming through the train window, glistened on a ring. It was a gold ring set with a ruby and small diamonds on either side. As he slipped it on my finger I started to cry softly. We were breathing hard and our hands were interlocked. Jesus God, I thought, will this train never get to Indianapolis?

A small hotel near Indianapolis' Union Station was the setting. As soon as the door was locked behind us I threw my arms around him and kissed him until we were both on fire. I found myself shaking almost uncontrollably as we undressed. Then I smelled his bareness as tiny rays of sunlight from the tattered blind fell on him. I looked at his magnificent maleness as his body descended to meet mine. I had a moment of fear. A question raced through my mind. Could I absorb this much man?

In no uncertain fashion I found that I could.

Chapter 3

PHIL AND I arrived back from Indianapolis at twilight, and I went directly home. Unfortunately, when Mama and Pa returned from the Noblesville celebration they went to Leona's home to pick me up in the phaeton. When they found I hadn't been there, they began to suspect I had been using Leona as an alibi for my clandestine meetings with Phil, but I confused the issue that day by being fast asleep in my own bed by the time they arrived home. Nothing was said to me, but I felt the air charged with tension.

Pa had evidently been hearing some rumors and his suspicions were running strong; his solution to the "Phil problem" was to get me out of town until it was time for me to enter DePauw University in the fall. He decided I should visit his sister, Martha Shumacher, who lived in Malone, New York.

I was determined not to go. I felt that if I had to leave Phil at this time I would surely die. I tried to scheme a method whereby Pa would keep me at home, and the best tactic I could arrive at was to act as if I wanted to go. I believed that if I appeared excited over the prospect of the trip, Pa would think I was over my infatuation with Phil and would devise a last-minute reason for me not to visit the Shumachers. I wrote a letter to my aunt and uncle, whom I had never met, and to my cousin, Martha Adele, asking her what type of clothes I should bring. The response from her was ideal for my purposes: she stated I would need a goodly selection of daytime and evening dresses, various informal outfits, a tennis costume, and a riding habit! I felt victorious because I knew Pa wouldn't want to spend a lot of money on clothes just for the trip. And, Martha Adele went on to say she had long-standing plans for a ten-day outing to Indian Lake, Saranac, and Lake Placid. She said I was welcome to accompany her on the outing, but she implied that I should be financially prepared if I wanted to go.

Martha Adele's letter affected Pa and Mama exactly the way I had thought it would: there was a dead silence when I read it to them before supper. I tried not to overplay my hand, but I couldn't keep from commenting on what fun it was going to be to visit such exciting and "high society" people. I also made a point of saying how stimulating it would be to shop for, and buy, all the necessary clothes in order not to look like a poor country cousin.

Then Mama said she agreed completely. I was stunned when she asked Pa for $500 to go on a clothes-buying expedition to Indianapolis. Until then I didn't realize that Mama was on to my scheme. When she took me to the stores in Indianapolis she went buying crazy; there were nine silk daytime dresses, two traveling suits, two evening gowns, four new hats, and five pairs of shoes.

The night before I left, Phil and I met under the covered bridge. It was a sorrowful parting, but we kept our spirits high by talking about our future. He thought he had a job possibility in Cincinnati, and his mother was thinking about moving back there. It would be a good opportunity to save money for our marriage.

Mama was up early the morning of my departure, getting all my belongings together. Andy filled the wagon with my luggage and followed the phaeton, driven by Mama, to the depot. Pa was waiting for us. He gave me my railroad tickets and two hundred dollars. I cried as I kissed him goodbye. "Have a good time, Helen, and if you need more money, just let me know," he said tearfully. This was to be the first time I had been parted from them since I was a child and living with Grandma and Grandpa Joseph.

Much to my surprise, Mama announced that she was going to accompany me to Indianapolis and see that I got on the correct through train for Utica, New York. I was pleased, even though I suspected she and Pa thought I would be meeting Phil in Indianapolis—possibly to get married. But since no such plans had been made, I was glad for the opportunity to be alone with Mama for a few hours.

As the train pulled slowly away from the station I took a left-hand seat next to a window. And sure enough, there was Phil at the first crossing. He waved and blew me a kiss, and I placed my hand over my heart to let him know that I had his ring on a chain around my neck. Mama observed the whole scene.

"He's very attractive," said Mama. "He's one of the best-looking men I've ever seen in my life."

I smiled when I asked, "But not as good-looking as Harry Levinson, is he?"

Mama laughed outright, "No, not as good-looking as Harry Levinson, and that's exactly who I was thinking about. You're pretty smart for a sixteen-year-old, aren't you?"

"Almost seventeen."

"Yes, you're almost seventeen."

"You were married when you were eighteen."

Mama sighed and said, "Helen, your father will never get over it if you marry Philip."

"I know it, Mama."

"Give yourself some time. Think it through."*

"I'm going to, Mama."

"When you're married, you stay married for a long time."

"I know it."

"I can see why you're not head over heels in love with Roy Dale. But Roy is such a nice boy, nice family."

"Roy is one of my best friends."

"And don't overlook George Eaton from Potter's Dam. He's rich. A real catch, and you could get him if you wanted him."

"You had a chance for a catch. Are you sorry you didn't take it, Mama?"

Mama laughed again and patted my hand as she said, "No, not really."

We didn't discuss Philip Cappel or my romantic future again. From then on we talked of trivialities and what I would wear to "high society doings" in New York State.

Auntie Shumacher walked ahead of Martha Adele and me. Her driver was collecting my luggage and trying to get all of it into the carriage.

"It was a lovely trip up from Utica, cousin Martha Adele, I changed trains there," I said.

"Just Martha Adele, or better, just Adele. Please no 'cousin,'" she stated.

"My ears popped practically all the way."

"You were over four thousand feet above sea level on the way here," said Adele. "But now you'll stop popping and start having fun."

Everything was going well. I wasn't too crazy about Auntie, but Adele was sharp. She was one of the smoothest-looking blondes I'd ever seen—just like one of the fashion drawings from *Ladies Home Journal*. I knew I would like her as soon as I saw her. She had just turned eighteen.

Adele surveyed me from head to toe. "You're not at all what I expected. I expected someone farmery-looking and pregnant."

"Pregnant!" I exclaimed.

"Well, it's no secret that your folks wrote my Mommy that you were involved in a passionate love affair. Naturally, I expected you to be pregnant. I thought you were coming up here to have an illegitimate you-know-what." Adele spoke matter-of-factly as she smoothed back her gorgeous blonde hair.

I was stunned.

Adele went on, "I don't mind telling you that I'm glad you're pretty. I loathe ugly people. We'll have fun. Just remember one thing; don't tell Mommy a thing, not one damned thing about your 'affair' or anything else. Understand? Not one damned thing. She'll try to find out everything."

"I understand, Adele."

The screeching of Auntie was audible all over the train station, "Martha Adele, darling, yoo-hoo, Helen, yoo-hoo, we're ready to leave. The luggage is loaded. Yoo-hoo."

Adele and I marched toward the fancy carriage arm-in-arm. As we walked she said, "Remember, dear cousin Helen, not one damned thing."

"Whatever you say, dear cousin Martha Adele, not one damned thing."

The Shumacher home was a many-turreted affair with a large veranda wrapped around three sides. It was painted a glossy white and was impressive. The rooms were elegantly furnished with mahogany Victorian furniture and English silver. The Shumachers were important people in that town, and Aunt Martha didn't want anyone to forget it. Uncle Clyde Shumacher owned a large factory and was considered a business whiz; but he was the very picture of a hen-pecked husband: short, balding, and constantly clearing his throat. I liked him immediately, or maybe I felt sorry for him for having to live with Aunt Martha. She had immediately antagonized me as soon as we arrived home from the depot by trying to get me to reveal details on what she referred to as "your unfortunate affair." I didn't know just what Mama had written her, but I stuck to Adele's advice about "not telling one damned thing."

The Shumacher's after-dinner ritual was to sit on their large veranda and watch early-evening strollers wander to a nearby park. Aunt Martha would comment on and gossip about everyone who passed. Uncle Clyde would only grunt and clear his throat. After about twenty minutes of that boring routine, I excused myself with the explanation that I wanted to write Mama and Pa about my safe arrival.

I went to the room I was to share with Adele, rummaged through my luggage to find my stationery, and, after admiring my ruby and diamond ring (which I had placed on the third finger of my left hand as soon as I left Mama in Indianapolis), proceeded to write Phil—describing the trip and telling him how much I loved him. Suddenly in the midst of the letter I was so overcome with emotion I rested my head on my arm and cried. I didn't hear Adele enter the room.

"Surely no man can be worth all that," she said.

I quickly dried my eyes. "Mine is."

Adele went to her dresser drawer and pulled out a cigarette. She lit it and inhaled deeply; then quickly locked the door leading to the hallway. I had never seen a woman smoke.

"Want a cigarette?"

"I've never had one."

"There's a first time for everything."

"All right." She held a match and I puffed. I wound up coughing.

"You'll get used to them," she said.

"I'm not sure I want to."

As Adele went around opening all the windows in the room she asked, "Is the man good-looking?"

"Very. The best-looking man I've ever seen."

"Dark hair?"

"No, he's very blond."

"Have you had sex with him?"

I was stunned by such a question; I could feel myself blushing. I stammered, "Uh, that's a strange question to ask someone."

"It's not so strange. Yes or No?"

At first I started to lie to her; then I decided to tell the truth. "Yes."

"Was it good?"

Again I was stunned. But for some reason I kept answering her truthfully.

"Yes."

"Every time?"

"There was only one time."

"Really?"

"Really!"

"Have you had other men?"

"No."

"Then you have nothing to compare him with."

Jesus God, I thought, what a conversation for newly-met cousins to be engaged in! "No."

"I've had five men."

"Five?"

"Five. All brunets. Hairy brunets. I'd like to try a blond sometime."

This time I was dumbfounded; but she kept the conversation alive by saying, "Speaking of hairy brunets reminds me of David Ardman. My favorite."

"Are you in love with him?" I wanted to get off the subject of sex.

"No. Only 'infatuated' as Mommy would say. Fortunately, Mommy has no idea of my kind of 'infatuation.'"

She walked to the dresser and mashed the cigarette into her pin tray. She held the pin tray toward me and I mashed my cigarette beside hers. Then she dumped both butts into the chamber pot with the comment, "The maid knows I smoke."

Adele proceeded to talk about sex. She said David Ardman was not only a millionaire but a "divine fuck" and that she was out to hook him. She told me how she had forged a letter to her mother and signed David Ardman's mother's name to it. It was a fake invitation to be Mrs. Ardman's guest at a resort known as the Mountain View Hotel. Aunt Martha had been delighted because she was vastly impressed with the Ardmans' money—they owned one of New York's great department stores—and nothing would please her more than to have Adele marry David. And, furthermore, Mrs. Ardman was in Europe and could cause no trouble. The whole thing was neatly planned and wrapped up with a ribbon.

I had been so shocked with Adele's language I had lost the gist of the plan and asked, "Will anyone you know be at the hotel?"

"You're goddamed right," she said, smiling sweetly and sweeping a hand across her gorgeous hair. "David's going to be there with several of his New York friends! I hope there's a nice blond among them, for variety's sake. God, I'm dying to get fucked by a big blond man." She gave a suggestive laugh and started toward the door, then stopped momentarily at her dressing table and atomized some cologne into her open mouth.

What a conversation! I had never heard such language—shocking. And the business about "getting fucked by a big blond man"! Suddenly I felt myself getting excited. If Phil had walked through the door I would have had him on the floor! Or, as Adele put it, given him a "divine fuck."

Just as Adele started to leave the room she turned and said, "Oh, Mommy sent me up here to check and see whether you're really writing your folks. And since I never lie to Mommy," she giggled, "please drop them a line." With that the door closed. So I wrote Mama and Pa a quick note:

"Dear Mama and Pa,

My trip was grand. Everything is lovely here. Cousin Martha Adele is so friendly, beautiful and refined ...."

Adele was inspecting my clothes and allowed as how they were passable enough for her chic crowd at the Mountain View Hotel, but she said it was necessary to have a bathing costume, so we went shopping. The bathing costume I chose at Malone's swankiest shop was lavender and pink polka dots on a gray background. There were tight bloomers that came to the knees, gray knee socks, and gray sneakers. The blouse had elbow-length sleeves. A matching frilled cap and parasol completed the ensemble. Nothing showed but my face and lower arms, but I felt terribly risqué in it.

"Sensational!" cried Adele when I came out of the fitting room. "You'll have to watch out for David Ardman after he sees you in that."

"Why? Do you think he'll try to fuck me?" I asked laughingly. I was having a goddamed good visit with Adele and had started picking up some of her terms of speech.

"I know damned well he will! He will put this 'great love' of yours for Phil to a real test. If you can refuse that hunk of stuff you can refuse anything. But if you decide to accept, do be my guest. It might be fun to compare notes on him."

I telegraphed Pa that more money was needed and he sent me three hundred dollars. Then we took off for the Mountain View Hotel at Indian Lake. If the hotel management thought it strange for two unchaperoned young ladies to be registering into one of their most expensive suites, they certainly didn't let on. As a matter of fact, after Adele inquired if Mr. David Ardman and his party had arrived, the management couldn't have been more solicitous. We had arrived dressed fit to kill and they thought us wealthy young socialites—which Adele was, in her own way.

David's group wasn't expected until late the following day so that gave us over twenty-four hours to, as Adele put it, "size the place up." And that's where the blond young man came into play. Was he blond! As blond as the Dutch can make them. Adele spied him as soon as we entered the elaborate dining room for lunch— exactly forty-five minutes after our arrival. Adele indicated to the head waiter that we preferred a table by the window. It had taken her only a split second to see that the only available window table was right next to Mr. Blond. I'll tell you something, there were no flies on Adele's fast ass! Within minutes Stanton Van Rensselaer had joined us and he and Adele were engaged in a witty conversation.

Van got me a date for an afternoon of doubles at tennis and a swim in the lake. Later, my date escorted me to dinner and dancing on the terrace. When he started getting romantic I told him I was engaged, showed him the ring, and he went his way. I was back in our suite by midnight and dropped off to sleep within minutes.

I awoke momentarily and noticed that Adele's bed was untouched; then at seven-thirty when I awoke for good, Adele was sleeping peacefully in the bed next to mine. I breakfasted alone in the hotel dining room and when I returned Adele was up, dressed, and sipping coffee in the sitting room of our suite. She looked fresh as a daisy and more beautiful than I had ever seen her. There was nothing like a good fuck to bring Adele into her own.

Adele kept no details from me. She had spent practically all night in Stanton Van Rensselaer's room. He had been "divine" and tutored her in some unusual and marvelous practices he had learned in Holland. I was speechless. I couldn't believe it. What seemed to please Adele was to have the blond binge out of the way so she could concentrate on the brunets who were arriving that day.

Evidently Adele proved to be completely satisfying to Mr. Van Rensselaer also. We learned, through the friend, that Van had checked out of the hotel prior to lunch and had taken off for parts unknown. He probably had had enough to hold him until the next trip to Amsterdam. Which was fine with Adele; she was afraid he might be a friend of David's and things could have become complicated.

David and his crowd arrived just prior to dinner. Adele had left a note at the desk giving our room number, and as soon as David checked in our door started rattling. There were five boys in the group: students from assorted Eastern colleges. David was between his junior and senior year at Yale. He was all Adele had said he was and more; he exuded charm and sophistication. In that hey-day of playboys, stagedoor johnnies, and true rounders, David was the original boom-t-ra kid. And he was built like a Greek god and must have been hung like a bull—little wonder Adele considered him such a fabulous fuck. That night, once again, Adele failed to utilize her own bed until the wee hours of the next morning.

The days were a continuous round of little gaieties highly laced with champagne, cigarettes, and passes being made at me by David's darling friends. Some other girls, hot numbers from Vassar, had joined our group and we were having a ball all ways. I would write Phil a daily letter but otherwise the purpose of my visit was working the way Pa had hoped (wouldn't he have pissed in his pants if he could have seen me in that marvelous bathing costume trying to fend off some dry-humping Princeton junior?) because Phil was being relegated to the back of my mind momentarily. Foremost in my mind was wondering who was going to fuck whom that night. I must point out I did not accept any propositions. Now that I think back on it, I was a goddamed fool.

As a base of operations, the Mountain View Hotel couldn't have been more ideal. From there we branched out southward to Lake Placid and Saranac; if we'd hear about a party being planned anywhere in the vicinity, we'd crash it and always be welcomed because of David's prominence.

Adele's fondness for champagne almost smashed our idyllic trip. We had been invited to a "champagne cruise" aboard a gasoline launch at Lake Placid. Something intuitive told me to stay clear of that deal but Adele and David thought it would be loads of fun, so we went.

The host for the launch party was to be Mr. Alfred M---. He was the scion of one of America's great empire-building families, and his name was one that even I, from Cicero, was familiar with.

Adele, David, and I took the train down from Indian Lake and were met at the Lake Placid station by Alfred's black-lacquered carriage. Alfred had remained on the launch, probably gaining strength for the evening's entertainment. The launch was beautifully appointed; today it would probably be termed a yacht. It had its own captain, which left Alfred free for other activities. There were two other crewmen plus a combination cook-steward.

Alfred himself was somewhat handsome, graying, in his forties. He met us at the gangplank in full regalia: blue coat, white trousers, and yachting cap. Since Adele had David, and a second couple had each other, I had Alfred as a date. When I saw him I was glad I had come; but I changed my tune after the sun went down.

The additional couple were not my dish of tea. She was limpid and dull-looking and he had one of those too-finely-bred, incestuous-looking faces that one finds in abundance in higher social circles.

Champagne started flowing immediately. Although I hadn't cared for cigarettes, I had developed a taste for champagne. Adele was mad about it and couldn't get enough; David, too, downed more than his share.

The launch stayed tied to the dock until after dinner, which was served in a small dining cabin, then the motors started and away we cruised. The large dinner and fresh air that hit us when we came on deck put only a slight damper on everyone's "highness"; the glow was reestablished with large snifters of brandy followed by more champagne.

By ten o'clock our host was completely smashed. First, he tried to paw me, all the while whispering suggestive little tidbits into my ear. I asked him to keep his distance and he complied, surprisingly enough. Then he turned his attentions on the dull-looking girl and got quite a few feels in before she passed out in a deck chair. In the meantime, her escort (possibly they were married, I didn't care enough to inquire) had found a banjo and started singing raucous songs. He was joined by David and Alfred, and occasionally by Adele, when she knew the words.

After the singing got sloppier and the words got dirtier, Alfred made a suggestion that was enthusiastically received by his fellow vocalists: why not view a portfolio of his famous "Paris pictures"?

Alfred stumbled below deck and returned with a thin, black leather case filled with the most beautifully mounted prints and etchings of the most pornographic art imaginable. We crowded around the light of two lanterns attached to the exterior bulkhead as we looked, laughed, and sometimes even screamed our approval. I was completely bewildered. Only the pictures portraying the most mundane situations were within my comprehension. I turned one picture upside down trying to figure it out and they screamed how clever I was. They thought it had much more zing to it turned that way. I felt stupid and out of things. Nowadays, of course, I'm a world authority on positions!

David mumbled something about feeling dizzy and clomped down the ladder leading to the sleeping compartments; he was followed closely by our host, Alfred. Adele, Incestuous Face, and I collapsed on deck chairs; snoozing a bit, hardly speaking. The dull-looking woman was really gone and snoring loudly.

I felt sick. I wanted a wet towel to sponge off my face, but I couldn't move to get one. And the crewmen and the steward were too well trained to be wandering about the launch—they were in evidence only when Alfred needed more champagne or brandy.

So there we sat for fully ten minutes, half sleeping, spray blowing in our faces, cruising in circles in the limited confines of Lake Placid.

Suddenly from below deck there came a roar, a crash, a scream. Adele and I both hit the deck like sailors going to battle stations and I raced behind her down the ladder.

In the tiny passageway we saw Alfred, prone on the deck with his head against the corner of a door; his eyes closed, his face deathly white, and blood oozing from a gash at the very top of his scalp. The blood was running down his face and dripping off the back of his head at the same time. Peering down at him was David, completely nude except for shoes and socks.

"Good God! What's going on down here?" shouted Adele.

"The goddamed bastard," stated David.

"What happened to Alfred? What happened?" demanded Adele.

"He tried to fuck me—that's what happened!" shouted David back at her.

"He must have done a pretty good job of it," cried Adele, "judging by the way you're dressed!"

With that I took my eyes off Alfred and looked at David. Jesus God, I thought, what a hunk of man!

"The bastard undressed me! I was asleep—he undressed me! I socked him when I woke up!"

"Don't holler at me, you fool!" screamed Adele. "Do something!"

Incestuous Face had joined the group and was bending down examining Alfred. "I think he's dead," he said flatly. "Dead?" screamed Adele.

I decided to enter into the screaming, too. "Dead?" I inquired with all my lung power.

"Where's the skipper of this damned boat?" asked Incestuous Face.

"Right here," said the skipper in an authoritative voice. He was elderly, fatherly-looking. He put his ear against Alfred's chest and said, "His heart's beating, but he's losing blood quickly. Get me some rags."

There was much confusion, but within thirty seconds Adele and I had ripped up a sheet and the skipper had sopped up Alfred's blood as the men lifted him into a bunk. Everybody, including David, had forgotten about David's nudity. As we stood gazing down at Alfred, it suddenly dawned on David that he was naked and he scampered to the corner of the room and retrieved his trousers which had been tossed in a chair. It seems that the legs were turned inside out and we all—the skipper, Incestuous Face, Adele, and I—watched transfixed as he fumbled his way into them. Pity, I thought fleetingly, that dull-looking woman isn't sober enough to see this, too.

The skipper went out and shouted orders to the crewmen to pull into the first available landing. Then he came back and asked a general question.

"What happened?"

No one answered for a split second, then David said, "I socked him."

The skipper turned his eyes to David. "You socked him?"

"He tried to do me! I was asleep! I socked him!"

"Oh," said the Captain, "I'm afraid Mr. M--- is seriously injured."

"David, you're a goddamed fool," said Adele.

"What did you expect me to do? Just lie there and get done?" shouted David at Adele.

"Well, I'm sure it wouldn't have been the first time," screeched Adele. "Now look at the goddamed mess we're in! The son of a bitch looks dead to me!"

"Mr. M--- has lost a lot of blood, but he's not dead," said the old skipper gently.

"I don't care if he does die!" stated David defiantly.

That raised the old skipper's ire. "Listen here, sir, I'm paid to run this launch, not to condone Mr. M---'s behavior. However, not many people accept invitations on this boat without knowing something about Mr. M--- and his weaknesses. We have been cruising around Lake Placid for about four hours, and during that time I have heard your own voice in song. I know you didn't think you were at a church social."

David looked at the floor and didn't utter a word.

The skipper continued, "My advice is not to accept invitations to these cruises if you aren't prepared for certain eventualities."

"That's right, don't accept 'em," chipped in Incestuous Face as his eyes devoured David's fabulous bare chest.

Jesus God, I thought, Cicero was never like this!

The nearest dock wasn't anywhere close to where we had boarded the launch. It was just after midnight when they took Alfred off the boat. All of us wanted to leave also, but there was no place to go at that hour of the night. So we had to stay on the launch.

The skipper had taken all of our names and addresses and that so upset Adele she vented her fury on David once again. David tried to get her to share his bunk (the one Alfred's unconscious body had occupied) with him and she flatly refused.

There were only two sleeping compartments aside from the crew's quarters and Adele and I took one and left David to solve his own problem of where to sleep since Incestuous Face claimed he was going to sleep in Alfred's bunk, with or without David. The dull-faced woman evidently remained on deck until daybreak and then wandered into a crewman's room. She was not in sight when I went on deck at six-thirty but appeared about an hour later looking fully refreshed. I decided to take a good look at the crewman!

About nine-thirty the skipper dropped us off where we had boarded the launch. We called the little hospital where they had taken Alfred and found that he had regained consciousness and was not going to die. Adele left the message that we had enjoyed his champagne cruise tremendously and we were so sorry he had slipped down the ladder while going below deck. That was the last I saw of Mr. Alfred M---, but for many years his name would jump out at me from the gossip columns.

After telephoning the hospital, Adele reasoned that Alfred wouldn't be needing his black-lacquered carriage for a while, so she commandeered it for our return trip to the Mountain View Hotel. The poor driver had heard of Alfred's accident and recognized us from the previous afternoon, so he didn't question Adele's authority to order him on such a long trip. David thought that Adele was so clever to think of using Alfred's carriage that his compliments about her ingenuity soon thawed her ice and all was well again. After she told him she appreciated his "manly attitude" of the night before, everything became smooth as silk. As soon as we reached the hotel Adele and David disappeared and I didn't see either of them again until after breakfast the next morning.

Adele came dashing into our room at nine a.m. I had never seen her looking more beautiful. "Helen, Helen, guess what?"

"David has asked you to marry him," I stated flatly. I smiled as I continued, "I felt he was going to."

"Yes, yes, he did! We're going to be married in the spring! Just after his graduation from Yale." Adele sat down on the side of the bed and grinned wisely at me. "He said he couldn't bear to lose me. The next time I see Stanton Van Rensselaer remind me to give him a big kiss!"

That was when I realized it takes technique to get a gal into the big chips. That Adele was a smart worker; in later years I thought of her often and mused that she had missed her calling. She would have made a terrific hustler, and I could have used her in any number of spots. I told Al Capone once that she would fill the bill to a "T " when he was looking for someone elegant to work Chicago's Blackstone Hotel for him, but unfortunately for us, she was by that time the extremely social Mrs. David Ardman of New York, Newport, and snazzy European locations. (Ardman, of course, is not the real name of my cousin's famous husband! The real name is a household word in America.)

We left shortly for Malone. David went with us to ask Uncle Clyde for "Adele's hand." When we arrived, Aunt Martha was in such an elated tizzy she didn't pry into any details of our "outing." She was far too busy having parties and inviting friends in to meet David. It was a real coup de grace for her.

We had been back in Malone for about a week. "Here's a letter for you, Helen," said Aunt Martha with affected sweetness as she handed me an envelope from Phil. "I hope your exposure to the nice, cultured atmosphere of Indian Lake has changed your thinking about your infatuation with an unsuitable young man. I'm positive that Adele's culture is what drew David to her."

Horseshit to you, I thought, as I snatched Phil's letter from her hand. I could have told her what it was that got Adele a husband, and it sure wasn't culture even though it began with a "c."

Phil's letter stated he was working as a bartender in Cincinnati and that his mother had sold her home in Cicero and was moving back to Cincinnati with Frances, his oldest sister, and with Ed, the youngest brother. He said he couldn't wait for us to be united and as soon as I arrived home he would get off work for a day or two and meet me in Cicero. But he insisted that I follow my father's wishes and enter De Pauw University in the fall while he saved money for our marriage.

The excitement about Adele's engagement made me think increasingly of Phil. I wired Mama and Pa I was coming home; I couldn't wait to be with Phil. All that jazz had given me hot pants!

Chapter 4

AS THE TRAIN pulled into the Cicero station I saw Mama and Pa standing on the platform. While they hugged and kissed me, I answered dozens of questions about the trip, about Malone, and about the Schumachers. Then Pa piled as much of my baggage on the phaeton as he could and pulled the remainder of it into his telegraph office for Andy to bring home later. Mama drove me home.

We pulled up before our house just as I finished telling Mama about Adele's engagement to David Ardman and what a wonderful match it was—leaving out, of course, the more succulent bits of their romance. Mama turned to me with laughter dancing in her eyes and said, "Speaking of romances, Helen, your ring is beautiful. In all the excitement I don't think Pa noticed it. I would suggest putting it back on the chain for a while."

Phil came from Cincinnati on the second day I was home. I made some excuse about going to Leona's and met him at our spot under the covered bridge; the excuse probably wasn't believed by either Mama or Pa, but I didn't care. My passion had reached such a peak that nothing mattered but being with Phil. When we saw each other our desire broke all bounds and we had each other right there on a mossy knoll. The aphrodisiacal effect of being with Adele and David came to the fore and all inhibitions within me were unleashed.

In the weeks that followed, Phil came to Cicero whenever he could get away, and inevitably Mama and Pa found out about

< Cincinnati Taverns, 1900s.

our torrid affair. Everyone in the small town knew about it, and I didn't give a goddam. It had become common gossip among the people of Cicero, so I could stop using Leona as an excuse. Roy Dale was pitiful and lovable, asking me to marry him but knowing I wouldn't. And Katie Heinz snubbed me on the street and in Dale's, but nothing mattered to me except Phil.

The scenes at home were ghastly. Pa ranted and raved and even called me wanton. We had been so close to each other all my life I couldn't believe that my father wouldn't make some concessions, but he refused to reconcile himself to Phil. Religion did, of course, play a part in all this. Pa didn't want me to marry a Catholic, he claimed. Yet hadn't he married a woman who was half Jewish? Wasn't his own niece, Adele, engaged to a rich Jew from New York? I have always believed that Pa used the religion angle as a crutch for something else. Whatever the cause, the wonderful relationship between Pa and me was destroyed, never to be regained.

I promised Pa that I would go to the university as we had planned, and that somewhat quieted him down. In mid-September I left for college and decided to apply myself to my studies. I wanted the time to go quickly and to be worthwhile. Mathematics and English were my favorite subjects and every night I studied diligently after writing Phil his daily letter. My main concerns during those months were to receive letters from Phil and make the classroom's highest marks on the weekly tests.

Late in November Phil wrote me an exuberant letter saying that he was the manager of his own saloon! He had been set up in business by the wealthy Herancourt Brewery[4] to run a profitable place at Wade and Linn Streets—a good location for such a saloon. Now, he said, he was financially able to support me and asked me to hurry to him immediately. I didn't know what to do. Should I stay at DePauw until the mid-year examinations? I knew that my grades were going to be high. I felt I owed it to Pa to take the exams.

So I wrote Phil that I would join him in just a couple of months and that it was important to my family that I take the exams. He

---

4. George Herancourt erected his brewery in Cincinnati in 1847 that grew to one of the largest in Ohio. Herancourt died in 1880 and his namesake brewery closed in 1918.

wrote back that he understood, but to come to him as soon as possible. He said he had told his mother and his sister, Frances, that we were going to be married.

Our examinations were given just prior to the Christmas holidays, and our grades were released to us before I left for Cicero. I made the Dean's Honor Roll and had some of the highest grades made by any girl at the university. Pa received the official announcement a few hours before my train pulled in to Cicero. It was the second-best present I could have given him; the first best would have been to break off with Phil, an impossibility.

I expected Phil to show up in Cicero at any moment, and when the phone rang the next morning I grabbed at it eagerly. It was Henry, and he said he was calling from the depot. Phil had called him—knowing that any calls or letters to my home would probably be intercepted—and asked that Henry get in touch with me and tell me that with the pressures of his new saloon it would be impossible to leave Cincinnati during the holidays and for me to come there. I had been invited by Mrs. Cappel to stay at their home. It was while I was plotting a way to get to Cincinnati that Mama came into my room to talk to me.

Mama told me that she was on my side. She said she knew that I would surely be thinking of plans to slip away and join Phil during the Christmas season and she wished there was some way she could help me. But, she said, Pa had become almost maniacal every time Phil's name was mentioned by her. She said that she and Pa had had scenes over the whole business and that such arguments left them both terribly nervous for days, even weeks, and that she simply couldn't take such outbursts anymore. Mama cried and made me promise her that I wouldn't slip off to Cincinnati during the holidays. Also, she said she had heard about Phil's new saloon and she knew I would be marrying him soon but—please, please, she begged—return to Greencastle and the university and try to postpone the wedding until spring. It was really something to see Mama saying all this, and we fell into each other's arms sobbing.

The holidays seemed endless. I was glad when New Year's was over and time came for me to return to Greencastle. Pa had not mentioned Phil's name once during the entire vacation, and I was grateful for that. Mama and Pa kissed me goodbye at the station. As I kissed Mama she looked me directly in the eye and a wan smile touched her lips—I think she knew what was going to happen.

All the way to Indianapolis where I was to change trains for Greencastle I kept asking myself, "Should I return to DePauw University or go to Phil?" As my train pulled into the depot in Indianapolis, I asked the conductor when the next train left for Cincinnati and he replied, "In forty-five minutes."

The connecting train for Greencastle was leaving in forty-seven minutes. Those two minutes between the trains proved to be the most important two minutes of my life.

I'm sure my voice quavered when I told the man behind the counter that I wanted a refund on my ticket from Indianapolis to Greencastle and that I wanted to buy a ticket to Cincinnati.

When he handed me my ticket I knew the die was cast. I sent Phil a telegram to meet me at the station in Cincinnati, that I was on my way to marry him. I also wired my parents to tell them I was going to join Phil.

The closer I got to Cincinnati the more reservations I had about what I was doing. By the time I walked into Cincinnati's enormous Big Four Railroad Depot, I was miserable with indecision and on the verge of tears. "As soon as I see Phil," I comforted myself, "everything will be all right."

"Helen, Helen dear!" I was swept into feminine arms. It was Frances, Phil's sister. "Oh, Helen, Mother and I are so pleased about you and Phil planning to get married. We'll take good care of you until the wedding!"

I looked around wildly. "Where's Phil, Frances?"

"He couldn't leave his saloon, Helen. The place is jammed with customers, and we couldn't find our cousin, Pete. There was no one to mind the saloon."

The dammed-up tears overflowed. I had never been so disappointed in my life. I didn't want to see Frances, I wanted to be met by Phil.

Father Lipski was kind and gentle as he spoke. "Are you sure, in your own mind, that you are doing the right thing, Helen?" Father Lipski was the Polish priest at the Catholic church on Liberty Street. He had become not only my instructor in Catholicism, but my friend and confidant. This particular church was not the one regularly attended by the Cappel family—they went to St. Joseph's—but for some reason they didn't want St. Joseph's involved in the wedding. "Yes, yes, Father, I'm sure. I love Phil very much."

"I know you do, child. But think of your own parents. Your father still objects to Phil. You are from a privileged family, Helen. You've had things that have been denied to Mrs. Cappel's family. If you marry Phil your way of life will be different from what it has been up to now." He paused, then continued, "Will you make a good Roman Catholic, Helen?"

"I don't know, Father." Then I added, "I doubt it."

His kindly eyes peered into mine. "I doubt it, too."

"But what does that matter, Father? When we have children, they'll be raised Catholic."

"Yes, they'll have to be, Helen. That's not what concerns me at this time. It's you I'm worried about. Just being 'in love' is not enough in life's long, hard pull."

"What do you mean, Father?"

"I think you should give a great deal of thought to this marriage. You must be absolutely certain that it's the thing to do."

"I have already given a great deal of thought to it. I know what I'm going to do." There was a moment of silence before Father Lipski spoke.

"If that is the case, then I'll marry you, Helen. Here, in my parlor."

I wrote Mama and Pa and begged them to come to my wedding. Mama wrote back that she would always love me, but her hands were tied. A separate letter came from Pa. It was very brief. It stated that as far as he was concerned I was dead. He warned me that it would be useless to contact him or Mama again. He said I was headed for damnation and that I was a wanton whore.

I stayed in my room for two days and two nights, foolishly clinging to the hope that at the last minute Mama and Pa would buy me a wedding dress and come to the ceremony in Cincinnati. Everything about my life as I had known it was butchered. I felt as if I, too, had been slaughtered. But when I had sobbed myself to a standstill, I came out of my room and flung myself into Phil's arms. He was my whole world now. There was no turning back.

We promised Phil's mother that we'd live with her and Frances for a few months after our marriage, so about a week before the wedding Phil and I went shopping and bought all new furniture for the large second-floor room which we were to occupy. After the furniture selection was completed Phil said, "Helen, I know it isn't considered customary, but I'd like to buy you a wedding gown."

I was touched. Phil realized how Pa's bitter letter had affected me. I started to cry. He took me in his arms. "Would you like a white wedding gown, Helen?" he asked gently.

I laughed through my tears. "I would love a white wedding gown," I said, "but I think we should watch our pennies. If you really want to buy me an outfit, how about something that I can use for other occasions as well?"

"You name it, Helen, and you'll get it."

We left the house together. While Phil stopped for a beer at a downtown saloon, I went to H.P. Jonap's shop and picked out a handsome brown wool suit and a matching hat topped off with pheasant feathers. The suit was a perfect fit. Not one alteration was needed. When Phil came to Jonap's to get me the two large packages were all wrapped up.

"Don't I get to see what I'm paying for?"

"No," I giggled. "You'll see it on our wedding day—and not before. Bad luck, you know!"

"We can have no bad luck, Helen! Our luck is all good."

I believed him and thought we were going to live happily ever after.

The wedding ceremony on February 2, 1903, was small but lovely. We were married in Father Lipski's church parlor at seven o'clock in the evening. Ed, Phil's younger brother, served as best man and Frances was my maid of honor. Mrs. Cappel cried, Henry looked ill at ease and Phil's cousin, Pete Cappel, looked bored. None of my hometown friends were present. I had invited Leona Neal, and she had written that she would accept, then she wrote that she wouldn't be able to attend; but Leona did send me one of her blue handkerchiefs—"something borrowed and something blue"—to use at the wedding. My "something old" was the cameo bracelet that had belonged to Grandma Joseph.

After the wedding ceremony we all returned to the Cappel home for a large neighborhood reception and dinner. After the last guests had departed, Mother Cappel and Frances quickly cleared the food and dishes away, then left with small overnight cases—they had arranged to spend a few days with obscure relatives in Covington.

Phil lifted me into his arms and carried me up to the large second-floor bedroom. We clung hungrily together and devoured each other.

Chapter 5

FOR THE FIRST few months after our marriage, I was content and happy to be Mrs. Phil Cappel. For me, it was enough to be near him, love him, share our marriage bed. Then as the summer heat waves hit Cincinnati, I became bored and restless. I felt cooped up in Mrs. Cappel's home; she and Frances were such thorough, immaculate housekeepers that there was little housework for me to do besides keeping our own room in order. Time hung heavy on my hands.

As a saloon keeper, Phil worked late at night; and as he worked he was constantly surrounded and entertained by the merriment of his find-fun-or-die-in-the-attempt patrons. I had no such associations or stimuli. Anyone in a business such as Phil's can tell you that you have to have a few peaceful hours a day away from high-key nightlife or you go berserk. Phil's home life with me were his restful hours. We would make love, then he would sleep until afternoon, arise, and get ready to go back to the saloon. We'd have our dinner together about four-thirty, and after he had eaten I wouldn't see him again until four o'clock the next morning. I scheduled my waking hours to fit his; the hours prior to, and just after, midnight seemed endless as I watched by our front window for him to come home.

Our social life was nil; Phil didn't have time to take me out, and my unusual schedule made it impossible to spend much time with the other young wives in the neighborhood. Not that I particularly enjoyed their company when I did see them, because most of them were of foreign extraction and we had little in common.

< Foucar's Bar.

This was the period when Cincinnati was known as "The Paris of America." Beer gardens and saloons were everywhere; it was often quoted that there were only three truly glorious streets in the United States: Broadway in New York, Market Street in San Francisco, and Vine Street in Cincinnati. The after-dark shenanigans and revelry of Vine, Fifth, and Walnut Streets were supposed to be surpassed only by a few capitals of Europe, but I knew of this only through hearsay. I decided to see for myself.

Phil and I were having our usual early dinner one Saturday afternoon in August when I broached the subject. "Phil?"

"Yeah, Helen."

"I want to go to Foucar's[5] tonight." I had heard that Foucar's Saloon was one of the city's most famous bistros.

"Foucar's? On Saturday night? You know that Saturday is our biggest night at the saloon."

"It's also the biggest night at Foucar's—that's why I want to go tonight." My voice held a certain determination.

"I'll be needed at the saloon."

"Pete can handle it." Pete ran a meat market but occasionally helped out at Phil's bar.

"Helen, I don't trust Pete: I think he pockets some of the take."

"Well, I'm glad to hear you say it! I haven't trusted him from the moment I laid eyes on him. But that doesn't matter—let him do it tonight. Will you take me to Foucar's—yes or no?"

"What if I say 'no'?"

"Then I'll go alone."

He laughed outright. "Like hell you will!"

"That's right—like hell I will."

"You've been bored lately, haven't you, Helen?"

"Yes."

He arose and came around to my side of the table and hugged me. "I'm sorry, my love. We'll probably be robbed by Pete

---

5 In 1902 , Theodore Foucar opened Foucar's Café at 429 Walnut St. The interior boasted of gold-gilt mirrors and a polished mahogany bar trimmed with Brazilian onyx and Vermont marble. Free roast beef lunches were given out. One room was called the rathskeller. It was styled in eighteenth-century Flemish with black oak walls, mounted elk heads and a large fireplace dominating one end of the room. It closed at the beginning of Prohibition.

tonight—but what the hell. All right, we'll go to Foucar's—and to The Mecca[6], too."

I spent over an hour getting dressed; it was the first time I had been "out" since our wedding. I wore a purple silk suit, white gloves, and two large white plumes in my bouffant hair-do. As a final fillip, I pinned on a large amethyst-colored brooch. I felt as if I looked good, and I knew it for sure when I saw the admiring glances from the mass of men in Cappel's Bar as I walked in to meet Phil.

"You're looking even better than usual tonight, Helen," said cousin Pete Cappel with a rather evil smirk as he surveyed me from head to toe.

"I knew you'd be here, Pete—that's why I wanted to look especially fetching," I said, giving him a smile I didn't feel.

"Hmmmm ... we'll have to discuss that further at a later date," returned Pete suggestively.

"Much later, Pete," I said coldly. "Where's Phil?"

"He's washing up. He'll be right here."

"Good. By the way, Pete, Phil has taken in over $150 the last two Saturday nights—I trust tonight will be an equally profitable night."

Pete looked surprised, then caught himself quickly. "It should be. It has started off right good."

"That's fine. I'll be interested in comparing the figures." At that moment Phil appeared.

"What are you two talking about so intently?"

"Just a little 'cousin talk,' eh, Pete?" I laughed.

"That's right, Helen, a little 'cousin talk.'"

"Not kissin' cousin' talk I hope," teased Phil—but I could tell that his eyes weren't laughing.

"Hardly," I stated flatly.

"We'll be at Foucar's or The Mecca if you want me—just send for me," Phil told Pete. Phil was leery of leaving the saloon in Pete's hands, but I only had thoughts of seeing the after-dark majesties of the Queen City.

---

6 Next door to Foucar's, The Mecca was a bar that served as the unofficial office of Mayor George Cox, Cincinnati political boss. His 'organization' paved the way for William McKinley to become Governor of Ohio and later President of the United States.

As we walked into the foyer of Foucar's we were greeted first by the babble of voices, second by the aroma of expensive whiskey, and third by Theodore Foucar. Mr. Foucar was the most elegantly dressed man I had ever seen. The sheen of his brocade vest matched the sheen of his hair, and the glitter of his twenty-carat diamond-solitaire stickpin was a companion piece for the glitter of his own eyes. He welcomed us warmly and waved us into the care of his continental headwaiter.

There was so much to see I didn't know where to look first. The walls were covered with European paintings. As one of Cincinnati's foremost art patrons, proprietor Theodore Foucar used his collection of paintings as decorations for his saloon. The blaze of candles in great Dore bronze sconces reflected the blaze of damask, silverware, and the customers' jewels. This was where visiting celebrities came to feast upon gourmet foods, imported liquors, lively conversation, and the impressive art exhibit.

Phil had told the headwaiter that we wished to be seated in the rear bar, and as we snaked our way around the tables and through the aisles, from room to room, I saw faces made familiar to me by billboards, newspapers, and my few visits to the theatre: Julia Marlow[7], Maggie Cline[8], E.H. Sothern[9], and the elder Tyrone Power[10]. As long as I live I'll never forget that eye-into-eye encounter with the magnificent Mr. Power. I recognized him immediately and just as I swept by his table our eyes met and hung together in split-second intensity. This was the first of three such eye encounters with him during the next few years: the following two were in theatres, when he was on the stage and I in the audience. We never met, but I could tell he knew about me and I knew about him.

---

7 Julia Marlow (August 17, 1865 – November 12, 1950) was an English-born American actress and suffragist, known for her interpretations of William Shakespeare.

8 Maggie Cline (January 1, 1857 – June 11, 1934) was an American vaudeville singer, active across the United States in the late nineteenth century, known as "The Irish Queen" and "The Bowery Brunhilde."

9 E.H. Sothern (December 6, 1859 – October 28, 1933) was an American actor who specialized in dashing, romantic leading roles and particularly in Shakespeare roles.

10 Tyrone Power (May 1869 – 23 December 1931) was an English-born American stage and screen actor, known professionally as Tyrone Power. He is now usually referred to as Tyrone Power Sr. to differentiate him from his son, actor Tyrone Power.

The waiter placed us at a small table in the bar and I was so dazzled I was speechless. Phil leaned over and whispered in my ear, "I've heard the bar cost $150,000." Then I saw the floor and did a double-take. Phil noticed my gaze and said, "Yep, that's what they are—twenty-dollar gold pieces!" The entire floor was embedded with them. My head was swimming to the rhythm of the orchestra which had begun to play.

"So you're taking a fisherman's holiday, too, huh, Phil?" I jumped, startled, as the booming bass voice came from directly behind and above me. Phil sprang to his feet. I turned in my chair and stared up at a rather short man who was completely encrusted in diamonds: diamonds were on both hands, both cuffs, both lapels, and on his necktie.

Phil's voice was nervous and he said, "Hello, Mr. Pittner … eh, Jake… how are you?"

"Fine, my boy. Fine." He looked down at me and beamed, "And, who is this lovely young lady, my boy?"

Phil introduced us, and I learned quickly that Jake Pittner[11] was the owner of an elegant saloon at Eighth and Vine Streets … and had a connection with the Herancourt Brewery[12] which had set Phil up in business. I glanced inquisitively at two rather crude-looking men who stood silently about six feet behind Jake Pittner. No effort was made to introduce them. Jake Pittner accepted Phil's invitation to join us, and pulled up a chair to our table. Still the two men stood quietly against the wall. Jake looked up, saw them there, and waved them away with the command, "Wait for me on the street." Then Mr. Pittner turned his charms on me.

"How do you like our city, Mrs. Cappel?"

"I love it, Mr. Pittner. Actually, though, this is the first time I've visited this area. It is fascinating."

Jake Pittner giggled. "It is a rather imposing array of saloons.

---

11 Pittner was a successful Cincinnati tavern keeper and was considered a 'boss' of the German, Over-the-Rhine neighborhood.

12 George Herancourt erected his brewery in Cincinnati in 1847. He brewed 14 barrels a day. By 1851 he began to brew lager beer and the business increased dramatically. It was also known as the Philadelphia Brewery and closed in 1918.

Almost like Paris ... or Vienna. Wettest city between New York and Chicago." He twisted a large diamond ring on his little finger until it caught the light to his satisfaction, then shot a question at Phil, "How would you like to run a place along this street ... or on Vine ... I hear you've done wonders with that place at Wade and Linn?"

Phil almost dropped his glass. He swallowed so hard his Adam's apple bobbed up and down. He didn't say a word. I piped up, "Phil would be a success in this area."

Jake Pittner placed his jeweled hand over mine and patted it. "I think he would be, too, my dear." He glanced up and saw a gentleman standing at the bar and exclaimed, "There's Ed Branagan ... I was supposed to meet him here. I hope you'll excuse me." He arose, and just as he was ready to leave he turned and said, "Why don't you two meet me at the Bay Horse Café for supper about eleven?" Without waiting for an answer he exclaimed, "Good! I'll see you there." And he was across the room talking to his friend at the bar.

"Well!" exclaimed Phil.

"Looks like you might be set up in business on Walnut or Vine Streets," I whispered excitedly.

"I didn't like the way he patted your hand."

"Don't be silly, Phil. That old goat!"

"That 'old goat' has had more eighteen-year-old girls running in and out of his saloon's back rooms than you could shake a stick at. He likes 'em young."

"So do I," I intoned as I patted Phil's hand.

Phil looked up at me and a smile flitted across his face. "What are we doing here when we could be at home making the bed rattle?"

I looked at him—loving him desperately—and laughed, "We can make the bed rattle any time ... right now I'd rather see Cincinnati, the real Cincinnati."

"Are you sure?" I felt Phil's hand reaching under the table and I slipped one hand under the table and gave him a mock slap on the face with the other. I looked over at the bar and realized that Jake Pittner and Ed Branagan had witnessed the entire vignette.

They were both smiling. I felt myself blushing.

"Phil, who is Ed Branagan?"

"The biggest politician in Cincinnati. He got George B. Cox elected mayor."

"Oh."

"Phil, who were those funny-looking men standing behind Jake Pittner when he was sitting here?"

"His bodyguards. Jake wears over $60,000 worth of diamonds."

"Oh." My boredom in Cincinnati had ceased.

The hour and a half before we were to meet Jake Pittner flew by. We stopped by the Mecca where the prism-glass chandeliers were reflected in the beveled-mirrored walls; where brown-derbied men vied with one another for the gaudiest vests and the flashiest stick-pins. Then we went to The Stag where we saw the massive painting, called *The Sirens*, that had been shipped from France. As we stared at the painting, which showed three nymphs lolling by the sea, Phil once again suggested the "bed rattling" business. Phil was serious; he would forego an opportunity to dine with Jake Pittner, and perhaps gain a prosperous business, to fulfill an immediate sexual urge. Of all the men I've ever known, Phil was the most easily aroused. I changed the subject by asking him to show me the famous bullet hole in the painting, and sure enough we found one. Supposedly, some gentleman had shot his wife's lover through the head and the bullet had continued on into the painting.

We wandered down Vine Street, listening to the music floating on the night air, peering into the beer gardens, watching the hawkers selling their wieners, bratwurst, and frankfurters, and generally mingling with the conglomeration of gamblers, trollops, con men, and ward heelers. I felt as if I had discovered Cincinnati.

The Bay Horse Café was on Fifth Street between Main and Sycamore and was surrounded by at least twenty other bistros. Right in the middle of the street, directly across from the café, was an actual horse market, and even at this hour of the night horse trading was in progress.

We pushed our way through the throngs of merry-makers and saw Jake Pittner coming toward us with both arms extended. You would have thought he was welcoming long-lost relatives.

"I came early to get the gin fizzes going," he gushed.

"Gin fizzes?' I questioned. I had never heard of them.

"Yes. It's a marvelous drink. And the bartenders here shake them for ten minutes, a full ten minutes!"

When the drinks were served, I could see why the gin fizzes at the Bay Horse Café were known the world over. They had a quality unlike anything I've ever tasted since. And another thing that makes them memorable is that they were served by a humorous, cross-eyed waiter who became well-known in later years as the ogler of Mack Sennett's[13] bathing beauties. Our waiter was Ben Turpin[14].

By the time a large brass tea cart was rolled to our table, and our plates filled from copper and silver tureens, Phil and Jake Pittner had reached a deal: Phil was a partner of the Capitol Café.

When we stopped by Cappel's Bar on the way home, Pete was closing up. I sat quietly at the table as Phil and Pete went over the night's receipts. I could tell that Phil was surprised to find that the amount taken in was even greater than it had been the previous Saturday night. He whispered to me later, "Pete must be getting religious. He evidently didn't swipe any money." I had no comment.

It had been a grand night; Phil thought so, too. The minute we closed our door, I could tell by his breathing that Phil's mind was on subjects other than Cincinnati's bar business.

---

13 Mack Sennett (January 17, 1880 – November 5, 1960) was an American film director and producer, known as the King of Comedy.

Born in Canada, he started in films in the Biograph company of New York, he opened Keystone Studios in Edendale, California in 1912. It was the first fully enclosed film stage, and Sennett became famous as the originator of slapstick routines such as pie-throwing and car-chases, as seen in the Keystone Cops films. He also produced short features that displayed his Bathing Beauties, many of whom went on to develop successful acting careers.

14 Ben Turpin (September 19, 1869 – July 1, 1940) was an American comedian and actor, best remembered for his work in silent films. His trademarks were his cross-eyed appearance and adeptness at vigorous physical comedy. Turpin worked with notable performers such as Charlie Chaplin and Laurel and Hardy, and was a part of the Mack Sennett studio team.

North, East, South or West, our SLOE GIN FIZZ is the best!

B-412

Chapter 6

IT ALL really began with a whore named Ella, but she didn't come into the picture until much later. What happened first was that I suddenly wanted to be part of the outside world and told Phil I would like to take a job. I had always been interested in clothes. Back in Cicero Mama had taught me how to sew and I was very good at alterations.

Phil was furious at the idea. He said he was making an adequate income and my place was in the home. But I explained that I needed some outside stimulation. I wanted to meet people. I was lonely.

With all the fantastic events which have happened since, I have never stopped being amazed at the way things somehow tied up. Who would ever have thought that a whore named Ella would become part of the Cappel family? And who would ever have thought that my job in selling ready-to-wear at a place called The Hub would indirectly lead to a whore named Helen?

With the added income, Phil and I moved out of his mother's home and took an apartment of our own. I was no longer bored. I liked my work, I had a feeling of achievement, and the bond between Phil and me was even stronger when I discovered that I was pregnant.

I stayed at The Hub until a few months before our first son, Phil Jr., was born at noon on May 27, 1904.

Phil was thrilled with the baby. I had worried for fear he wouldn't relish being a father, but my fears were groundless. For

< Over-the-Rhine neighborhood, 1905.

several months I did nothing but take care of the baby and bask in the glory of being an ideal wife and mother.

Directly across the hall from our apartment lived a widow, Mrs. Tatewilder, who had little interest in life; she had a small income, but no family, no outside activities. Mrs. Tatewilder and I became close friends. We would sit throughout the day talking and playing with the baby. Mrs. Tatewilder had never been around a child before and she fell head-over-heels in love with Phil, Jr. It was Mrs. Tatewilder who suggested I go back to work. "Helen, you love the ready-to-wear business and you're obviously bored when you spend so much time at home. You know I'd treat little Phil just like my own. Why don't you leave him in my care during the day and resume your job at The Hub?"

"I'd love to, Tate, but Phil wouldn't hear of it. He didn't think I should work before the baby was born; he wouldn't consider such a thing now!"

"Let me talk to him, Helen." Phil didn't see as much of Mrs. Tatewilder as I did, but he admired her enormously. She was middle-aged, well-bred, highly educated. I don't know how she did it, but she convinced Phil that I would be better humored if I continued my former job. Phil actually suggested to me that I go back to work, if I wanted to. And, of course, I did.

The next few years were the most "normal" of my entire adult life. I was an everyday, garden-variety housewife and working mother. I was busy and happy. One of my greatest attributes is an ability for organization; I had my life highly timed and organized. I would do the laundry every Sunday after Phil and I returned from church (although I did accompany him to church, I was never, in my own mind, a real Catholic); on Sunday evenings I would iron and prepare my wardrobe for the coming week. During the week, I had my time organized to spend a maximum number of hours at home. My employer at The Hub was generous in giving me time off if I needed it. Neither my husband nor my child suffered from my outside work, or at least I didn't think so at the time.

Phil, too, had been extremely busy with his work. He had acquired another saloon called the German Village in the teeming German colony known as "Over-the-Rhine." This section of one time or another, by every resident of Cincinnati as he pushed a cart through the streets collecting rags and junk from garbage pails. His hobby of collecting litter was not his sole source of income. He owned practically every house on George Street and nearly all of the squalid tenements in the West End, and he made the rounds of his tenants every week, perched languidly on a sway-back white horse.

Just when and how my husband's cousin, Pete, became infatuated with Ella after her association with Devon had ended, I never learned, but Frances told me that she had heard that he was her pimp and that's why he married her. In any case, they did marry and he moved her from George Street to a more discreet apartment on Smith Street. When I first met Ella—Pete brought her to dinner at Mother Cappel's one Sunday—I thought she was disgusting-looking and loathed her almost as much as I loathed Pete. They deserved each other.

Four or five months after Pete took up with Ella, I was preparing, one morning, to go to work. It was a Wednesday—the day I always sent clothes to the dry cleaners. Phil hadn't gotten home until after five o'clock and was sound asleep in our bed; I hesitated to awaken him for breakfast, and decided I'd ask Mrs. Tatewilder if she'd mind fixing him something to eat when she heard him stirring around. Then I picked up the suit that he had worn the previous day and emptied the pockets before putting the suit in a cleaning bag. The note was in a side pocket. It was brief:

"Phil,
I'll see you tonight at 10:30.
Florence."

I was puzzled. Whom did Phil know named Florence? I didn't recall anyone by that name. I assumed it to be someone connected with his business and thought no more about it. I put the note, along with Phil's wallet and loose change, on the dresser.

That evening Little Phil and I ate dinner with Mother Cappel and Frances at their home. Mother Cappel was reading the baby a story in the parlor and Frances and I were in the kitchen.

Cincinnati was north of lower Central Parkway and contained hundreds of drinking places, many of which were open around the clock. Over-the-Rhine was noted for "a free wienerwurst with every drink," and its Oom-pa-pa bands.

A favorite saying of this era was "I love my wife, but oh you kid!" ... I could not guess then that it had become Phil's philosophy, too.

The whore known as Ella was big and hippy, with the hands and feet of a farm worker. If Ella had had a rag about her head and a hoe in her hands she might have had a certain attractiveness; but with brittle, bleached hair and a voluminous, uncorseted figure under a sleazy dress, she left much to be desired. However, it was reported that she was one of the biggest moneymakers on George Street.

George Street was as much a part of pre-World War I Cincinnati's night scene as Vine Street or Over-the-Rhine. Wedged between West Sixth and West Seventh Streets were three blocks of neat brick houses which, during the day, looked like any other middle-class neighborhood. With dusk, the area came alive with red lights, music from negro orchestras, painted women, and business-minded madams. Door signs on the bordellos proclaimed who resided inside: Claire, Nellie, Ada, Maude, May, and, of course, Ella.

For a price anything was available on George Street. Name your pleasure, gentlemen: white girl, colored girl, high-yellow girl—or any combination thereof. And for the ladies: white men, colored men—in any group to suit the fancy. Or why chance a ride in the woods with your regular lover? Bring her, or him, to George Street where you can scintillate the eye and the imagination with red plush chairs, ornate beds, French chandeliers, silk brocade, and velvet draperies.

George Street was, in a nutshell, the Queen City's Temple of Aphrodite and Adonis. Tenderloin was readily available to fit any pocketbook.

Ella was notorious in Cincinnati and was considered a favorite of the street. She had been, in her time, the companion of William P. Devon, until he married a colored woman. Mr. Devon was one of the richest men west of the Alleghenies but had been seen, at

She was drying the dishes as I washed them. Even though I sometimes became bored with her, when I was around her too much, I loved her dearly and she was devoted to me. Without Frances' companionship, I don't know how I could have survived my lonely early years in Cincinnati. Frances was a big one for family reunions, and it was only through her efforts that the Cappel family and assorted relatives were infrequently pulled together for a family dinner. She had asked me if I would help her with the food for one that was coming up in two weeks.

"I just don't know what to do, Helen. Ham would be a lot simpler to prepare, but we had it the last time. Turkey would be better, but I've never yet had one turn out good; they're either undercooked or overcooked. What do you think I should do?"

"You know me, Frances. I'd choose turkey over ham anytime. I like turkey best two or three days after the feast, when you can make ala king out of it. That's my favorite dish."

"Then you vote for turkey?" she said in a resigned voice.

"Yes, and I'll tell you what, I'll cook it at my apartment and bring it over here."

Frances brightened. "I was hoping you'd offer to do that."

"I know it," I said, laughing.

"You're a pretty nice sister-in-law, Helen."

I was glad that Frances liked me. "Why, thank you, Frances."

"Speaking of sisters-in-law reminds me of cousins-in-law, do you think we'll have to invite that ... that prostitute ... that Pete married?"

"Yes, I do. Pete has always come to the family dinners, and now that he's married, you'll have to ask his wife."

Frances dried and redried a dinner plate before she spoke. "I can hardly stand that Ella, and it has nothing to do with her morals. That's something that is her own concern—and Pete's. I don't like her as a person. She's so sour and disagreeable. And I despise her looks. I do believe she's the most unattractive woman I've ever seen."

"Maybe that's why she does what she does, Frances. I mean because she's so unattractive." I poured the dishpan of water into the wooden sink, shook my hands, and dried them on a towel.

"I don't know about that, Helen. You should see the woman Ella sometimes works for. She's a marvelous-looking creature, even if dyed red hair is considered vulgar. I understand she's in thick with all the city's big wigs. She lives in a swanky apartment at Sixth and Smith Streets. You must have heard about her, Helen. Her name is Florence—Florence Gossett."

The thunderbolt struck. Florence. The name on the note I had found in Phil's pocket. I folded the towel carefully and hung it on the rack before asking, "Does Phil know Florence, Frances?"

"I imagine so. I should think every saloon keeper in the city would know her; she's supposed to be Cincinnati's most famous call madam. You know what that is? That's when men call up on the telephone and the madam directs them to certain prostitutes, then the prostitutes give the madam some of the money. Awful. Well, anyway, Ed told me one time that Ella works for that Gossett woman. And I've heard she wears the most expensive clothes in Cincinnati. I got up enough nerve to ask Ella that Sunday she and Pete came for dinner, and Ella enjoyed talking about her. Ella says that practically all of Florence's clothes come from Chicago or New York."

I was glad I had finished the dishes. My hands were shaking. The note was like a pistol-shot.

Phil didn't get home until after three. I was awake staring into the darkness of our room. He came in quietly and was undressing without lighting a lamp. I had decided on the direct approach and I asked, "Phil, do you know Florence Gossett?"

It was a moment before he spoke and I couldn't see his expression in the dark. "I didn't know you were awake, Helen."

"Do you know Florence Gossett?"

"Sure, I know Florence Gossett. Every saloon owner in Cincinnati knows her. Why?" He had had his explanation ready. It was too logical, too pat. He knew I had read the note.

"Do you know her better than ... most saloon owners?"

His answer came quickly, too quickly. "Maybe. After all, she's Ella's best friend and Pete's married to Ella—and Pete still works for me on weekends and when things are rushed. Sure, I see them around." He had it all worked out too well, and I knew then, definitely, that he was running around with Florence.

As he sat down on his side of the bed I fired at random. I could not bear to lose him but he had to know that I knew.

"You've been stepping out on me, Phil. With that Florence. Please stop it. Promise. If you don't I'll take little Phil and leave you."

His voice was amused.

"Where do you think you'd go, Helen?"

"To Cicero."

"I don't think you'd be welcome there."

"I'd find a place."

"Don't you love me anymore, Helen?" His hands reached for me.

"I don't want to share you with anyone, Phil. Promise you'll stop seeing her. Please."

"You gave up your family for me, Helen. I'd never give you up for someone else."

"You promise then?"

"Yes, Helen. Come here." He pulled me toward him, eager as always. I had to believe him. I could not afford to do anything else.

Chapter 7

MY LIFE SEEMED to have straightened itself out. The crisis over
Florence Gossett appeared to have resolved itself. At first I had
a desire to see her; I merely wanted a glimpse of the woman. I
would occasionally hire a hack and have the driver go slowly as
we approached the corner of Sixth and Smith Streets. I never did
see anyone who might be Florence Gossett and, in time, I stopped
thinking about her.

Phil, Jr., was no longer a baby; he was walking, talking—a
real little boy. I had again quit my job at The Hub, and Little Phil
received too much attention. Even though Mrs. Tatewilder no
longer had the role of official baby sitter, she was still with him,
and me, from morning to night. After a few months I decided to
go back to work; once again I searched the classified section of
the Sunday paper and the ad that appealed to me was small and
inconspicuous:

EXPERIENCED SALESWOMAN WANTED
Outlet for N.Y. mfg. of exceptional apparel.
Sample Coat & Suit Co.
3rd floor Lyric Bldg.
WALK A FLIGHT AND SAVE A DOLLAR

I had never heard of this firm but the next morning I climbed
to the third floor of the Lyric Theatre Building and applied for the
job. Several women had already arrived and there was an hour's

< Fifth Street Cincinnati, 1907.

wait before I had my interview. All the interviewing was being handled by one man. I looked at the other women; they were poorly dressed. I had worn my best black suit accessorized with white. This no-color scheme was to become my uniform in the ready-to-wear field. My experience at The Hub had taught me that in order to sell women's clothes, one must wear good clothes. Customers want, and expect, a clothing saleswoman to look the part.

A tall gentleman said to me, "I'm Walter Wise, owner of the shop. I'm sorry to have kept you waiting—I had no idea so many ladies would answer my small ad."

I looked at him and smiled. "I think it was the word 'exceptional' and the slogan 'Walk a Flight and Save a Dollar'— no woman could pass that by!" I had struck the correct chord because his face suddenly glowed and his eyes danced with self-satisfaction.

"Do you like my slogan?"

"Very much. As I said, no woman could pass it by."

"I made it up as I wrote that ad." He was pleased with himself.

Walter Wise studied the small white card I had filled out. "I hope you realize, Mrs. Cappel, that this room you're in is the extent of the shop." I looked around at a bare space that was only about twenty feet square as he continued, "The garments will be hung on plain metal racks around the room; there will be no fluff, no decorations—only some of the most ordinary, and also some of the most beautiful, ladies' suits and coats ever manufactured in New York. All samples."

"I like clothes, especially good clothes," I said.

"I can see that, Mrs. Cappel. That's one reason I'd like you to work for me. The other reason is that you've had selling experience in ready-to-wear."

"Yes, over three years."

"You're the only woman I've interviewed this morning with more than a few months of sales experience, and I notice that you're experienced at alterations." He glanced again at my card.

"Not that you'd be expected to do alterations, but it's important to know what can be altered and what can't be." He again studied my card, this time in silence. "I'd like very much for you to work here, but I'm afraid the salary I have to offer won't be satisfactory to you."

"What is the salary?"

"Fourteen dollars a week."

"Plus commission?"

"Of course."

"Then I'd be pleased to work here, Mr. Wise ... if you want to hire me." The salary was considerably lower than I had been making at The Hub, but at The Hub I hadn't been on commission. I knew that the commission arrangement was my cup of tea; it added more spice to the job. I liked Walter Wise's frankness and I liked the prospects of the whole set-up.

At that moment the door of the shop opened and one of the most stunning auburn-haired women I had ever seen entered and took a chair. She, too, was dressed in black.

"Could you start the day after tomorrow?" he asked.

"Yes."

"The hours will be eight-thirty until six—with an hour for lunch. Later we might stay open one or two evenings a week and your salary would be adjusted accordingly."

"That will be fine. How many employees will you have, Mr. Wise?"

"Only two salespeople, and a girl for alterations. I'll handle my own bookkeeping ... at least for the time being. We'll all have to pitch in on the housekeeping."

I arose and extended my hand. "Goodbye Mr. Wise, I'll see you the day after tomorrow. .. at eight-thirty."

"Goodbye, Mrs. Cappel."

I turned and looked once again at the auburn-haired lady. I nodded and smiled at her and she returned the greeting. I had no doubt that she would be my selling associate—previous sales experience or not.

Monta Risk was not only lovely to look at, she was lovely to be around. She was stylish, humorous, and a hard worker. I later found she had a knack for selling—even without previous sales experience. Walter Wise, Monta, and I developed into a coordinated team that first week on the job. Each of us felt that the Sample Coat & Suit Company was our baby and we all coddled, fed, and nursed it to radiant health. We worked long hours unpacking all the cumbersome boxes from New York, pricing all garments, and cleaning up the space. As Walter had said, some of the coats and suits were mediocre; but most of them had style, and a few of them had extraordinary hand-tailoring and exquisite details.

"Walk a Flight and Save a Dollar" evidently had great appeal to the women of Cincinnati. Exactly eleven days after we opened the shop every garment in the place was gone—at prices ranging from $18 to $100. Walter wired New York and another shipment was rushed to us; that shipment of thousands of garments vanished from the racks as quickly as had the first. The store's reputation for bargains was made. Monta and I became walking advertisements for Walter Wise. He allowed us to take our pick of the finest garments and buy them at his cost, which was ridiculously low. Within a matter of weeks Monta Risk and I were the most splendidly dressed women in Cincinnati—and we were never seen in anything but suits.

The Sample Coat & Suit Company mushroomed. It was a thrill to us all. Here was selling and excitement and growth. Our salaries were increased, our commissions were larger, and Walter gave Monta and me bonuses and free suits. We had to take over additional space on our floor of the building and hire a full-time stock and clean-up boy. Then we added a second alterations girl and hired another saleswoman.

Time passed swiftly. Within a few short years the company had expanded to three entire floors in the Lyric Building and the personnel roster had grown to thirty-five persons.

My income was good and Phil's income was excellent; it was Phil who suggested that we move to a spacious new apartment on Chateau Avenue in the Price Hill section of the city. Mrs. Tatewilder insisted on moving into a small apartment close to us—she couldn't stand the prospect of not being able to oversee the upbringing of little Phil even though I did have a full-time hired girl to come in every day. So, we all moved to Price Hill—a cloister of upper-middle-class Catholic families.

It had been a busy day at the Sample Coat & Suit Company. I was glad to get home. My head ached and I was afraid I was getting the flu. This, combined with my second pregnancy and Phil's failure to show up for dinner without telephoning, made me terribly irritable. Phil, Jr. must have sensed my feelings because he was good as gold during dinner and even accepted my proposal to read him two bedtime stories the following night rather than the usual one story on this particular night. He went to sleep like a little lamb as soon as I tucked him in bed. The apartment was quiet, and for the first time in twelve hours I felt relaxed as I curled up on the living room sofa with one of my favorite newspapers—the *Chicago Tribune*.

The nausea and churning within me gradually ceased as I read the news articles, the editorials, and looked at the tantalizing advertisements of Marshall Field's, Mandel's, and the other huge stores. The telephone rang and I thought: It's Phil; I hope he's calling to say he'll be home soon; but he's probably calling to say they're having a busy night at the Capitol and he'll stay there overnight on his cot in the back room. Deep within me I knew the Capitol wasn't that busy during the week and I knew he didn't stay on his cot, but I believed him because I didn't want not to believe him.

"I'd like to speak to Phil," said the feminine voice in the telephone. Although I had never heard that voice before, my woman's intuition came rushing at me with the realization that this unidentified voice belonged to my longtime foe, Florence Gossett. How dare she call Phil's home? I felt my breath coming in quick spurts, my heart began to rush wildly and my skin prickled. I was ready to plunge into battle with her.

"He's not home, Miss Gossett," I hissed into the mouthpiece. There was a moment of silence, then a short laugh at the other end of the line. I continued, "I had assumed he was at your place." A quick glance showed me it was a little after 10 p.m.

"So you know who I am?"

"Of course. I've known about you for several years."

"Oh. Did Phil tell you?"

"No. Not intentionally."

"If you know about me, why don't you get out of my way?" Blood began to pound at my temples; I could hardly breathe. If Florence Gossett had been in the room with me, I would have killed her. I tried to keep my voice smooth as I said, "What do you mean 'out of your way'? I'm Mrs. Philip Cappel. I'm married to him!"

"He doesn't love you. He loves me. Why don't you divorce him before the baby is born?"

If a horsewhip had been lashed around my body I couldn't have flinched more. My control was gone. I screamed at her, "Did Phil tell you about the baby?" It was too much; I couldn't believe that Phil had discussed my baby with this woman.

"He didn't have to tell me, I have eyes," she laughed. Her voice was coarse, the rasp of gravel against gravel.

"Eyes?"

"I bought a suit from you recently. I wanted to see you up close. Phil paid for the suit." Again, the gravelly laugh.

I was actually trembling; a pain shot through me. I'm dying, I thought. Should I tell her that I'm dying or should I just die here alone with little Phil asleep in his bed?

"Be wise. Get out, Helen," said the voice and, once more, the horrible laugh. Then the click of the phone as she hung up.

My hand was cemented to the ear piece. I was suspended in space; I stood holding the black mechanism, knowing I was clutching it but unable to let go. Then a crash of cymbals exploded in my head and blaring at me, ricocheting around me came: Helen, Helen, Helen, Helen. She had called me Helen. What right had this creature to call me Helen? Then it passed and I placed the ear piece back in its cradle and turned and went to the sofa and stretched out.

My mind was clear. I didn't sob, I didn't cry. I tried to think of nothing. When that didn't work I concentrated on the pain which was still in my stomach. In order to make that particular pain less I tried to relive the birth of Phil, Jr. I dozed off for a few minutes. When I awoke I went to a drawer of the desk and found a cigarette that had been there for months; someone had dropped it, and I had put it away. I'm thrifty that way.

As I smoked the cigarette I tried to remember customers at the store who had bought suits. There had been hundreds over the past few weeks. What did Florence Gossett look like? I had heard she was red-headed. What red-headed customers had I waited on? Was she tall or short? I believe someone had said she was tall. Tall and red-headed. I remembered a stunning henna-haired woman. Could that have been Florence Gossett?

"Be wise. Get out, Helen!" That's what she had said. Wise or unwise, I decided to go to Florence's. I went to the phone and called Phil's mother's home. Ed answered the telephone and I asked for Frances. She was asleep. I said to wake her up, it was important. Frances' voice was weak, drowsy, when I told her to get dressed, I was coming by in a hack to get her and I wanted her to go somewhere with me. Frances sensed the urgency in my request and didn't even inquire where we were going. She said she'd be ready in twenty minutes. Then I telephoned Mrs. Tatewilder.

"What's wrong, Helen?" she inquired drowsily. Then she became alarmed. "Helen, you're not losing the baby!"

"No, Tate. Everything is all right, I've got to see Frances. It's important. Could you come up here and stay with Phil? He may wake up and be frightened. I'll be back in an hour."

Mrs. Tatewilder knew something was happening. She pleaded with me to tell her, but I didn't. She, too, realized it was something urgent—and maybe she guessed what it was. She said she'd come right up and wait in my apartment until I returned.

A hack was lingering at the corner. It had been exactly twenty minutes from the time of my call to Frances to the time when the cab pulled up in front of the Cappel home. Frances came running out the door.

"Where are we going, Helen?" asked Frances gently.

"To Florence Gossett's."

"Oh, God, no. Mama was right. She said that's where you were going. The telephone woke her."

"Does Mother Cappel know about Florence, too?"

"Yes."

"Then everyone knows."

Frances didn't say anything more for a few moments. Then

she started crying. "Please don't go, Helen."

"I have to."

"He might be there. Oh, God, it will be awful."

"He's not there."

"How do you know?"

"She called the apartment."

Frances was incredulous. "Called the apartment? Florence called you?"

"Yes."

"God. Oh, Helen." Frances took my hand in hers and raised it to her lips and kissed it. "It's hard to believe. I just can't believe that Phil is doing this." I felt her tears on my fingers.

"It's hard to believe, Frances. But it's true. Now I know it for sure."

The hack stopped in front of the darkened drugstore at the corner of Sixth and Smith Streets. The apartment above the drugstore, on the second floor, was ablaze with light. I had been by this same corner many times, over two years before this, trying to catch a glimpse of Florence Gossett—wanting to see what she looked like. Now I had to know.

Frances followed me up the uncarpeted stairs to the hall landing. She was terrified. As I stood looking at the bare wooden door at the head of the stairs I thought: This door leads to the apartment where my first love, my only love, spends his nights; behind it is a woman who knows him as I know him. Then I knocked on the door.

The shock I had suffered when Florence Gossett telephoned my apartment was minor compared to the shock I received when the door opened and I stared up at her. Of course I remembered waiting on her at the store. I even remembered that exact suit she bought. No one could forget a woman that handsome. The hennaed hair, the heavy make-up only played up her stately innate elegance. She was thin, yet well-proportioned. She looked about thirty-five. Older than Phil, I thought.

She smiled as she said, "Now don't tell me you've never seen me before? Monta Risk knows who I am. Didn't she tell you after I left your dress shop?"

I couldn't speak; I shook my head to indicate no. I had even asked Monta who the slick redhead was, but Monta had played dumb.

Florence Gosset was dressed in a deep green velvet dress cut low in front, exposing a creamy white throat and the foothills of an expansive bosom. She toyed at the neckline of the dress with a long, slender hand; on the third finger was an immense, fiery diamond ring. I was transfixed by the glitter and dancing light of the diamond. I still had not been able to utter one word.

The gravel laugh I remembered from the telephone call resounded in my ears once again as she said, "I see you like my diamond. Phil gave it to me."

I had come to see Florence Gossett. Just to see her. But her laugh turned me into a madwoman. This time it was her turn to get a shock. I had been standing there docile, inanimate; then suddenly I was a female animal fighting to protect her cubs and lair. I jumped at Florence with bared fingernails which dug into her hennaed scalp; then I pulled my fingernails down her face with a strength I had never known I possessed. Ribbons of open flesh were cut down each side of her face. When my fingers converged at her chin I continued the powerful fingernail stroke down her bare neck and bosom to the very points of her breasts.

My hands were covered with blood as they reached the velvet neckline of her gown. I yanked with a second wave of strength and ripped the dress down the front and spun her around until her back was facing the stairs—then I pushed her. Head over heels, yelling, screaming, thump, bump, she tumbled. She barely missed Frances who was cringing on the stairs, petrified. Then she landed at the bottom, her feet sticking out the open door to the street.

We stared at the crumpled silent Florence piled in a green velvet heap: I, with my back to the open door of the apartment, and Frances down about three steps clinging to the bannister. Without a word, Frances fled down the stairs and out into the street.

I turned to see Florence's flat. Again, I was in for a surprise; the place was furnished elaborately. It was much finer than my apartment. My eyes landed on a long library table close to the door and there stood a large photograph of Phil in a heavy silver frame. It was a good likeness, one I had never seen before. I stared at it for a split second then grabbed it and slammed it against the wall.

With that act I gained yet another volley of untapped, maddened strength and dashed farther into the living room. I yanked and pulled at the brocaded draperies, tearing rods and all from the windows. Next came a matching pair of hand-painted oil lamps: one crashed against a wall and the other went sailing through a closed window, smashing the glass panes. I was wild, furious in my attempt to destroy Florence Gossett's possessions.

An immense china cabinet came in my furry vision. Behind the curved glass front was row on row of cut glass. I flung a straight-back chair directly at it and the cabinet and its contents exploded like a rocket. Grabbing a decanter of wine, I emptied the contents over the tufted satin loveseat. I retreated toward the still-open front door, then turned to survey my work. At my feet was the photograph of Phil; I snatched it up and ripped the picture from behind its broken glass and carried it with me down the steps.

The heap that was Florence had remained in the same position at the foot of the stairs. I hoped she was dead. As I stepped over her body I saw the diamond ring. The arm that connected to the hand was limp. I put my foot on her wrist, the way farm wives put a foot on the neck of a chicken when they are about to pull off the chicken's head, then I reached down and yanked off the ring and clutched it in my hand. With that I turned and stepped out into the fresh air of the night.

Two policemen came running toward me; one of them blew a whistle. Then I saw Frances behind them. They stopped a few feet in front of me and I held the picture of Phil up like a shield. The street lamp shone directly on it.

"Look, Frances," was all I said. Frances burst into tears.

The police saw Florence Gossett's feet sticking from the doorway and dashed toward her. A hack came around the corner and I flagged it down; then I pulled Frances into the closed cab beside me.

I was never contacted by the police about the episode.

Obviously Phil had taken care of them.

Less than an hour. That is all it had taken. I told Mrs. Tatewilder I would be home within an hour and I was. The pain in my stomach was gone, and I knew I'd sleep well.

Mrs. Tatewilder asked me no questions and I gave no explanations. I washed the dried blood from my hands and ran scalding water over Florence's diamond ring. Then I opened a jar of Mother Cappel's homemade preserves and dropped the ring into it. Next I tore Phil's picture into four equal parts and threw them on the floor in front of our bedroom door. I went into the room, closed the door, and went to bed.

It was almost seven o'clock when I awoke the next morning. I could hear little Phil talking and laughing to himself in his baby bed in the adjoining room. My general routine was to wear a dressing robe until I had dressed little Phil and both of us had had breakfast, then I would dress myself and by that time the hired girl would either have arrived, or I'd leave him at Tate's apartment down the street.

This morning was different; I wanted to digest the events of the previous evening before I got to the store. Since little Phil seemed contented enough, I decided to leave him in bed and let Mrs. Tatewilder dress him and prepare his breakfast. I thought that I would eat downtown. I dressed slowly. My best black suit, tailored black hat with a long narrow feather and white gloves. I was ready to face the world when I opened the door to the living room.

Phil was on the sofa, fully clothed, staring at the ceiling. He needed a shave.

I walked past him without speaking and had my hand on the doorknob of the hall when he said, "You almost killed Florence."

Spinning around, I glared at him, but he continued to stare at the ceiling. "Almost? You mean the bitch isn't dead? Pity. Tell her that the next time I see her I'll finish her off … Imagine her telling me 'Be wise. Get out Helen!'" Then I gave a nasty laugh that was a perfect imitation of one I associated with Florence Gossett.

Phil sprang from the sofa and ran at me, grabbing both of my arms with his big hands. The furies of hell shot from his eyes.

"Get your hands off of me, Phil," I said quietly. He immediately dropped his hands to his sides. The line between our eyes was bared of love. There was nothing but hate between us.

"What are you trying to prove, Helen?"

"I'm not trying to prove anything, Phil. It has already been proved."

"Did breaking Florence's arm and scratching her beyond recognition help you prove it?"

"It did indeed. It proved to me that no two-bit whore is going to get my husband unless I want her to have him. And I want her to have you. I'm getting a divorce."

"Catholics don't get divorced."

"What's that to me? I'm not a Catholic!"

"You're going to stay married to me!"

"Like hell I am. Get out of my way—I'm going to work!"

He grabbed me once again and shook me. I tried to control my voice as I whispered, "What are you trying to do? Kill your unborn baby?" He released me and stood paralyzed with fury.

"Until my divorce, I'd appreciate it if you'd stay out of my sight. Go sit in the hospital with your two-bit whore!"

Phil exploded. "You think you've gotten pretty goddamed smart, don't you? You were a country girl when I married you and you're still a country girl—a slow country girl!"

I clenched my fists. The wrath I felt toward Florence Gossett returned, but now it was directed toward Phil. "Oh, so I'm slow am I? Well, let me tell you something, big shot! When you're at Fifth and Race Streets, I'll be at Seventh and Race Streets. That's how far I'll be ahead of you, you fucking bastard." I unclenched my fist, swung my arm up and slapped him across the face.

Then I opened the door and left.

DOES IT PAY?

The Confessions of MRS. EDDIE MACK, Wife of the Pickpocket and Bank Robber. As Told to HARRIET FERRILL

What sort of a woman is a bank robber's wife?
What sort of child is a bank robber's daughter?
What society do they move in?
What sort of life do they live?
What is the home of a bandit like?
How did they start wrong?
Can a thief ever be happy? Or his wife? Or his baby?
DOES IT PAY?

Eddie Mack (John Jorge) thought himself the cleverest crook in the world. Many times he had long stretches of life, a convict in penitentiaries, and many times he barely escaped them. This last time he just saved himself from being locked away from society by turning squealer. After the Washington Park bank robbery he "squawked" on his pals—as they would have "squawked" on him—to preserve his freedom.

Here is the story of crime and its cast as told by Mrs. Eddie Mack.

Eddie Mack

THE first thing I can remember is that one day a number of strange people came to our house. They walked softly in and out. My mother was asleep, with her arms folded. I cried because she wouldn't wake up. Then they told me she really was dead.

I was Blanche Austin, the baby of the seven Austin children—four sisters and three brothers. We lived in Haytood, near Bloomington, Ill. The relatives came for us children, and we were passed about from one uncle and aunt to another.

I was just 6 then. I remember at one of my aunts' homes my father would romp with a big collie between jobs of carpentry in the village. Once he brought us some thick material for my aunt to make up in dresses. I always cried to be taken away with him, but he had no home for us.

Courtship on the Back Porch.

Eddie was witty and big—he weighed more than 200 pounds then—and the landlady was jealous of me. She told Eddie how my brother-in-law had driven me from his home because of bad hoodoos. Tom and I tried to give a wrong impression of me. But Eddie didn't believe her story. When I knew him better he told me he didn't suppose so innocent a woman as I had ever lived.

The Big City Calls.

When I was 15 I began thinking about opportunities I had heard of from other girls who had gone to the city.

Mack Her First Friend.

There was a woman named Ruby who lived in Lincoln parkway.

Two Weeks of Happiness.

They ran away and Eddie asked me to come to our resting place on the veranda.

He Falls in Love Here.

Then one evening I waited for Eddie to come home from work. The dinner was cold.

Mack Serves His Term.

I was ashamed and humiliated at first when I met some one who knew where my husband was.

Another Home and a Factory Job.

Once when they had let me visit him at central asylum Eddie told me that he had gone into the forgery because he wanted to get money enough to furnish a flat of our own. Then he said, I would be removed from the evil influence of Ruby, the familiar.

Booked on Suspicion.

Eddie had bought a baby buggy, the best he could afford, for $29, and selected the little carriage to say boldly.

Using His Wits.

His work showed the effects of the strain and he lost his job again. For three weeks he looked for a position. The landlady was asking for her rent, the doctors' bills were heavy.

Police Watch the House.

A pickpocket's wife knows no peace if her lover be hunted. Any night he may be brought home dead.

Out in the Street.

I was not strong enough to go to work. I eyed the laundry for the rent, but was too weak to go on long terms.

Eddie Mack in the Mask He Wore the Morning He Participated in the Washington Park Bank Robbery.

Chapter 8

I DIDN'T GO to the store. My body was a mass of raw, vibrating nerves. I needed consolation. Suddenly I thought of Father Lipski; I hadn't seen him since my wedding day. He would have the strength that I needed and could guide me.

Father Lipski talked me out of my divorce plans—not on religious grounds, but for the sake of Phil, Jr., and the unborn child. He pointed out that time would heal my wounds and I should try to find the goodness within me to forgive Phil. When I left Father Lipski's study, I had promised him that I would do nothing until the baby was born, and even after that time I would try to hold onto my marriage.

Don was born on May 1, 1907. I tried not to think of the future as I recuperated from childbirth, but I couldn't focus my mind on anything else.

I decided not to go back to work. The thought haunted me that perhaps my job was at the root of my domestic troubles. I kept reviling myself for accepting the position at the store; perhaps Phil thought I didn't care for my home, my husband, my children. Does a mother really care for these things if she leaves them for ten hours every day when she doesn't need the financial compensation? Yes, I decided, my job was the evil seed that had sprouted in my life, choking off the oxygen of our happiness.

I wouldn't return to the Sample Coat & Suit Company; it was selfishness to even want to return. Pure selfishness to want to gossip, giggle, and idle lunch hours away listening to Monta

Risk and Eleanor Wilson talk of their dates, their nightlife, their plans on what to wear here and there. Ridiculous. Wasteful. Even improper. Hadn't Mother Cappel and Frances given veiled, and then unveiled, hints that nice women didn't work unless someone in the family was starving? Maybe I was depriving some deserving woman of a much needed job. Was I keeping some poor child from getting proper food because I had a job that his widowed mother should be filling? Was I really necessary at the store? Did I really have the sense of style in ready-to-wear that I thought I had? No, of course not, it was selfishness. I liked to be there when the shipping boxes were unpacked because I loved beautiful clothes. I liked to see them, feel them, even hear them. That's why I worked. Selfishness.

Was I really attractive? Did my own appearance have the sophistication that I thought it had? Does an attractive wife lose her husband to a common whore? What is the importance to a woman to be attractive? Does it make her children love her any the better? No, of course not. Immoral. Ridiculous. Am I losing my sanity? Yes. Am I breaking under this emotional strain? Yes. Would it help matters if I killed Phil? Yes. How should I do it? I don't know. Forget it. Concentrate on a project at home—something you've always said you didn't have time to do.

What could occupy my mind? The apartment was looking worn and shabby. Why not redecorate it? Funny I hadn't noticed before how gloomy everything looked. Where to start? The dining room was the worst; there was even a large stain on the ceiling. Probably a leak during the blowing rains last March. How could I have missed seeing that stain before?

It was the year of the Golden Oak Look. Why not have it? The days were fun; searching all the furniture stores to find just the right round table with a diameter split that extended, with leaves added, into a large oval for big-scale dinners. I must remember to tell Frances that the next family reunion could be held at my place. What about the walls? The *Chicago Tribune* had stated that everyone on the Gold Coast had a red dining room; red walls inspired charming dinner conversation. Fruit prints, yes, fruit prints in gilt frames to match the shimmering brass of the new electric chandelier that was to hang rather low over the round Golden Oak table. Could I possibly be frivolous enough to buy a player piano? Wouldn't it be grand? A player piano in that beautiful red dining room. A week was spent comparing player pianos; the choice was a Farney. How nice for the children and for Phil. Phil would love the room; it was really stylish. And with the music—how wonderful our family dinners would be. Just Phil, little Phil, Donnie, and me.

Yes, the days were fun—shopping for furniture, fabrics, and wallpapers. But the nights were lonely. I hated to see the children drop off to sleep in their own room for it meant that I, too, would have to go to bed soon and lie in the darkness, hearing and seeing nothing, only thinking of Florence Gossett's white breasts pressed tautly against my Phil. For over a month Phil had not been home to sleep; Phil had not had a meal in his grand dining room and had never heard the Farney Player Piano.

A second month went by without Phil. I lived from day to day continually muttering a half-formulated prayer directed vaguely upward to a deity as loosely defined as the prayer itself. Then, again, I found myself thinking of ways to kill Phil. Hadn't he killed the spirit that I had hoped would reunite us?

It was all too useless. My love for Phil, along with my deflated spirit, slipped to the bottom of my heart and lay there and sagged. Finally, I accepted the fact: his affair with Florence Gossett had reached the point of no return.

I went back to work. And it was during this bitter period that I encountered Eddie Mack[15].

"May I help you, sir?" The distinguished-looking gentleman was the morning's first customer. Neither Monta nor Eleanor had arrived yet. There had been an unusual snow storm the night before, and I was surprised to see a customer at all.

"Yes, thank you. I'd like to buy a suit for my wife." He explained that they were stopping at the Hotel Sinton en route to New

---

15 Eddie Mack was one of the many names used by the notorious gangster. His real name was John Jerge. He was a skilled bank robber who operated throughout the Midwest and East coast doing jobs for hire from the early 1900s until his death in 1928. His murder, run down by a car in the middle near Times Square in New York City, was never solved and rumored to be a hit.

Orleans for the Mardi Gras; he had all the necessary sizes and measurements and we spent a half hour looking at possibilities, but we couldn't find anything in her exact size.

"I'm sorry, but there doesn't seem to be anything that would fit your wife without alterations."

"Is there one that would be close enough to her measurements that only minor alterations would be required?" He was reexamining a $100 rust wool suit—one of the finest suits we had in stock.

"Yes, sir ... that suit you have there would be about the nearest thing. The waist would need to be taken in and the hem shortened. The jacket seems to be about right—according to the measurements you've given me. However, that is our most expensive suit... ."

"How much is it?"

"A hundred dollars."

"That'll be fine. We'll need it today though. Could it be altered and delivered to our suite at the Sinton this afternoon?"

"Well..." I glanced at the clock. It was almost ten and not another soul had shown up at the shop. Even Walter Wise was missing—and he hadn't called in. The telephone lines must have been down. "I don't really know what to say, sir. None of our other employees have shown up. If the alterations girl and delivery boy don't come, I'm afraid we could never get it to you today." He looked disappointed. Before I knew what I was saying I heard myself telling him, "It doesn't look like I'm going to be very busy today so I'll alter it myself—and deliver it, too, if necessary."

His face exploded into a grin and he said, "Say, that's darned nice of you!" He paid for the suit in cash, and wrote his name and hotel room number on a slip of paper. The name he wrote ... and the name I shall call him ... was Ed Mack. "Thank you, Mr. Mack. Your wife will have her suit by six o'clock this evening."

I had one additional customer that day but no employees.

Walter Wise finally got a call through to me saying he was snowbound at home; no one else even bothered to call.

I spent the entire afternoon altering the wool suit. At five o'clock it was alarmingly dark and still snowing. I was surprised that I was able to get a telephone call through to Mrs. Tatewilder. Tate said everybody was snug at home and not to worry. I told her that I hadn't been out all day, and didn't know what the transportation situation was, so if I didn't get home at all, not to worry because I'd stay at a downtown hotel. Then I folded the suit in tissue paper, placed it in a box, and sloshed out in the snow.

Mr. Mack opened the door of the suite himself. He was surprised to see me. "I can't believe that anyone would go out in this weather to deliver a suit!"

"Well, I told you I would—and here it is." Then Mrs. Mack came to the door and introduced herself. She was plain and pale, but sweet-looking. I liked her.

"Do come in, Mrs. Cappel, you must be half frozen after being out in all that snow." She turned to her husband. "Eddie, get Mrs. Cappel a glass of sherry."

I stepped into the parlor of their suite and handed Mrs. Mack the suit box. We were soon talking and sipping sherry as if we had known each other for years. Mrs. Mack excused herself and tried on her new suit; it fit perfectly. When they asked me to stay to dinner I accepted readily. We had dinner in their suite, simple and friendly. When I left them, Ed Mack insisted on my accepting an extra ten dollars, and I accepted it because I knew I would have to get myself a room at the Sinton. A real blizzard had hit Cincinnati. That was my first encounter with Eddie Mack.

My second encounter with Eddie was to be after Christmas of 1913; I was reading the *Chicago Tribune* and his photograph stared at me from the front page. It was the headline story: a large South Side bank had been robbed of $250,000 cash by a lone bandit. The bandit was suave, beautifully tailored. He was polite to the bank personnel and to the customers who happened to be about. He wore no disguise. He was well known as a companion to various political figures. He was easily identified as Mack.

He had vanished with his haul. Where was Mack? There was no way of knowing then that the man I call Eddie Mack would one day play a significant role in the bizarre pattern of my life.

The years of 1910, 1911, and 1912 were barren and painful. For months at a time I'm sure Phil gave up Florence, but he always returned to her. He couldn't break away from her sorcery. Frances and Mother Cappel comforted me in my loneliness and Monta became my only contact with laughter. Phil, Jr. was in the third grade at school and Donnie was in kindergarten. I had been married for nine years, and many of these years had been a trial of my own personal strength.

That is the way matters stood on that day when Monta asked me to double date with her and I accepted the invitation. She had been trying for several years to get me to go out with her traveling salesmen companions and I had always refused. But not this time.

I couldn't concentrate on my work. Several times I had to ask a customer to repeat what she had just said. Everything was set, little Phil and Donnie were both going to spend the night at Tate's apartment, but it was no use, I decided I couldn't go through with the date. If Phil had no regard for our marriage, I did. It was something sacred—even if it was a one-sided deal in the Cappel home. I hadn't looked at another man in nine years. But here I was with a date. In less than six hours I was to meet him at the Hotel Gibson. I would be stepping out on my husband.

Even as upset as I was, I had to smile sourly to myself. Stepping out on my husband, indeed! Sometimes days would go by without my even seeing Phil. Where he stayed I didn't inquire; Florence's, I suppose. I would have divorced him months ago, even over the objections and arguments of Father Lipski and Mother Cappel, had it not been for one obstacle: In Ohio, at that time, when parents got a divorce, the boys always went to the father and the girls went to the mother. I couldn't bear the thought of being separated from my babies; that may sound strange coming from me, but it's true.

The frayed ribbons of our marriage were strained to the snapping point, but still I held some shreds of hope. If only Phil would say, "Forgive me, Helen," it could all still turn out differently. I had vented my wrath, which stemmed from crushed pride, on him. I had told him I hated and despised him, but deep within me I knew that I still wanted him. I had to try one more time.

"Idiot!" I cried aloud to myself as I stood alone in a deserted corner of the store. "Go to him! Beg him to come back!"

It was two o'clock in the afternoon when I reached that decision. I had my hat and coat on when I told Monta I was sorry but I couldn't go on the date. She gave me an amused smile and said, "Well, it's too late to get anyone else, so if you change your mind we'll see you at the Gibson Bar. Seven o'clock."

I told Walter Wise I was feeling faint and was leaving for the afternoon. I went to a phone and called the saloon.

"Is Phil there, Ed?"

"No, Helen. He's never here this early." Then his voice became anxious. "Anything wrong?"

"Nothing's wrong, I just want to see Phil a moment." I'm sure my voice revealed disappointment.

"He'll be in about four and I'll tell him you ... wait a minute, Helen, he just walked in!"

"Tell him I'm coming right over." I hung up the phone. As I walked hurriedly to the Capitol, I prayed that what I was about to do would be the salvation of the union between Phil and me.

Phil was sitting at a rear table by himself. An open ledger was before him. About five or six men were standing at the bar talking to Ed. Ed spoke as I walked by and I murmured a greeting without looking at him. I went directly to Phil.

"Phil, I want to talk to you. It's important to me—to us."

As I looked at his unsmiling face I noticed how strained he looked. There were lines about the mouth and eyes. His hair had grown darker. But he was still the most attractive man I had ever seen.

"You know I don't like you to come here," he snapped. He remained seated.

I sat down in a chair next to his as I said, "I know, I know. But it's important! Phil, let's try again."

He looked down at the ledger, slowly closed it and pushed it to one side before answering. Without looking at me he asked, "Don't you think it's too late for that?"

My voice came out in a high pitch that carried to the bar, "No! No, it's not too late! Come back to me! I want you back! Let's start again, please!" The men at the bar turned and looked at us. A flush rose up Phil's face.

He gritted his teeth and whispered angrily. "This is a hell of a place for this conversation. We'll talk about it later."

"I don't want to talk about it later! I want to talk about it now—today—Now!"

"Shut up, Helen, and get out of here. I'm in a rush. I have an appointment." He was mad. He arose.

I grabbed his hand and held onto it tightly. I whispered, "Please, Phil, please!" Then I blurted out, "I have a date tonight. I don't want to go. Please, don't make me go."

A sarcastic smile flitted across his mouth, but his eyes were cold as steel. "So you have a date? Well, now, I didn't know slow little country girls had dates after they were married! Don't be a fool, Helen. Go home."

He took the ledger and walked to the bar, tossing the book toward Ed. One of the men standing at the bar gave a loud guffaw and bellowed, "I hope your luck's better at the racetrack than it is here!" All the patrons snickered. Phil walked to the little room at the rear and slammed the door. He didn't look in my direction. I pulled myself to my feet and walked to the entrance. Ed came running up and as I passed him he said, "I'm awful sorry, Helen."

I blinked as I stepped into the brilliant sunlight. It had gone badly. Just like a second-rate, showboat melodrama: the poor wife coming to a saloon, begging the wayward husband to come home. God, it had gone badly. I'm not as important as his appointment. He's going to the racetrack, probably with Jake Pittner and Ed Branagan. Well, I'm not defeated. I'm going to make him come back to me. I've got to. I want him.

My explanation to Walter Wise for leaving the store had been that I was feeling faint. Now I really did feel faint. I had never fainted before in my life. The fourth building down from the Capitol Bar was empty. The recessed entrance had a boarded-up door. It was just back a few feet from the sidewalk, but it was secluded. I leaned against the boarded-up door and then stared blankly as a hack stopped in front of the Capitol Bar and Phil walked briskly to it. He placed his hand on the knob. He had on his best suit and a brand new hat. The hack door flew open and as

Phil climbed inside I saw the great, green cloak and the hennaed hair. The hack rolled away.

Time stood still. The racetrack. He was taking her to Latonia. I had never been to Latonia Racetrack. A slow country girl. Now I knew what to do.

I walked to Jonap's Store. I had seen the hat and had admired the color, but I didn't think it was for me. Now I bought it. I stopped at the cosmetic counter on the way out and bought brilliant lipstick and a new product containing belladonna advertised "to make the eyes glitter with fire." Then up the familiar flights of stairs to the Sample Coat & Suit Company. I walked to a rack next to the wall and pulled the suit off the hanger. I had tried it on before; I knew it fit perfectly. I folded it into a box. Monta walked up to me and asked, "What's up? You feeling better?'

"I'm feeling fine, Monta. Please make a ticket out for me and charge this suit to my account."

"Oh. The time is now, huh?'

"The time is now. I'll see you in the Gibson Bar at seven." At five-thirty I was in the tub. Then I sprayed myself with cologne and pulled the red sheer wool suit from the box, thinking: A scarlet suit for a scarlet woman.

The hat was exactly the same color with a mound of red plumes falling into a sweep by my face. Into each eye went one drop of belladonna and then on my pale lips was slashed the red lipstick. I went to the kitchen and poured the jar of Mother Cappel's homemade preserves into the sink and held Florence Gossett's diamond under the hot water tap. I dropped my small ruby ring with its petite diamonds onto the slush of the water-sodden preserves and slipped on the gigantic diamond that once was Florence's. It was my only accessory, my only relief to the smash of scarlet.

Standing before my mirror I spoke to the memory of Phil, as he looked when he had glared at me that afternoon. "Slow country girl, hell, I can be a fancy woman, too, Phil."

Then I turned and walked...no, strutted...down the primrose path.

Chapter 9

MONTA INTRODUCED Nate Lehman to me. As I had walked up to their table he had inspected me from head to foot. He evidently approved of what he saw. I had expected someone bald, middle-aged—what I considered the typical New York ready-to-wear representative. Instead, I was face-to-face with a combination, in looks, of Harry Levinson and David Ardman. The thought flitted through my mind: I'm glad I came.

I bent my head over the match he held for my cigarette. I still didn't care for smoking, but "fancy women" always smoked, just as they wore lipstick. "Did anyone ever tell you you're beautiful, Helen?" His voice was low, husky.

"Not in a long time, Nate." I gave him what I hoped was a coquettish smile. "We slow, country girls, in Cincinnati, aren't used to such gallantry."

"You're about as un-slow and un-country as anyone I've ever seen." This was all nothing but talk, traveling salesman talk, but it was salve to the wounds of my pride. I was young again, whereas I had been old at twenty-seven. Life was fun again!

"What do you want to drink, Helen?"

I glanced at the low glasses before Monta and her date. "What are you drinking, Monta?"

"A Sazarac—discovered in New Orleans and made New York style—to make you forget your troubles," laughed Monta.

"Sounds marvelous—that's what I'll have, Nate."

Sazarac cocktails and I developed a quick friendship. We went from the Gibson across the river to the fabulous Coty's: laughing, dancing, teasing, drinking the hours away. Just before midnight we returned to Cincinnati and Foucar's for supper.

I knew as our party entered that, of all the bistros in Cincinnati, this was the most likely location for running into Phil's friends, or even Phil himself. It was sure to get back to Phil that I had been at Foucar's. Perhaps I should suggest going somewhere else! Then it came to me: That's why I came tonight; that's why I'm dressed this way; I want Phil to know I accepted this date; I want to hurt his pride the way he has hurt me.

I saw Florence Gossett before she saw me. Both Phil and Jake Pittner had their backs to the entrance. Florence was waving her hands animatedly as punctuation for whatever she was saying. Her green cloak was draped about her shoulders and her mouth was open in speech. Then she saw me and froze; her mouth remained open and her slender hands remained poised in the air.

I had my right arm through Nate's as we walked smartly behind the headwaiter, absorbed in each other. Phil and Jake Pittner turned in their chairs to see what had stunned Florence. I directed my full attention to Nate. Just as we passed their table I extended my left arm in a wide sweep and ran my fingers down the plumes of my hat, knowing that the large diamond would catch the light of the candles and dazzle Florence—just as it had dazzled me the first time I had seen it! Nate said something and I laughed—the loud, deep, hoarse, gravelly laugh of Florence Gossett.

It was my moment, my performance. And I knew, without looking at my audience, the effect it had on them.

Each time there was a movement close to our table I hoped it would be Phil: jealous, ready to smash his fist into Nate's face, ready even to strike me! I wanted him to create a scene, to fight for me. But he didn't even enter the room we were in. He's glad, I mused to myself; glad to be set free with his Florence. Then I shut off my mind to Phil and concentrated on Nate and a steady procession of Sazarac cocktails. I was getting drunk and I didn't care.

Phil and Florence had evidently gone; perhaps they had left as soon as we arrived. As our party prepared to leave the restaurant

I saw Ed Branagan standing at the bar. His eyes twinkled and an amused smile flirted across his face as he bowed, ever so slightly, at me.

Nate's hand held my elbow in a firm grip as we said goodnight to Monta and her escort on the sidewalk in front of Foucar's. As their hack pulled away, I felt a moment of terror. I was alone with Nate Lehman. I wasn't dumb enough to think that a large amount of money had been spent on me that evening merely because Nate wanted a nightclub companion. The glow of the streetlight fell into his eyes. The way he looked at me left no doubt as to what he wanted. When Phil had first looked at me that way it had meaning. We had been in love. But this was not love. This was just for raw, plain fucking. I hesitated, but for a moment. I had been alone too long. I returned Nate's look. Raw, plain fucking was fine with me. But where could we go?

My home? Never. The room he was sharing with his partner? No, Monta might be there. Only one place seemed logical—George Street—and luckily Nate had heard of it too. He whispered to the cab driver and we were taken to an establishment called Isabelle's. We were directed to a sumptuous, private bedroom. The decoration of the room surpassed the descriptions I had heard of the lavish bordellos; there was a great Aubusson rug, tapestried French furniture, a pier mirror flanked by black and gold winged figures holding sconces with dozens of candles—but only a few were lighted.

I had pangs of conscience when I awoke, but I rejected them. I refused to have regrets. Nate was sleeping heavily. There was no way to know what time it was. I dressed quickly, then reached for my hat. As I lifted the hat, five $10 bills fluttered to the floor. Fury rose within me. I looked at Nate; then back at the paper money. I stared at it for seconds. Slowly, I stooped, reached for the money, and stuffed it into the bodice of my suit.

As I slipped out the side door of Isabelle's the early morning sun was rising over Cincinnati. I remembered the letter in which Pa had called me a whore. But my eyes were dry and I felt a sense of elation. I liked being valued. Nobody would ever call me a slow country girl again.

I have found throughout my life that when you are ready for something, that something is also ready for you. As though I had beamed out a message to the world that I was ready to become a woman of pleasure—and rewards—the first call came on the same day, in the late afternoon while I was still at the store. The caller was none other than the powerful Ed Branagan. He had seen me the night before at Foucar's and he wanted to grasp his opportunity quickly. He asked me to have dinner with him.

"I'd love to, Ed, but I'm tired. How about giving me a raincheck?"

"All right, I'll give you a raincheck until midnight. Instead of dinner, we'll have midnight supper. That'll give you a few hours to get rested. What do you say?"

"I say that sounds grand. Tell me where and I'll meet you."

"Would you prefer some ... uh, out-of-the-way place across the river, or somewhere in Cincinnati?"

"I think I'd prefer some out-of-the-way place in Cincinnati, such as The Mecca."

He roared with laughter. "Where have you been all these years, Helen?"

"Getting myself prepared for you, Ed. The Mecca, then, at midnight." I hung up the phone.

I found a teal blue faille suit that had come in a recent shipment. I told one of the alterations girls to stop whatever she was doing and work on my new suit. Then I made out a ticket and charged it to myself. That's when I decided there's overhead expense to being a party girl.

I was bold and shameless in my relationship with Ed Branagan. In no way did I care for him, and I exploited him to the fullest extent. At times, during the affair, I had great remorse, not only because of my conduct, but because I knew that I was only using Ed as a weapon to strike back at Phil.

Of all the powerful and cruel weapons I could have chosen, Ed was at the top of the list on both counts. He was powerful because of his financial interests, along with Jake Pittner, in Phil's businesses; a mere request to Ed would have pulled the skids from beneath Phil's bars. He was also powerful because of his political pull. Many of the prominent citizens of Cincinnati were demanding that George and Smith Streets be wiped clean of their girls; I could have said, "Ed, get rid of Florence Gossett," and she would have been on the first train out of Cincinnati. He was a cruel weapon because of all the men that Phil had known, Ed was his ideal; he admired Ed for his forthrightness, his great sense of business, and his personal style. So here was this ideal ... this man on a pedestal ... the paramour of Phil's own wife. Sheer irony, I thought.

Ed Branagan lavished gifts on me: jewelry, furs, money. I used his personal hack to go to and from the store. I even sat in his private box at Latonia Racetrack.

It was at Latonia during the fall meet that an incident occurred which, in some strange way, shaped the direction of my life. It was the day when two famous jockeys, brothers known as "Goose" and "Ganz," were ruled off the tracks forever. A stable boy was riding a thirty-to-one longshot named Silklady; as the horses came into the home stretch, in full view of the clubhouse and grandstand patrons, Silklady was ahead by half a length. Then "Goose" and "Ganz" closed up on either side of Silklady and enclosed her in a pocket. The brothers both whipped her with their crops and she fell. The crowd of spectators were shocked, then indignant, then enraged. People climbed the low fences and spilled from the grandstand walls in a mass of thousands—all intent on getting at "Goose" and "Ganz." The two jockeys were mauled by the mob but escaped with their lives.

The unruly crowds were screaming insults at the jockeys when, suddenly, a shot rang out and a stillness descended on the racetrack. Silklady had broken her front legs and the officials had shot her where she lay on the track in front of the clubhouse. That silence, from the group that had been hysterical only moments before, was a tribute to a spirited horse and a gallant, unknown little stable boy who, for the first time, had ridden a winner.

I was possessed by the memory of that racetrack incident. I dreamed about it night after night; in my dream I was Silklady —racing, racing toward a victorious finish—then, suddenly, I was being whipped by riding crops on both sides and being pushed, crowded, smothered. Then I would trip and fall down, down, down ... At this point I always awoke. It was horrifying.

If psychiatrists had been as plentiful in those days as they are now, perhaps I could have gotten myself straightened out. Instead I tried to analyze the dream myself and in doing so it was on my mind continually. Finally, I theorized that it was Phil whipping me and the life I was living with Ed Branagan that was smothering me. Phil had not made a single move to reach me. It was time to leave Cincinnati, it was time to make a definite break. I hired a lawyer to start divorce proceedings. Sooner or later, I was certain, Phil would try to get custody of the children. I knew instinctively that I had to act fast. I also knew that I would have to make a terribly hard decision.

There was no one to turn to. It was something I had to work out on my own. I couldn't deprive Phil of both our children. I would leave him one and take the other.

It was March and very cold. I made arrangements for little Phil, whose stern mind always made me think of Pa, to spend the weekend with his Grandmother Cappel. Of course I did not explain that it was a weekend that would last for years. Ed came to get little Phil, and as soon as they left I finished my packing. I held back my tears. I was leaving my first-born, perhaps never to see him again. My heart hammered violently as I bundled Donnie up in his winter coat and toboggan cap. I slipped Florence Gossett's diamond ring in with the rest of my jewelry, and took one last look at the apartment I had refurnished with such high hopes of a reunion with my husband.

I turned the front door key but left it in the lock. I've often wondered whatever happened to the goddamed Farney Player Piano.

Chapter 10

DURING THE FIRST PART of the Twentieth Century it seems that everyone who wanted to disappear "went West." Well, why not? I didn't know where I wanted to go—just West; but I did know that Chicago was the changing point for all the westbound trains. I purchased tickets for Donnie and myself to Chicago and we left on the midnight train. That first night in the sleeping car I didn't close my eyes; I foundered with self-pity. The next morning, after arriving in Chicago, I looked at one of those big train boards and decided on Tucson, probably because it sounded warm compared to the Chicago weather that day. Next, I came to a resolution that I've kept for over fifty years: Live a little, Helen, things could get worse!

With that resolution planted firmly in mind, I took Donnie to the washroom and brushed his hair; then I turned my attention on myself. I couldn't have chosen a more somber hat for traveling West! It was dark and tailored, too severe for a girl who had decided to "live a little." I pinked my lips with rouge, slipped on Florence Gossett's diamond ring, and took Donnie with me to the hat salon at Marshall Field & Company. I had already learned something that many women never wake up to: if you want service and courtesy in a store, wear diamonds.

I had never been in Marshall Field's. I loved the place. The hat I bought cost sixty dollars; it was huge and topaz-colored. I threw the old dark one in a wastebasket. At one-thirty we got on the "Golden State Limited" that was to take us to Tucson, and I took stock of my money. My purse had contained about three hundred dollars when I walked out the door of my apartment; our train tickets had cost a hundred and twenty-five and the hat had been sixty. I had just a little over a hundred dollars to see us through. Through to what? Damn it, I thought, looking at Ed Branagan's sable wrap, I can sell that if I have to. Oh, well, if I sell it there'll probably be more of them available where that one came from!

Early in the evening Donnie dropped off to sleep in our compartment and I wandered into the parlor car. The place was filled with traveling men from all walks of business life. They were smoking and laughing—obviously telling jokes. I took them by surprise; they all stopped talking. In the stillness that followed you could have heard a pin drop. I spoke up quickly and said, "Carry on, gentlemen, I enjoy a good joke, too!" They all arose in a single group and each one offered me his individual seat. Laughingly I said, "Perhaps I had better take this vacant seat." The men sitting on either side of the vacant seat thought I had made a wise choice. From the many conversations that I had, which lasted until after midnight, I knew that I had passed my first test in learning how to "live a little."

I couldn't wait to arrive in Tucson; everyone said it would be so warm and colorful. It turned out to be warm, but not particularly colorful. It was late in the afternoon when Donnie and I got off the train and made our way into the adobe depot. A lone man sat behind the ticket counter and he scrutinized us as we entered. I left Donnie sitting on a bench and walked to the counter.

From beneath layers of leathery wrinkles, his mouth moved and he gave me the warm greeting of the Old West: "Yes'm?"

"I'm a stranger to Tucson; I would like to get a room for my son and myself. Could you please direct me to the city's nicest hotel?" I smiled pleasantly.

His eyes darted to Donnie and then back to me. "Yes'm."

Then he walked to the window and pointed to a large frame hotel about two blocks down the street. "The Grand. Good as any."

There were no women at all in the lobby; the handful of men scattered around the room gave me their undivided attention as I marched straight toward the registration desk.

The man behind the desk just stared at me as I said, "My son and I want a room. The station agent at the depot sent us over here." Without a word he turned a huge ledger around and pushed it toward me. As I was registering—Mrs. Helen Cappel & Son, Don, Chicago—the desk clerk spoke his first words.

"From the East, huh?"

"Yes."

"How long are you staying?"

"I don't know."

He handed me a key and said, "Room 217 at the head of the stairs."

Donnie and I found our room without help of a bellboy, since they didn't seem to have one. The room had two large beds, one chair, a big table, and small chest of drawers.

Poor, tired little Donnie sat on the side of a bed and immediately went to sleep. Gently, he fell back onto the bed. I covered him with blankets and let him sleep peacefully. I looked at Donnie and decided he needed sleep more than food. I dressed myself in fresh clothes and descended to the "grand" lobby of the Grand Hotel.

Only one man was seated in the dining section and as I sat down at a table only a few feet from him, memory stirred through me like a swizzle stick in a sazarac—it was Eddie!

Eddie who had bought a suit in Cincinnati for his wife; Eddie, still looking as distinguished as he had some years before.

A waiter came over and asked me what I'd have; I asked for a chicken sandwich and he allowed that the only kind of sandwich they had was beef. I told him that would be all right. He started toward the kitchen and was called by Eddie M.

Eddie whispered a few words, then both of the men looked at me. The waiter came back to my table and said the gentleman, he nodded toward Eddie, would like to join me and did I mind? I told him it was agreeable and he relayed my message to Eddie. I assumed that Eddie had recognized me, too.

"Thank you for allowing me to join you." He was standing directly in front of me.

I motioned toward a chair and said, "Please sit down."

He introduced himself by a fictitious name and said he was

a cattle man from Colorado. I did not offer my name. After a few moments of talking to him I realized that he had not recognized me. As we talked of generalities—mainly war news and the pleasant weather—I decided to let him know that I knew who he was, and I took the surprise tactic. "How long have you been here . . . Mr. M---?"

Every muscle of his body flinched. He made a motion as if to rise, thought better of it, and stared at me in silence. Then he said, "I know you from somewhere, don't I?"

"Yes."

"Where?"

"Cincinnati. Years ago. You and your wife—at least you introduced her as your wife—were going to New Orleans. I sold you a suit for her."

"Yes, I remember now. It was snowing."

"One of the biggest snows ever to hit Cincinnati."

"It was my wife."

"I thought it was. Is she well?"

"No. She's very ill."

"Is she in Chicago?"

He looked at me searchingly. "You have a real memory, don't you?"

"Yes. I have a fine memory. I never forget a face."

Eddie looked down at the tablecloth for a moment then looked up at me. "I remember it all now. We had a pleasant evening with you."

"I had a pleasant evening with you, too." I smiled at him and said, "If it will ease your mind, I'll confide that I prefer not to be recognized in Tucson, too."

Soon I was telling him the whole story of why and how I had left Cincinnati. Our food came, and as he was finishing his second cup of coffee, and I was draining my second glass of milk, he told me in veiled terms that he had been connected with the Chicago bank robbery. He didn't go into any details and I asked him no questions; I had learned from Ed Branagan never to ask questions.

"What are your plans, Helen? Where do you intend to go from here?"

"I don't really know, Eddie. I want to vanish for a while. Maybe I'll stay right here. I'm not broke, but I will be soon. But as my Pa used to say, 'I've made my bed, now I'll have to lie in it.'"

The waiter poured Eddie another cup of coffee and he sipped it in silence. I felt warm and comfortable and the shaking and rattling of the train seemed to be ebbing out of me. I was tired and nothing seemed important but crawling into bed and getting about twelve hours of sleep. Eddie stirred in his chair and said, "Helen, I have a proposition for you."

"I'm afraid I'm not interested in a proposition, Eddie. I'm far too tired for such a thing." I actually yawned.

"I don't mean that; I mean for the next few months." He leaned his elbows on the table and spoke softly. "I'm staying at a fishing cabin on the Old Gold Rush Trail out of Carpentersville, Colorado. It's way up in the mountains. I'm dying of boredom. That's why I took this chance and came to Tucson for a few days. If you'll return to the cabin and keep me company, I'll make it worth your while. You said you wanted to vanish for a while. Here's your chance."

"Eddie, do you realize I have a seven-year-old son asleep upstairs?"

"Yes, of course. I saw you as you came in."

"Do you suggest that I take my son to some Colorado fishing cabin in the middle of March?" I asked incredulously.

"No, we'll enter him in a private boarding school; a fine military school that I know of. They have what they call a junior school for boys entering the primary grades. I would pay his tuition."

I didn't know what to say.

Eddie must have taken my silence as a refusal because he continued, "It is a wonderful school, Helen. It would be good for the boy—really much better than … traveling with you." I was still thinking about the possibilities as he pressed on urgently, "I'll pay four full years of tuition for him; if you don't want to send him back there after the summer, you can always get a refund on the money."

"Do you mean, Eddie, that you will pay Donnie's tuition to a military school for four years if I'll stay at a fishing cabin with you?"

"Yes, if you'll stay until ... well, maybe the first of September."

"What about during the summer? Schools are usually out about the first week of June. Where will he go then?"

"They have a summer camp right there during June, July, and August. He can stay until you get him. I'll pay the entire tuition for four full years."

"What would all this tuition be worth in cold cash, Eddie?"

"Several thousand dollars a year, I'd estimate. About ten thousand dollars for four years."

"Then, in other words, you'd give me approximately ten thousand dollars to stay until the first of September with you?"

"Yes."

"Would I be able to see Donnie frequently?"

He didn't answer for a moment. Then he said quietly, "I'm afraid not, Helen. Once we get to the cabin I'm afraid we'd have to stay put for a while. But you could see him in late May—about that time the summer season opens up around those parts and your coming and going wouldn't create suspicion."

Eddie's proposition had some definite appeal to it. It would, at least, assure Donnie of being in a proper atmosphere while I collected and coordinated my own life. "Is the cabin comfortable?"

Again, Eddie hesitated before answering. "Yes," he stated flatly. "It's not what you're used to, but it could be considered comfortable."

I toyed with the salt shaker, moving it first on one side of the pepper shaker and then on the other. Suddenly, Eddie leaned across the table and whispered, "I'll pay your son's tuition and also give you six thousand cash if you'll go with me—that will add up to about eighteen thousand dollars. But I want you to know before you go that it's terribly cold and lonely in those mountains. I don't think I could stand to return there alone."

I looked at Eddie and wondered what distressed fate had brought me into an alliance with a bank robber. In my mind's eye I caught a volatile glimpse of the Helen that ought to be, but wasn't, and so I said in a firm voice, "It's a deal, Eddie. I'll see you in the morning at the breakfast table. I've got to go to bed now—my own bed."

The next morning Eddie gave me an envelope containing eighteen thousand dollars in large bills. I was flabbergasted. I was touched to think that he trusted me enough to give me all of it at one time. Before Donnie and I left for the military school I gave Eddie my word that I would join him in Denver in exactly ten days. My new life had started on a high note. I felt alive and optimistic.

Donnie liked the school from the very beginning. I received permission from the headmaster—or commandant, as they called him—to attend classes and take my meals in the "mess hall" for two days to get Donnie settled in his new surroundings. I left word at the registrar's office that I could always be reached at general delivery in Denver. Then I took the train for Denver, just as I had promised Eddie I would, and he met me at the depot

We spent the first night in Denver and started the next morning for the hideaway cabin. It took the better part of the day to reach it—and what a trip! If you've never been in a mule cart—and all uphill—you won't appreciate the shaking up that went on. I could name some odd places of assignation, but this one topped them all. I don't mind being shaken up—but not on—a half-assed hill.

If you'll think of an all-white picture with one dot of color, you'll see us going up the side of our mountain in that cart. The dot of color was my topaz hat. I was dressed for traveling: my suit, my quarter-length coat, Ed Branagan's sable wrap, and, of course, the Marshall Field's hat. It was a stunning outfit, but not intended for mule carts. Large, pristine flakes of snow began falling and soon covered everything but my hat (I kept shaking the snow off of it). God damn it, I thought, this beats all. You've done some stupid things, Helen, but accepting this arrangement takes the cake! After an hour of brushing and shaking snow off my hat, I delved into a suitcase and pulled out a blouse. I managed to wrap the blouse around my head (hat and all) and tie the sleeves under my chin; then I sort of buttoned up the buttons until nothing was exposed but my nose and eyes. Cold, Jesus! Eddie and I had ceased trying to talk. Words seemed to freeze in the air, then blow back into our numb faces.

Finally, Eddie shouted at me and pointed upward. "There it is, Helen!" Directly above us, skewered to the side of the mountain, was the face of a little cabin barely visible under tons of snow. Home, I thought sourly, what a hell of a place to be holed up in!

Actually, the cabin wasn't too bad. After a few days, when I got myself thoroughly thawed out, I cleaned it completely and it was quite livable. During the days that followed I was more relaxed, more rested than I had been in years. I put everything out of my mind except the problem at hand: melting snow to make water for drinking, cooking, and cleaning; trying to make interesting meals out of the uninspired stock of food staples; dreaming up new ways to prepare brook trout. Brook trout! I can hardly think of trout without gagging. Eddie was crazy about fishing and every day he would plow and flounder through the snow to a trout stream he had discovered and every evening I would have a new batch of brook trout to cook. We ate it day after day for almost five months.

Eddie and I became good friends; and friends is the correct term. Never once during our entire association were we ever intimate. Strange? I thought so too. But restful, very restful. In the evenings, after supper, Eddie and I would sit before the rough-stone fireplace and tell each other about our lives. He was deeply in love with his wife and devoted to his daughter; he talked about them for hours on end. It was only a matter of time until Eddie confided the whole story of the Chicago bank robbery to me; I didn't prod him on, I allowed him to tell it when he was ready to tell it.

The robbery had been committed with the blessings of some highly placed Chicago officials. They had actually planned it for Eddie, including his getaway from Chicago and his hiding place. Two brothers were hired, at a price of twenty-five thousand dollars each, to drive the getaway car and take the rap, if caught, for aiding a fugitive from justice (they weren't caught). The price to the officials: twenty-five thousand, plus high rental on the gang-owned fishing cabin. The head official among this group of schemers gave Eddie his "word of honor" that the whole episode would die a natural death and there would be no further investigation if Eddie would lie low at the cabin for a period of time not to exceed six months. They were to write Eddie a coded message, in care of Denver general delivery, when the heat had blown off and everything was under control. At that time Eddie would be free to return to Chicago and lead a respectable life with his wife and daughter until time for a future and similar job.

Eddie made himself miserable worrying about his wife's poor health. Some friends of his were supposed to keep him posted on Mrs. M---'s welfare, but failed to keep the bargain. Every two weeks Eddie would make a big excursion into Denver to check the post office general delivery, buy the Chicago newspapers (which he read and reread until they were limp), and stock up on food supplies. Each time he would return to the cabin discouraged—no word from the "officials" nor from his friends. But one encouraging sign was evident: the newspapers had ceased mentioning the unsolved robbery.

In late Spring, after the snows melted, our isolated area became nonisolated and fairly buzzed with activity. Various lodges were reopened for the season and owners began arriving to enjoy their cabins and "Springtime in the Rockies." There were many wagons and carriages on the roads and getting into Denver wasn't much of a problem.

The first of June I received a letter from the commandant of Donnie's military school saying that Donnie appeared to enjoy his friends and was showing promise as a good student. The commandant also wrote that the summer camp was commencing the middle of June and that Donnie was pleased he was getting to stay on. I went to Denver and bought some Spring and Summer clothes, then took a train to visit Donnie for two days. He was fine; suntanned and healthy-looking. I wanted to stay longer, but Eddie was expecting his letter from Chicago, so I hurried back to the mountain cabin.

We were at the cabin practically all summer. We had both begun to lose all hope of ever leaving when, on a late evening in the middle of August, Eddie returned from his now-weekly trip to Denver. "It's here, Helen, it's here!" He grabbed me and we danced a jig in the clearing at the side of the cabin. "Now I can go back to Chicago!" he hollered joyously. After our supper of the usual brook trout, he became serious. "What about you, Helen? Where are you going?"

"I haven't decided, Eddie."

"Want to go back to Chicago with me? I think you'd like that town." Now that his own future seemed to be secure, Eddie was worried about mine.

"No, I don't think I want to go anywhere East yet. I think maybe I'll go to the West Coast." I really didn't know where I would go.

"What about San Francisco? That's one of the greatest places on earth."

"All right, I'll go to San Francisco." I was relieved that Eddie had helped me decide where to go.

"I'll go with you, Helen. I'll take you out there, then I'll turn around and go back to Chicago. I want to be sure you're halfway settled." He smiled at me and continued, "I feel a certain responsibility for you, Helen. Without you, I couldn't have lived through the last months. You're a good friend."

I was glad that Eddie felt that way about me because I had a great feeling—not to be confused with love—for him.

We left the cabin at five o'clock the next morning.

Eddie stayed only two days with me in San Francisco. He got me a beautiful apartment on Russian Hill and paid two months' rent ("to repay you for the rustic cabin"). He made me promise him that I'd take a secretarial course ("I want you to be able to take care of yourself"). Then he was gone. I hated to see him leave because once again I was alone. But there are worse things than being alone in San Francisco with a paid-up apartment, and six thousand dollars in your purse.

Chapter 11

SAN FRANCISCO: the Lord Above made that place for girls like me! There are views in the daytime and there are views at night, each surpassing the other. It was a city recently rebuilt after the earthquake, rebuilt just for me. I wanted to see the town and I wanted to see it quickly—and I did. The heavy richness, the heady formality, the guffawing informality left me with the gasping feeling of wanting to unlace my stays—and I did.

I bought silk underwear (to hell with that cotton stuff). Skirts were up six inches off the floor and I bought new dresses and had the older things redone. With my shorter skirts came sheer stockings and low-cut pumps. This was the newly arrived New Freedom and I was in San Francisco!

The spot I liked the best was the Palace Hotel. Off the great court was an assortment of the most fabulous dining rooms and bars I had ever seen. It was in one of those bars that I met Mr. Harold C--.

It was a mild evening and I was in gray wool with a larkspur-blue hat with matching gloves and shoes. Mr. C-- and I sort of bumped into each other (you know how it is). He was unattractive, but he had a certain charm (money). He responded to my attributes with a subtle suggestion that echoed throughout the bar: "Let's have some fun, Helen!" We had fun all night.

The next morning we were breakfasting in the main dining room and he asked me what I did for a living—what a question

since he had, not an hour before, forked over a crisp one-hundred
-dollar bill!

"I'm a private secretary, Harold," I answered.

"The hell you say!" he bellowed.

"Yes, I'm just a little business woman," I said in a voice I hoped
was sincere.

"That's what I need—a private secretary. Why don't you work
for me in Canada?" His eyes gleamed.

I started backing down immediately. "Well, you see, Harold,
what I mean is I'm studying to be a private secretary."

"When do you finish studying?"

"Well ... I haven't really and truly started yet."

"You haven't started yet?"

"No, you see ... it costs lots of money."

"How much?"

I had no idea, so I chanced a guess. "About five hundred
dollars." (It turned out to cost only a hundred and forty.)

"If I pay for your studying, will you be my private secretary in
Canada?"

"I most certainly would, Harold."

"All right, I'll pay for your studying." He pulled five one-
hundred-dollar bills from his wallet and pushed them toward me.

"When will you finish studying?" I had no idea how long such
a course would take, so I asked him to keep his money until I made
a telephone call. I remembered seeing a sign in a second-story
window on Sutter Street called "The Carlisle Business School."

I called them and they told me that they started a new class
every Monday and the entire course took ninety days. I returned
to Harold and told him what I had learned.

"All right, Helen, in ninety days you send me a wire and I'll
send you the money to come to Vancouver."

"Excellent, Harold, I'll do it." I tucked the five bills into my
bodice next to the one given me earlier. "By the way, Harold, what
business are you in?"

"Timber. Lots of timber. Lots of logging camps."

A secretary. A real live secretary. It was wonderful to think
that I had actually passed the ninety-day course and was equipped

for business. Now the ready-to-wear field was not my only forte; I was prepared to do all sorts of things in and around an office.

The day of graduation Miss Lorna Carlisle, the dean of the school, singled me out and said, "Helen, your typing is not good and in most cases I wouldn't think of giving a diploma to a girl whose typing isn't up to our standards, but," she ran her eyes down my Irene Castle-type shantung dress, "I really don't think you'll have too hard a time finding employment."

"I already have a job, Miss Carlisle," I stated matter-of-factly.

"Oh, where?" she asked patronizingly.

"In Vancouver. I'm going to be the private secretary to a lumber czar."

"A lumber czar. My, my, how fascinating. How on earth did you ever acquire such a position?"

"I met him in the bar off the court at the Palace and he offered me a job."

"The Palace—oh, oh. When did you meet him?"

"About three months ago."

"You mean before you started your secretarial course?" Miss Carlisle was more than fascinated now, she was hanging on my every word.

"Yes, in fact he suggested that I take the course."

"Did he ... uh, help with your tuition?"

"Why, of course. He paid the entire amount." I couldn't conceive of any red-blooded girl paying for a secretarial course out of her own pocketbook.

The left side of Miss Carlisle's lips were twitching as she asked, "Please don't think I'm rude but ... is he your lover?" She was sort of gasping for breath. "Is he, oh, is he?" She was pleading for a positive answer and I decided to give her one.

"I guess you could call him that. Yes, he's my lover."

Miss Carlisle's face was flushed and her words were almost incoherent. "Tell me about him! Oh, please, tell me about him!"

"Well, he's big, very big, all over." At this point Miss Carlisle had to put a hand on the wall to brace herself. "You know—the rugged, northwoods type. And virile, and powerful." Miss Carlisle smothered a slight groan. "Rich, too. Very rich."

It took a moment for Miss Carlisle to pull herself together, then she said, "Helen, you have certainly been one of the most brilliant students we've ever had here and I do wish I could have known you better. We could have had such fun, but what with all the duties here I don't have much time for ... social activities."

"I understand, Miss Carlisle."

"And," she tittered, "don't forget your friend Lorna if you ever hear of another lumber czar who needs a private secretary."

"I certainly won't forget my friend Lorna, Miss Carlisle."

"Don't worry about your typing, Helen. Maybe the job won't require any." She opened her mouth halfway and winked provocatively. "Maybe I'll have dinner at the Palace tonight myself."

Whether or not Miss Carlisle had dinner at the Palace I'll never know, but what I do know is that Miss Carlisle was right when she said my job might not require typing.

I telegraphed Mr. Czar that I was ready and waiting to be his private and personal secretary, and he wired me three hundred dollars to make the journey to Vancouver.

I had already decided that I'd marry Mr. Czar. He hadn't asked me yet, but there were no problems on that score. Move over, Mrs. Potter Palmer[16], I thought, you've had it, kiddo. The leader of international society is now going to be Helen Worley Cappel Czar! What does one wear when she is a czarina in Vancouver? I began with a purple velvet slit-to-the-knee dress with dangling ermine tails; I got it at the "City of Paris" and told them to send the bill to Mr. Czar in Vancouver. I was sure it would be just the thing for entertaining in Vancouver, and I did expect to entertain.

I booked passage on the ship that ran between San Francisco and some places called Astoria, Hoquiam, Port Angeles, and finally to Vancouver. I went, of course, first class, and was elated to

---

16 Bertha Palmer (May 22, 1849 – May 5, 1918) was an American businesswoman, socialite, and philanthropist. Bertha Honoré married the Chicago millionaire Potter Palmer in 1870. She was twenty-one and he was forty-four. In Chicago he learned to please his customers, many of whom were women. He made customer service a priority and carried everything from dry goods to the latest French fashions for ladies. Palmer sold his vast store to a consortium and it would eventually become Marshall Field's. Palmer then opened a luxury hotel, Palmer House, and invested in real estate, eventually owning a vast portfolio of properties.

find that we (there were about two dozen other passengers) could "dress" for dinner if we so desired. I was dying to check the effect of the purple-and-ermine deal. Coupled with Florence Gossett's diamond, the outfit was a knockout. It was almost too impressive; at first some of the more attractive gentlemen travelers thought I couldn't be reached, but it didn't take long for us to overcome that barrier. The trip was fun and I found, on docking, that I had more ready cash than I had had when I boarded. It's amazing what a sea voyage does for one's outlook and pocketbook!

Mr. Czar was at the pier with a hungry look in both eyeballs. I had forgotten just how ugly he was. But, after all, I said to myself, it's the inner man that really counts—and this inner man was just filled with tall, tall fir trees and umpteen logging camps. He was glad to see me; he kept laughing, laughing, laughing. His big Stetson hat was just above his bushy eyebrows and across his tight vest, just above his rather pot-ish belly, was stretched a gold chain with an antler's horn fob dangling from it. I'm sure that when John L. Lewis[17] was fifty years old, he and Mr. Czar could have passed for twin brothers.

For the hundredth time Mr. Czar repeated his greeting, "Can't tell you how great it is to see you up here in the wide-open spaces, Helen."

"I'm glad to be here, Harold. To see you in your own surroundings really does my heart good!" I, too, had repeated this dozens of times.

We were in his buggy; it wasn't very good-looking but it had possibilities for repainting—at least it would do until we got a horseless carriage. The house was just like the buggy; a bit run down, but it was big and had scads of revamping possibilities. The furniture was awful, but what the hell, a good interior decorator from San Francisco with a boatload of golden oak could make the place look like something from Nob Hill.

I had expected some servants in a place that big, but none

---

17 John L. Lewis (February 12, 1880 – June 11, 1969) was an American leader of organized labor who served as president of the United Mine Workers of America (UMW) from 1920 to 1960. A major player in the history of coal mining, he was the driving force behind the founding of the Congress of Industrial Organizations (CIO), which established the United Steel Workers of America and helped organize millions of other industrial workers in the 1930s.

seemed to be about. "Harold, don't you have servants in this gigantic place?"

"Only my cook from Medicine Hat. I'm not here much." "Medicine Hat? What do you mean you're not here much?" "I'm usually at the logging camps and at my place at Medicine Hat. I don't come to Vancouver but about every three months."

"Do you mean you're going to leave me alone in Vancouver, in this big place, without servants!"

"Hell, no, Helen, I'm going to take you with me. We'll travel a lot. To all the camps and to Medicine Hat."

"What will we do in Medicine Hat?"

"The same thing we do in Vancouver!" With that he swept me up in his arms and dumped me in a bed with a solid walnut headboard nine feet high. He didn't even remove his vest and I had a black-and-blue mark for a week—those antlers' tips can really gouge a gal.

I had promised myself that I would practice typing in Medicine Hat until I could truly perform on the machine. Fortunately or otherwise, Harold didn't have a typewriter—and besides it was forty-five degrees below zero—so I never did learn to type.

Being a private secretary to a lumber czar in wintertime Canada doesn't require many business school skills. But there were requirements and I was well paid for them. Saving money became my hobby; Mr. Czar paid me five hundred dollars a month and all of it went into my stocking.

By this time the prospect of being Mrs. Czar was the farthest thing from my mind. After seeing Medicine Hat, I wouldn't have married Harold Czar if he had been the last man on earth—and as far as my life was concerned, he just about was. The lumber camps were literally filled with man-type men, but Harold kept me under constant surveillance; and when he wasn't around, his cook—the one he had mentioned in Vancouver—took over the patrol. To make matters even worse, the cook was an Indian about sixty years old and hardly spoke English.

Harold was jealous, but not cruel to me. Every six months I'd go to visit Donnie at his military school and Harold would make me promise to return, which I did for almost four years. Each time

I'd wonder why anyone would, of their own free will, return to Medicine Hat.

Going to Medicine Hat is like going to hell. The only difference is that instead of being hot, Medicine Hat is cold. Do you know where Medicine Hat is? Well, it is sort of on a line between Elkwater and Kininvie, a little northeast of Etzikom (which is close to Manyberries and Seven Persons) and a bit southeast of Iddesleigh.

I shall never forget our first train ride from Vancouver to Medicine Hat via Calgary. We left the morning after I arrived in Vancouver, just as Harold said we would. The night had been extremely taxing, but he insisted that we catch the dawn train; he couldn't wait for me to see Medicine Hat. The ride was torturous. It took days.

The train backed up more than it went forward; but that would have been all right if our "sitting car" (there were only two cars of passengers, fifty cars of freight) had had any heat. It was rather a prehistoric arrangement. The "sitting car" was the coach section and it was also where the people with berth accommodations spent their daylight hours along with the passengers who were sitting up the entire way. The reasoning behind this was for the sake of comfort; the sleeping cars had no heat whatsoever. It was bad enough to be freezing to death in a crowded little slab of a bed separated only by a green curtain from the other people; what made things worse was for Harold to bellow in his moose voice, "Let's have lots of fun!" I hope our activities helped warm up the other passengers.

The "sitting car" had a squat, rotund stove, with a pendulous overhang at the top, tucked far back in a corner. The shape of the stove reminded me of cousin Pete's charming Ella; it was constructed exactly like her. This bit of picturesque antiquity would have served its designated purpose had it not acted up soon out of Vancouver. Every human being on the train tried his hand at adjusting dampers and various other gimcracks on the stove, but it was useless. The stove smoked horrendously and several of our fellow passengers were overcome with smoke inhalation. The stove was fired by a quaint fuel known as "coke" which went out of style about the time Mrs. Josephus Daniels made her Secretary-of-the-Navy husband pass the rule that all sailors had to sleep in pajamas (no connection between these two episodes whatsoever). In any case, it was impossible to heat the "sitting car" without asphyxiating ourselves; so the passenger complement of the train sat huddling and shivering under blankets. Everyone considered it a ghastly experience except Mr. Czar—it gave him a good excuse to keep me in the berth for the entire trip and "have lots of fun." When we finally arrived in Medicine Hat, I wished I had been back on the train—the train was warmer.

I know exactly what you're wondering: what happened to the purple dress with the ermine tails? Did I wear it? Hell, yes, but not in Medicine Hat. You must realize that while I was a "private secretary" in the wilds of Canada the world was clanging and crashing elsewhere. Those people had been shot while gadding around Sarajevo; the first World War was in full regalia and I hadn't done one damn thing to help the boys in khaki. I wanted some wartime action and I decided to get it.

"Do you love me, Harold?" It was a cold, horrible night and I had gone to bed with my fur parka on.

"I sure do. Want me to show you?"

"Easy there, Laddie, I merely want to ask a favor of you."

"Anything you want, Helen. Want some more money?"

"That's just it, Harold … dear … you pile money on me and yet I have no way to spend it. I want to go to Calgary and buy some pretty clothes."

"You don't need pretty clothes, Helen. You've got suitcases full of them. And that purple dress—the one I paid for—I ain't never even seen it on you."

"I know Harold … dear … I don't really need new clothes, but they keep me from wishing that I … uh, could leave this place and go back to Cincinnati or Chicago or somewhere. You know, clothes are good for a woman's soul." I knew the talk about leaving would unclog his drain.

"Sure, we'll go to Calgary. I'll buy you anything you want."

"I want to go alone, Harold … dear … I want to shop and shop and shop, and have my hair done a dozen ways until I get it just the way I want it ... for you."

"All right. When do you want to go?"

"Early in the morning." I was already packed. The velvet dress was on top, nicely wrapped in tissue paper.

Just outside of Calgary was one of the biggest army camps in all of Canada. And the town itself was jam-pack full of delightful doughboys (or whatever the Canadians called them). I, of course, knew this before arriving there absolutely bursting with patriotic energy.

I am not one for class distinction, but I decided to start with the officers. They were, after all, the ones "up front" during the skirmishes. I was definitely in the mood for skirmishes. If the truth were known, I was damn tired of Harold.

"I'm very sorry, Mrs. Cappel, but we can't allow anyone on the post without a pass. Orders you know." The gate sentry had referred me to the officer-of-the-day. The OOD was rather cute in his leggings and cavalry hat and he obviously thought I was rather cute in my Irene Castle[18]-type shantung dress which I kept warm with my dark Canadian mink (very small strips) coat which Harold ... dear ... had given me for Christmas. I had acquired some long topaz gloves to match the Marshall Field's hat.

"I know all about orders, and I understand. It was orders which took my dear husband—Captain Cappel—from here to the battleground of France." I pulled out a filmy hankie edged with

---

18 Irene Castle (April 17, 1893 - January 25, 1969) was born in New Rochelle, New York. She studied dancing and performed in several amateur theatricals before meeting Vernon Castle at the New Rochelle Rowing Club in 1910. On May 28, 1911 in New Rochelle, New York, over her father's objections, the two were married. The couple reached the peak of their popularity in Irving Berlin's first Broadway show, *Watch Your Step* (1914), in which they refined and popularized the Foxtrot. They also helped to promote ragtime, jazz rhythms and African-American music for dance. Irene became a fashion icon through her appearances on stage and in early movies, and both Castles were in demand as teachers and writers on dance. After serving with distinction as a pilot in the British Royal Flying Corps during World War I, Vernon died in a plane crash on a flight training base near Fort Worth, Texas, in 1918. Irene starred solo in about a dozen silent films between 1917 and 1924, including *Patria* (1917), and appeared in several more stage productions before retiring from show business. She married three more times, to Robert E. Treman, the scion of a prominent Ithaca, New York family. Treman reportedly invested Castle's money and lost it in the stock market. They divorced in 1923. The same year, she married Frederic McLaughlin (a man 16 years her elder), and two years after he died in 1944, she married George Enzinger (died 1959), an advertising executive from Chicago. During her marriage to "Major" McLaughlin, who was the owner of the Chicago Blackhawks, she is credited with designing the original sweater for the Blackhawks Colosimo Hockey Club.

topaz lace and fluttered it across my face. I spoke quietly. "And now I have no husband. He was one of your countrymen—French Canadien—he courted me while visiting in Chicago. We married there, you know. Together only a few weeks. Then he was sent here. He loved this post; he wrote me all about it. I came here—hoping beyond hope—that I could catch some of the flavor of this place he loved so, even see some of his favorite spots—such as the officers' club. He was a captain, just like you. In fact, you remind me of him: so young, handsome, and … vital. Yes, it was a place he loved—the officers' club, I mean."

The captain who was the officer-of-the-day was sympathetic, kind, and rather excited. He reasoned that since I was an officer's widow (and had left all my identification in Chicago) he could see no reason why I shouldn't have a pass to the officers' club to use anytime that week I wanted to use it.

"You're so dear," I told him. "Yes, just to sit in the officers' club and reflect—perhaps sip a glass of Bordeaux (he was French, you know)—that would make my journey worthwhile." I left the OOD room with a gate pass and a date to meet the Captain later at the officers' club—and perhaps share a small bottle of Bordeaux.

I wore my purple velvet number with the ermine tails and the captain shared more than a bottle. He was dear, and so was the regiment or battalion or whatever they call it. From private to general, they were dears, and insisted on showering me with remembrances: seven hundred and fifty dollars total.

When I left for Medicine Hat a week later, I felt much more entitled to hum "Over There."

There was much ranting and raving from Harold when I told him I was leaving his "employment." He begged me to marry him (I had forgotten we weren't married) and said we could live all the time in Vancouver (I told him I had had Medicine Hat). I had been with him for over three and a half years, and I felt that for someone who had wanted to "Live a little" I had certainly been in cold storage for a hell of a long time. Nothing he could say could persuade me to stay on with him. I told the Indian cook to kiss my ass and left for civilization. I could well afford the trip; I had over thirty thousand dollars saved up.

I went to Vancouver and from there back to San Francisco for two days—as trite as it might sound, I wanted to see the sun set on San Francisco Bay just once more before I started East. It was the first week of August, 1918, and Donnie's summer camp was scheduled to be over the last of the month. I decided to go to Chicago before it was time to pick up Donnie. Eddie's tuition fees had run out.

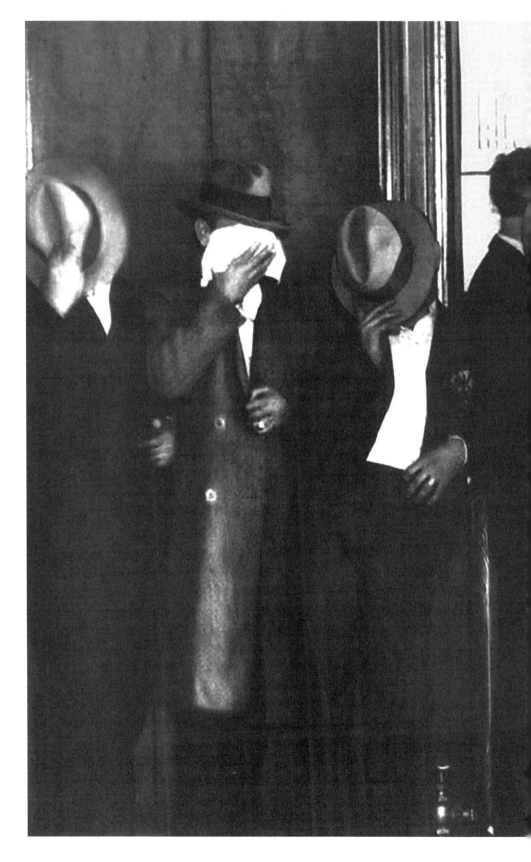

Chapter 12

AS SOON AS the bellboy finished fussing with my luggage, switching on and off lights, and doing the countless things that bellboys feel they must do, I called Eddie M. He had given me his telephone number when we had parted four years before in San Francisco, and I still remembered it. I was almost breathless as I heard the telephone ringing on the other end of the line. Will Eddie be in Chicago? Will he mind my calling him? Maybe he's not even alive! Finally, the telephone was answered, and I recognized the voice of my sweet Eddie.

"Hello, Eddie," I announced, "This is someone from your past; have you any idea who it is?'

"I'd know your voice anywhere, Helen!" he cried. "Where are you?"

"At the LaSalle Hotel, I just checked in."

"I'll be there within thirty minutes. See you in the lobby." It were as if four years of my life's slate had been wiped off. I sat in the lobby watching the minute hand of the big clock jump each sixty seconds; I could hardly wait to see him. I saw Eddie when he entered the LaSalle Street entrance. The past years had been kind to him and he was even better-looking than he had been before. Then he saw me and came bounding toward me. He kissed me, then hugged me; then he kissed me again. "I've never been so glad to see anyone in my life, Helen," he exclaimed over and over.

As we sat on a sofa in a back corner of the lobby, I told him briefly what had taken place since we had parted in San Francisco.

We had dinner together in the dining room and Eddie kept looking at his watch; he said he was going on a business trip to Detroit and had to catch the night train.

"Why don't you come with me?" he asked. "We'll be back day after tomorrow."

"If you really want me to come, I'd love it, Eddie." Within an hour I had repacked my luggage and we were in his drawing room on the train. Early the next morning we checked into Detroit's old Pontchartrain Hotel. In those days, the Pontchartrain was considered to be one of the most elegant hotels in America. The decorations and the service were copied along the lines of Europe's great hotels.

"We're invited to a private dinner party in the hotel dining room tonight," Eddie said. "Everything is formal here in the evenings. Do you have an evening dress?" he asked. He had bathed, dressed, and was on his way out of the hotel suite.

"No. I don't believe I have anything with me that could even pass for one." Eddie gave me two hundred dollars and told me to spend the morning finding an evening dress that I liked, and he would see me in the suite after lunch. I went to store after store, and finally chose a pale blue satin for a hundred and eighty-five dollars. Then another search of the stores produced a red-beaded evening bag and matching red satin slippers. I arrived back in our hotel suite about three-thirty and within five minutes Eddie came through the door followed by two swarthy men. Eddie carried a large leather valise. The trio merely nodded at me, then proceeded into the bedroom. Minutes later the two strangers strolled through the living room and out the door to the corridor. They each had a wrapped package tucked tightly under their left arms. Eddie called to me from the bedroom. "Come here, Helen, I want to show you something."

I walked into the room and there—spread on the bed like a gigantic green body—was the largest pile of money I had ever seen. I stared at it in disbelief, saying nothing. I opened my mouth to speak, thought better of it, and closed my mouth.

"The payoff was terrific," Eddie said quietly. "But I think I have almost seventy-five thousand for myself." I still didn't say anything. What was there to say? I turned and walked back into the living room as Eddie stacked the packages of money in his valise. My curiosity was killing me and I would have given anything for a rundown on what had transpired that day, but I knew better than to ask questions. Eddie soon joined me in the living room. "Did you find an evening dress that you liked?"

"Yes. It's lovely. Pale blue." I thought my voice sounded strange. How could people discuss evening dresses with that in the next room?

"May I see it?" asked Eddie. The next five minutes were spent discussing the merits of the dress. Eddie liked good clothes and was interested in examining the construction of the dress. Then he excused himself, saying he had to go out for about an hour and hoped I didn't mind being left alone. I did mind! I didn't like the idea of being alone in a hotel suite with seventy-five thousand dollars, particularly if it were hot, which I knew it was. But what could I do? I nodded my head to indicate that it was all right and Eddie left the suite.

I decided that if I were to be robbed or arrested, whichever the case might be, I might as well be tidy, so I was still soaking in a tubful of hot water when Eddie returned. He spoke through the closed bathroom door and said, "I'm going to rest for about thirty minutes. Please wake me about six o'clock." Eddie had had a busy day.

No man could have looked more handsome than Eddie did in his evening clothes. He appeared to be the graying, debonair, high-income business man. Just as we were leaving the suite he handed me a small packet and asked off-handedly, "Helen, would you mind keeping this in your evening bag?" I placed the little package in my new red-beaded evening bag, took Eddie by the arm, and we descended in the elevator.

At exactly ten minutes after seven we entered the magnificent dining room of the Pontchartrain Hotel and were seated at a large, reserved table. The orchestra was playing a beautiful song I had never heard before and I asked Eddie to find out what the name of it was. He motioned to the headwaiter, who informed us the title of the song was "Ah, Sweet Mystery of Life". Ever since that evening, that particular song has been one of my favorites. As the last strains of the song floated through the vast room, other dinner guests arrived.

The two dark-complexioned men who had been in our suite earlier in the day looked much less ominous in their evening clothes; with them were two black-haired ladies whom they introduced as their wives. Both of the women had faint traces of European accents. The last members of the party arrived about five minutes later; as the imposing-looking gentleman and his elaborately attired wife were introduced to me I'm sure I appeared startled—his title was one of the highest of the Detroit city government.

The conversation seemed a little strained until the second round of cocktails was served. By the time the champagne and Chicken Parisienne were served the orchestra had started playing again and from then on our party was a group of laughing, friendly people. I danced first with Eddie, then with the city official, and in turn with the dark-complexioned men. We were still dancing and chatting at eleven p.m. when Eddie announced that he and I had to change clothes and gather our luggage to catch the midnight sleeper for Chicago. The group waited in our living room, then took us to the depot in the city official's long, black limousine. A porter at the entrance to the train depot took all of our luggage, including Eddie's valise.

As Eddie and I walked across the large, empty waiting room of the depot, he stopped at a newsstand and bought an early edition of the next morning's paper. I saw the headline as he slowly folded the paper and tucked it under his arm: "$200,000 PAYROLL ROBBERY!"

Early the next morning we entered the lobby of the LaSalle Hotel in Chicago. I sent my suitcases up to my room and we had breakfast in the coffee shop.

"I'm afraid I won't be able to see you again for some time, Helen," Eddie said.

"I know, Eddie, but this trip to Detroit has been fun—just like old times."

"Do you need anything, Helen?"

"Not a thing, Eddie."

"If you ever need anything, Helen, you know you can count on me."

I patted Eddie's hand as I said, "I know that, Eddie. You're the best friend I have."

"Life's funny, isn't it?"

"Yes, Eddie, life is funny."

'Things could have turned out differently for us—for you and me—couldn't they have!"

"Yes, but they didn't. Maybe that's why we'll always be friends."

Eddie and I were saying goodbye in front of the elevators when he asked suddenly, "Oh, Helen, where is that small package I gave you last night?"

"Small package?"

"The one you put in your red evening bag."

"I had forgotten about it. It's still in the beaded bag. Upstairs in my suitcase." Eddie went up to my room with me and I found him the package. He took off the rubber band and opened up the brown paper folder, then poured the contents into the palm of his left hand. He had a handful of glistening, unset diamonds.

"Just a little something I picked up while you were taking your bath yesterday. I imagine they are worth about seventy-five thousand. The newspaper said a hundred and twenty-five, but they always exaggerate." Just as yesterday, I was speechless; I asked no questions. He extended his hand toward me. "Do you want some?"

"No, Eddie, thank you. I don't want any." He poured the diamonds back into the small brown envelope, folded the flap over, and placed the rubber band on it again.

As Eddie kissed me goodbye he asked, "We'll always be friends, won't we?"

"Always, Eddie." He knew what I meant, just as I knew what he meant.

Donnie had grown into a big boy with a big boy's curiosity about automobiles, trains, travel, and cities. He was so interested in seeing things and going places, I decided to take him on a long trip.

After I picked him up at the military academy, we returned to Chicago and I spent several days getting him outfitted in "civilian" clothes. Then we left on the New York Central Railroad for Cleveland; we spent several sightseeing days there, then went to the Breakers Hotel at Cedar Point for two weeks. We visited Rochester, Syracuse, Buffalo, and Niagara Falls—taking our time, seeing whatever we wanted to see, and becoming acquainted again after our long absence from each other.

We were in Utica when the premature announcement of the Armistice hit the newspapers. It was November 7, 1918, and Utica went wild; then a gloom settled over the festivities when it was learned that the Germans hadn't really laid down their swords. I felt that the real armistice would be coming soon and I wanted to see the biggest celebration of all: that's when I decided to leave within the next few days for New York City. I wired the McAlpin Hotel for reservations and they were confirmed.

It was on the train that I saw Eddie M--- again—for the last time. I was sitting in a pullman seat with Donnie when Eddie came down the aisle. I was elated to see him and started to call him by name, when he motioned for me to keep quiet. As he passed my seat, he stooped and whispered in my ear, "Don't let on you know me. Tough deal." It must have been a tough deal, because Eddie was killed the following week; run down by a careening car at Thirty-fourth Street and Broadway. I read about it in the newspapers. There were speculations as to whether the hit-and-run had been engineered by the Chicago mob, the New York boys, or that treacherous Purple Gang from Detroit.

We arrived at Grand Central Station on November 11. The station was in turmoil; I hurriedly bought a *New York Times* and there it was: ARMISTICE SIGNED, END OF WAR! OUSTED KAISER FLEES TO HOLLAND. The article went on to say that the armistice had been signed in France at midnight and that the State Department in Washington had made the official announcement at 2:45 o'clock in the morning.

Demonstrators jammed the streets with wild celebrations. It

took us several hours to find a hack and get through the throngs of people. When we finally got to the McAlpin they showed us to a lovely two-bedroom suite. After we bathed and redressed, Donnie wanted to see more of the jubilant activities, so we plowed out into the surging mob. We returned to the hotel for dinner in the Rathskeller and after dinner made another tour up Broadway; I was determined to let Donnie see as much of the victory shenanigans as he wanted. (In all the time since we had left Cincinnati Donnie never questioned me about my reasons for taking him away with me. Perhaps he didn't want to know the answers, any more than I wanted to have to give them. Kids can be pretty goddamed smart.) Before midnight he admitted that he wanted to go to bed, and he was asleep before his head touched the pillow.

I was too keyed up to go to bed, but I wouldn't have thought of leaving Donnie alone in a strange hotel. Then I thought of a way of having someone to talk to; I called the desk and asked them to send up the house detective.

The house detective's name was Tim. He was about thirty-five, big, tall, and Irish-looking. When I saw him I thought I had just about hit the jackpot on finding someone to chat with. Tim didn't mind at all that I had called him up to my room for no particular reason. He was from Indiana and so was I and we had a good time shooting the breeze. I told him that I was too excited over being in New York to try to sleep, and he suggested that I take a night-life sightseeing tour that didn't begin until one-thirty a.m. He said it was a wonderful way to see the seamy side of the city and was perfectly safe since the bus was protected by guards. I explained to Tim that I couldn't leave Donnie, but he said he would keep an eye on my room and Donnie would be well taken care of. I remembered my money; I didn't want to leave it in my room and I certainly didn't want to take it with me. I asked Tim if he would have it put in the hotel safe for me. He almost fainted when I handed him eight thousand dollars in cash; I had the remainder in a Chicago bank.

"Wow! Where did you get this much money, Helen?"

"I'm a business woman, Tim."

"What kind of business?"

I decided to lay my cards on the table. "Bedroom business."

"Oh, maybe I can help get you some customers."

"'That's exactly what I had in mind, Tim." What better protection, I thought, than to have the house detective for a pimp.

"When do you want to start?" he asked.

"Not tonight," I laughed. "That sightseeing tour you mentioned intrigues me."

There were about twenty other people on the tour, plus the bus driver and four uniformed guards. I saw sights I can never forget: the East Side slums with rat-infested streets, Chinatown with its acrid smells, the Bowery with drunks asleep on the sidewalks covered only with old newspapers, and everywhere winos and dope addicts begging us for money before they were shooed away by the guards. The tour cost only five dollars, and it exposed a slice of life to me that I didn't know existed. At three-thirty I was back in the hotel with a sick feeling in the pit of my stomach.

In the months that followed, Tim made many contacts for me. Outstanding among these contacts was Mr. Bradford.

Brad lived in a large penthouse apartment at the McAlpin. He was wonderful to me, and to Donnie—who by this time was in a fine private boarding school. One of Brad's great pleasures was taking Donnie, on Saturdays, to Brooks Brothers or Rogers Peet and buying him clothes. Brad was a well-known Wall Street stockbroker, and I was a fool not to marry him when he asked me to. He first asked me to stop seeing my other contacts and settle down as his mistress; when I refused to do that, he asked me to marry him; when I refused to marry him, he stopped seeing me completely. Brad liked only exclusive rights.

I had gotten a job selling millinery at Renard's on Forty-Second Street near Fifth Avenue. I wanted Donnie and his friends to think of me as a respectable working mother. I also learned quickly that a call girl who has legitimate employment in the daytime is rarely bothered by the police at night. And since I loved beautiful hats, it was a pleasure to work at Renard's. The shop catered to wealthy customers, people who could afford expensive, imported hats and gloves. I was with the store for several years.

On weekends Tim and I would go to Atlantic City. I would get a nice suite at one of the large hotels and Tim would do the leg work of getting me customers. I always split fifty-fifty with him and when we'd leave for New York on Sunday evenings we'd both have hundreds of dollars. I think that maybe the key to our success in the call racket was that Tim was not the typical pimp and I wasn't the typical call girl. I had many opportunities to get my name on the lists of some of the big-name New York madams, but I shunned such connections. And my association with Tim was one of pure business; we both had legitimate jobs, we were never bed partners, and our undercover activities were merely a sideline ... a profitable sideline. My career as a woman of pleasure was paying splendid dividends—and I was never lonely.

Chapter 13

BAA-ROOM, BOOM boom boom, baa-room boom boom boom—damn, how I loved the tango! The tango is sort of like a savings and loan institution: the more you put into it, the more you get out of it. The only thing I liked better than the tango was a rich man. I had both the tango and a rich man tied up in a neat package and sealed with a diamond clip, an aquamarine bracelet, and a matching dinner ring.

It started innocently, but many interesting things do start innocently. It was almost six o'clock, the closing hour at Renard's. Mr. Gold, my boss, was shuffling around in the stock room and I was tidying up the merchandise in the show cases when the door opened and a tall gentleman in a Stetson hat entered. He was grubby-faced and obviously intoxicated … but also obviously rich. Money, like great heart, always shows through.

"Howdy, miss!" His voice made a sliding glass door of the glove case rattle.

"Good evening, sir," I returned in the voice I reserved for drunk business tycoons. "May I help you?"

"That would be nice," he slobbered in his Texas drawl. "That sure would be nice." He stared down at the gloves in the glass case. "I want a pair of those gloves—those right there." He pointed at a stack of ladies' full-length, white kid opera gloves.

"What size, sir?"

"Well, now, let's see. Let's see." He swept his eyes down my figure, stopping them here and there, then back up again. "Your size, yessiree, just your size."

I found a pair of eighteen-dollar gloves that fit me perfectly, and he said they'd do nicely. I asked him if he wanted them gift-wrapped, and he allowed as how he did. He had to hold onto the counter to keep from falling, but his eyes were certainly alert to my every movement as I tied a white satin bow around the long glove box. I handed him the box and he paid me. Then he handed me the box back and said it was a little gift just for me. Drunk or not, I knew I had a "live one."

He had seen me, he claimed, through the window and had decided I was "just his type." He gave me his name (I'll call him Tex) and asked if I would join him for dinner in his suite at the Murray Hill Hotel. I thought about it (for a second) and said "yes."

Tex was a mess, as were his apartment at the Murray Hill and his private railroad car (we went there later). Both the apartment and the railroad car were strewn with newspapers and empty whiskey bottles. Tex had been the victim of a tragedy; his wife had drowned in a horrible flood in Texas. He was in New York trying to forget his troubles. Oh, poor dear! He was, incidentally, the president of one of the West's great railroads. He wanted me to spend the weekend with him and I named my price; he said he'd double it, which was all right with me since I've never been one for messy men or messy private railroad cars. Tex was too drunk to cause me much activity or trouble, but I was glad when the weekend was over. Just as I was preparing to leave the Murray Hill on Monday morning, Tex sobered up enough to offer another invitation. "Wanna go to Argentina with me, Helen?"

"Go to Argentina? What are you talking about?"

"I'm gonna go down there and forget everything. Wanna go?"

Argentina! The Argentine! The Tango! "When are you going?" I asked.

"Soon as I can get tickets. Or whatever it is you get."

"I don't want to get stuck down there." I thought quickly and said, "If you'll pay my expenses, buy me a new wardrobe, and give me a thousand dollars I'll go."

"Okay." We sailed the following Thursday. Tex was still drunk and it took two stewards to get him into his bed, where he remained during the entire voyage. I had taken Tex's thousand dollars to the bank and had the teller give me a single one-thousand-dollar bill which I folded neatly and placed in my shoe. This was to be my "mad money" for getting home.

I was plenty mad. It was a ghastly trip. Tex apparently had said he wanted to leave on the first ship to the Argentine, and the first ship was a freighter of some type. There was no one interesting on the whole damned boat. I had spent my own money for some marvelous clothes and there was no one on the boat to appreciate them. One particularly fetching ensemble was sold to me as being just the thing for the promenade deck—it was lavender voile and silver fox—but if that boat had a promenade deck, I couldn't find it. Aside from Tex and myself, everyone on the boat were spicks (peasants really) with the exception of two pasty-faced young men who seemed to be on their toujours gay honeymoon. For this I had spent *beaucoup* money for the promenade costume!

Eons later we arrived in Buenos Aires (after many stops at various shitty little islands). By this time I was not speaking to Tex; he had been a perfectly stupid and intoxicated boor the entire voyage. As far as I was concerned, he could have taken all his trains and done you-know-what with them. Immediately upon docking I discarded Tex and made my way directly to the American Embassy. I told them there exactly what had happened; they kept passing me from hand to hand (as it were) and I had to tell my story to many sympathetic ears. I told it straightforward: I had been duped by the president of the Railroad into accompanying him to Argentina; he had misrepresented his intentions; he was an alcoholic; I was an American citizen stranded in the Argentine; I had a perfectly respectable position with Renard's in New York (I was on leave of absence) and I expected the Embassy to see that I was booked for passage on the first nice ship leaving for New York. Also, I told them I was broke (that thousand-dollar bill had practically worn a blister under my big toe).

The Under Secretary had passed me to the Secretary and soon after lunch (he was a true gentleman and asked me to lunch with him right there in the Embassy) he made some calls and informed me that everything was smoothed out and that passage had been booked for me on a ship that was sailing in two days. I told him that he was a dear as were all his "Under people" and it did my heart good, as an American, to know that my own government took such nice care of its own citizens when they were in distress. He giggled embarrassedly and said it was really nothing, and he only wished that the passage could have been first class rather than cabin.

"Cabin!" I cried. "I'm sorry, Mr. Secretary, but I cannot go cabin class." I shuddered visibly.

"But my dear Miss Worley," he said, "You must realize that this is truly an unusual situation for us to afford cabin class. Many times people are sent home by steerage."

"Steerage!" I screamed, practically dropping the eagle-crested spoon in the clear consomme. "I insist on first class or nothing." He said that such a request would have to be taken up with THE TOP PERSON and I insisted on seeing THE TOP PERSON. I waited almost three hours until THE TOP PERSON was available. He was really the nicest one employed there. We were still discussing my predicament at the closing hour, and THE TOP PERSON suggested that we continue our conversation over cocktails at an interesting little off-the-beaten-track bistro he knew of. We were driven there in a car with an American flag on each front fender and two perfectly cute marines in the front seat.

We had dinner at a very smart apartment which he kept to "get away from official duties." Since my luggage was still at the dock, and I had made no hotel arrangements, THE TOP PERSON said I was free to stay at his apartment until my ship sailed. And he told me that, of course, I would be sailing first class. After dinner we went to a rather wild type of frenzied nightclub where the gauchos danced the tango. I wanted to dance it, too, but the TOP PERSON didn't know how; I couldn't believe anyone could be much of a diplomat without knowing how to dance the tango! I pouted (just a little) and he asked one of the gauchos to give it a whirl with me—and hot damn!—it was worth the whole hectic trip.

The northbound voyage was more of what I had in mind. The ship had an orchestra and a promenade deck. My lavender voile with the silver fox served me well. Every night it was just tango, tango, tango. And for those gentlemen who didn't know how to tango I offered other pleasures that had to do with rhythm. By the time I arrived back in New York and unpacked in the McAlpin, my thousand-dollar bill had some interesting companion pieces. I decided to move from the hotel to a place of my own. But I still held on to my job at Renard's. I liked the busy life.

Tim found a nice apartment for me on West End Avenue at a Hundred and Tenth Street; it was just a block off Riverside Drive and very convenient to get to. By this time I knew New York thoroughly. Donnie loved his school and things seemed very rosy. Then I received word that while I was in Argentina my Pa had died. The realization that he was gone affected me more than I would have thought possible, even though we had never seen each other since I had left for Cincinnati years before.

I suddenly felt remorse about the past and sadness that Pa's feelings about Phil had been so correct. His death left me open to human comfort, and it was at this time that I met Bob.

It had been a busy day at the store and I decided to have dinner alone and go home alone; so I stopped at the St. Regis Restaurant at 42nd and Broadway. As I entered the restaurant and looked around for a table, a handsome young man in an Army lieutenant's uniform jumped to his feet and said quickly, "If you're by yourself, I'd love to have dinner with you. I'm a stranger here and I'm lonesome in the big city." It was such a direct, fresh approach I almost laughed. I sat down with him and while he was talking I simply stared into his big, young black eyes. As he talked on about his family in Chicago, being mustard-gassed in France, taking treatments at the veteran's hospital in New Jersey, all I could do was nod. By the time dinner was over, I knew what had happened: the hardened New York call girl had fallen in love with a beautiful lieutenant—a man considerably younger than she.

After dinner we went to the Claridge Hotel and danced. Then we went to the Moulin Rouge. It was after one o'clock a.m. when we left the Moulin Rouge and started toward the subway at Times Square. I began to feel panicky inside; I wanted him to come home with me, but I didn't want him to know what I was. Was it obvious what I was? Did it really matter that he not know? I wanted him. He had been direct with me, so I decided to be direct with him.

"I want you to come with me, Bob."

"Do you, Helen?"

"Yes, very much. You can stay with me as long as you want to."

I didn't go to work the next morning, but I felt I would be needed in the afternoon, so I woke Bob up at eleven-thirty by raining kisses all over him. He stretched and yawned like a drowsy child before he realized where he was. Then he looked at me and said hesitatingly, "Do I ... uh, give you money, Helen?"

I placed my index finger over his lips as I whispered, "No money, Bob. Now nor ever. This is for love." Then I showed him that I meant it.

Bob stayed with me for weeks. Every three days he had to go to the hospital for a treatment, then he would return to me. I told Tim that as long as Bob was in New York I was not accepting any calls. Tim said I was a goddamed fool and I asked him if he had ever been in love, and that shut him up; as brash as Tim was, he had a heart of gold, and had been in love with a little crippled girl from the Bronx for years—for some reason the girl refused to marry him, giving the ridiculous answer that she didn't want to be a millstone around his neck. In any case, Tim left me alone; but other men who had my phone number called me continuously until I finally stuffed a handkerchief between the bells.

I had found someone to fill the vacant place in my heart.

Chapter 14

A NEW DECADE, a new me—it was 1920. Once again I had someone to love. There were no secrets between us. Bob knew about Phil, about Branagan, about Eddie, about Mr. Czar, about Tim, and about the multitude of nameless and faceless men who had marched through the past few years of my life. I told him everything. I was what I was, and I wanted him to know it. Still, he wanted to marry me.

Bob was feeling a little better. The treatments at the veterans' hospital in New Jersey had helped, but the doctors hadn't tried to delude him; there was really no cure for the large dose of mustard gas he had inhaled. He returned to Chicago in February to join his father in their business. I promised to visit him in April.

It was early March and even the New York papers were filled with the hot Chicago news: Big Jim Colosimo[19], gangland chief and restaurateur extraordinaire, was divorcing his wife of many years, Victoria Moresco, to marry a youthful singer named Dale Winter[20].

---

19 James "Big Jim" or "Diamond Jim" Colosimo (February 16, 1878 – May 11, 1920), known as James "Big Jim" Colosimo or as "Diamond Jim," was an Italian-American Mafia crime boss who emigrated from Calabria, Italy, in 1895, and built a criminal empire in Chicago based on prostitution, gambling, and racketeering. He gained power through petty crime and by heading a chain of brothels. From about 1902 until his murder in 1920, he led a gang that became known after his death as the Chicago Outfit. Johnny Torrio was his nephew and an enforcer whom Colosimo imported in 1909 from New York and who seized control after his death. Al Capone, a Torrio henchman, allegedly was directly involved in the murder.

20 Dale Winter (1891–1985) became a teenage beauty and singing talent. She arrived in Chicago in 1915 and auditioned as a singer at Colosimo's Café. After Colosimo's assassination, she went on to a moderately successful career on Broadway, and occasionally, in film. She married again in 1924 and moved to California, where she and her husband operated a chain of theaters.

< Colosimo's menu.

Not much was known about Miss Winter except she was fairly good at singing light opera and had been an entertainer at Colosimo's Restaurant for several months. It was rumored that the Chicago underworld was furious at Big Jim; they felt that Jim's shedding of an old, devoted wife, who had struggled with him through lean years of small-time banditry, showed tremendous disloyalty and unpardonable bad taste. If nothing else, the Chicago underworld is big on loyalty and on family. It was noted in the papers that even Johnny Torrio, Colosimo's right-hand lieutenant, had stated, "Marry her if you must, Jim, but remember … it's your own funeral."

I had more than a casual interest in those news items because I knew Dale Winter. We had arrived in New York about the same time, and I had seen her around at various clubs, restaurants, and parties. Prior to leaving New York she had had a few bit parts in some musical plays and I admired her voice tremendously and told her so. We weren't close friends, but we were friends. We went shopping together at Steam's Store one Saturday. After she left Manhattan she went to San Francisco, and I didn't know where she finally landed until I saw the newspaper articles. The photographs in the papers didn't do justice to her sweet, smiling, pixie-like face.

My business was booming. The good-time charlies knew that Old John Barleycorn had only a few lingering months before Prohibition would put him to rest, and they were determined to enjoy John's last few days. My chosen profession went hand-in-hand with hard liquor; early in the evening came the drinks and later in the evening came a ring at my telephone or a knock on my door—if I was at home. If I was at the Claridge or Poppy Room it was an alcoholically polite "Would you care to join me for a drink?"

When Bob was in New York I was "true" to him, and I did have a great affection for him, but at thirty-four I had no illusions. I was a professional bed partner and although I truly wanted to marry Bob and settle into a respectable life, I didn't try to kid myself. I knew he might marry me and then again he might not. Until we were definitely married—and even the prospects of that state were dimmed by the fact that I wasn't sure if my divorce from Phil had ever been finalized—I couldn't afford to retire from "business." My salary and commissions from Renard's were good, but not enough to keep me in a handsome apartment and Donnie in an expensive private school. I wanted to make money and save a large chunk of it for the years when my services wouldn't bring such premiums on the open market. My fee was seventy-five to a hundred dollars, and there were plenty of takers.

Bars, drinking, dancing, parties in apartments, and then to bed with a doctor; same routine the next night except he was a lawyer; next night the pattern might vary by visiting an undercover bistro on the East Side with a broker. New York club keepers and restaurant owners had already started moving to unmarked locations in preparation of the enforcement of the Eighteenth Amendment. The Roaring Twenties had started to roar. I was tired. I was glad when the time came for me to visit Bob in Chicago.

Chicago has guts and verve and thrust. As Bob and I darted from the train station to the waiting limousine, I knew that I was in the town where I belonged, and I resolved to return there permanently whether he married me or not. The wind off Lake Michigan lashed at me with fury and I embraced it as a long-lost lover. Yes, I thought, here's where I belong.

From all that Bob had told me, I assumed his family was well-off; I didn't realize they were wealthy. He lived with his mother and father in their walled-in house in Hyde Park. Hyde Park was, in those days, one of the most elegant sections of Chicago. Bob and I had discussed the arrangements for my "visit" and had decided that since his mother wanted me to stay at their home, he would have a hotel room in the area for our amours. I was introduced to his parents as Helen Cappel, his fiancée. It was strange to hear my married name; I thought of myself as Helen Worley. I'd been using my maiden name for years. Bob had told his parents that I was a widow, that I worked at Renard's, and that I had a twelve-year-old son. And he also must have told them that he was violently in love with me, for they immediately accepted me into the family. His mother, a fragile woman with thin wispy hair, helped me unpack. She complimented my clothes and we discussed the current styles briefly before she launched into the core of her conversation.

"Helen, do you realize that Bob is a terribly ill young man?"

"Yes, I do. I've seen him when he's in the throes of an attack."

"And you still want to marry him?"

"Yes, if he wants me to."

"He wants you to more than anything."

"Then I will." Bob's mother was silent, and I added, "Unless you and Bob's father have objections—then I won't." She arose from her chair and put an arm around my shoulder.

"Oh, Helen, please don't think that! Our concern is for you — Bob doesn't have long to live. Has he told you?"

"I'm afraid it's obvious. Those attacks! Oh, God, those attacks! I don't know how he has lived through as many as he has!" I couldn't help myself; the tears welled up and overflowed. She began crying also. Then she stopped, dabbed at her eyes and smiled.

"Let's stop this foolishness," she said. "I haven't seen Bob so happy since before the war. You've changed him, Helen. You've taken away his depression and exchanged it for optimism. Please, Helen, if you love him, marry him."

"Would you want me to marry him if you knew I was a divorcee and not a widow?"

She pressed her lips together tight for a split second then opened them in a wide smile. "Yes. It makes no difference at all to me. I'd prefer for Bob's father not to know, so let's keep it a secret. Only one thing is important to me: Bob's happiness. And I'm sure he's found it. You have changed his outlook on life. I want you to know you have my blessings—and his dad's."

With that she slipped out of the room and I didn't see her again until Bob and I were ready to leave for a drive to the Chicago Loop. As we left the house, she waved and laughed, "Now don't forget, dinner will be at seven. After tonight you can dine anywhere you want, but tonight both of you are Dad's and mine!" A certain surge rushed through my body and I thought, oh, dear Lord in heaven, wash away my sins and let me be worthy of these magnificent people.

I think Bob's father saw through me. The real me. But it didn't matter to him. The dinner was fun. We laughed and talked. I told them about Cicero, Indiana, and about my memories of the boom there. Bob's dad knew of Mr. W.F. Modes who instigated the glass factory, and we laughed about how he changed the town. I knew that my future father-in-law would have me investigated and that he would find out everything, but I knew he would never tell, not even his wife, because his son's happiness, as short-lived as it might be, was the only thing he wanted now.

Bob and his father told me about their business. I knew, of course, they were importers of Oriental rugs and carpeting, but I didn't learn until that first dinner that their customers were primarily the big-income gangsters of Chicagoland. They were discussing a recent purchase made by Colosimo for his new home when the father said, "Bob, why don't you take Helen to Big Jim's for dinner tomorrow night? He's so crazy about those rugs he'll give you the biggest reception you've ever had there." He looked at me and said with a grin, "You'll think New York is a small town after you've seen Jim Colosimo's."

"Would you like to go there for dinner tomorrow, Helen?" asked Bob.

"I surely would," I responded quickly, "because I know Dale Winter." Everyone looked at me and I realized I had said something wrong. I tried to smooth things over by saying, "I mean I've seen her on the stage. She has a marvelous voice."

Bob's mother realized that they had embarrassed me and said, "I've never met Miss Winter … the new Mrs. Colosimo … so I can't judge her. And even though I don't generally care for the wives of most of the … er, gangsters, I do like Victoria Colosimo. She has a big heart. She's one of my best friends."

"I'm sorry. I read about the whole thing in the papers."

"There's nothing to be sorry about. I, personally, think Vick is better off. The sad part is that she doesn't think so."

"That has nothing to do with that grand food and wine," laughed Bob's dad. "Be sure and go there."

Big Jim Colosimo had done well. Born in the slums of the South Side he had become first a shoe-shine boy, a stealer of apples from pushcarts, then a small-time hoodlum, and finally, a big-time hoodlum. He ran one of the celebrated eating places of the world at Wabash Avenue and 22nd Street in Chicago. He knew everyone and most people liked him. He had many friends, but two of his closest friends were Caruso[21], the voice that shattered glass, and Big Bill Thompson[22], the widely discussed Mayor of Chicago. And he also liked my Bob.

Bob had made a reservation, and we had the best table in the place. Two dozen red roses were on the large table that ordinarily seated eight persons; there were only two place settings, side by side, facing the dance floor. Jim Colosimo himself brought us a bottle of champagne. As his owlish eyes peered at me from behind his steel-framed round glasses, I found it hard to believe that this man could create the terror attributed to him. He laughed continually behind the close-cropped mustache of a type made famous later by Adolph Hitler.

"Jim, Dad tells me you were pleased with the rugs," said Bob.

"I'm head over heels in love with them and so is Dale. They were delivered at the house while we were honeymooning in French Lick," He almost giggled, like a little boy.

"Helen knows Dale," stated Bob.

"I didn't know you were from Chicago."

"I'm not. I knew her in New York. We used to bargain-hunt the department stores together," I laughed. Then I added, "And I've seen her on the stage; her voice is so grand it gives me goose flesh."

From the way Big Jim Colosimo looked, and by the way he gushed on about her singing voice I could tell that he, too, was smitten with Dale's vocal ability. I'm sure he loved her. And my complimentary comments about her had made me his friend for life. Short as his was going to be.

---

21 Enrico Caruso (February 25, 1873 – August 2, 1921) was an Italian operatic tenor. He sang to great acclaim at the major opera houses of Europe and the Americas, appearing in a wide variety of roles from the Italian and French repertoires that ranged from the lyric to the dramatic.

22 Big Bill Thompson (May 14, 1869 – March 19, 1944) was an American politician, mayor of Chicago for three terms, from 1915 to 1923 and again from 1927 to 1931. Known as "Big Bill" Thompson, he is the last Republican to have served as mayor of Chicago to date. Historians rank Thompson among the most unethical mayors in American history, mainly for his open alliance with Al Capone.

"You're the first person I've ever met who knew Dale before she came to Chicago," he said. "I'm going to call her to come right over here and see you." He was half-way out of his chair.

"I really don't know her very well—please don't disturb her," I injected quickly.

"Truthfully, Helen, Dale doesn't have many friends, and she'd love to see you. Maybe she'll sing for us." Colosimo again reminded me of a little boy. A little boy about to receive a birthday present and knowing he's going to get just what he wants. I noticed, too, that he had called me Helen; up to that time it had been Miss Cappel.

"Okay, Jim, call her and tell her I'd really like to see her." As an afterthought I added, "But tell her it is Helen Worley, not Helen Cappel." He gave me a perplexed look, and I stated simply, "My stage name."

Colosimo returned just as the first course of the dinner was being served. "Dale said she'd be here in a half hour and that she's looking forward to seeing you, Helen. She also said to tell you not to tell anything about her until she arrived. What do you know about her?" His mouth smiled, but his eyes were somber, pleading not to be told anything.

"I know that she's a whiz of a singer, and a hell of a bargain hunter—and those are, after all, two of the most flattering things anybody can say about any gal." I could tell that he heard exactly what he wanted to hear.

"I like you, Helen Cappel Worley," stated Colosimo.

Bob laughed out loud. "My God, what a bunch of stuff! Big Jim, I'm very jealous of Helen, but since your wife will be here to chaperone you, why don't you join us for dinner?"

"Bob, I was really hoping you'd ask us to. Dale doesn't particularly like to come here … and sit with a group of my boys. She hasn't been here much since we were married."

At that moment a short man entered the restaurant and Colosimo sent a waiter for him. Colosimo turned to Bob and said, "I want you to meet one of my partners. He's a real good guy."

We were introduced to Johnny Torrio. It was a brief introduction. We discussed New York for a moment. Torrio was from there. He had been brought to Chicago by Colosimo to act as a bodyguard, just as Torrio himself later brought Al Capone from New York. Torrio was not invited to sit down, so left us after a few pleasantries. Maybe it was something psychic, but as Johnny Torrio turned from our table I knew that I'd have more encounters with him, somewhere, someplace.

Dale Winter looked lovely. Dale Winter was lovely. Big Jim and I both wanted her to sing, and she did. To me, her voice was perfection. It had improved since her days in New York. Colosimo had seen to it that she took lessons; even Caruso coached her. She had sung in a church choir for many months as a featured soloist until it had become known to the church elders just who she was, then she was booted. It had hurt her pride. Dale sang because we wanted her to, and then we did something that she wanted us to do: we visited her new home on Vernon Avenue. Dale wanted to show her house to friends, but not many people had been invited there; it was too risky for her husband.

Vernon Avenue was in the heart of the elite area. It was a stone's throw from Prairie Avenue. In this limited compound lived the Chicago greats in their opulent brick and stone townhouses.

We entered Dale's house on the street level and stepped into a black-and-white marbled entrance room; directly ahead was the stairway leading upward to a glass-ceilinged gallery. The walls of the gallery were hung with paintings and even after these many years I still recall a Titian madonna and child that has, as far as I know, never appeared in an art museum anywhere. The floors were covered with the beige and rose colored Persian rugs that had been acquired from Bob and his father. The narrow loveseats about the room were gold-leafed and covered in a beige background petit point. The wallpaper of the library had been removed from a French chateau and painstakingly reassembled to delight the eyes of the gentle overlord of Midwestern vice. I had been in many townhouses in New York, but I had never seen anything equal to what Big Jim Colosimo gave to his thrush, Dale Winter.

It's a shame he didn't get to enjoy his new home and his new wife longer. Exactly three weeks later, on May 11th, Big Jim was gunned down. Colosimo's assassin was possibly someone we had seen or met earlier that carefree evening.

As soon as I arrived back in New York, I wrote to the court in Cincinnati to find out if my divorce had ever been finalized. I had decided to marry Bob; I had wanted to all along, but I had felt that it would cause conflict between him and his parents. Now that I had their blessing, my uncertainty about the divorce from Phil was all that held me back. Bob and I were engaged; as proof, I had a ring. It was an antique amethyst surrounded by diamonds and had belonged to his mother.

Weeks turned into months and still I received no answer to my inquiry about the divorce. I wrote them again demanding an immediate reply. Still there was no answer. I considered taking the bull by the horns and going to Cincinnati; if the divorce had never gone through, I would start proceedings for another review. But then I would think about Donnie; even though he was in his private school I did see him often and we were quite close. He and Bob had been together frequently and they liked each other. If only I could marry Bob and have Donnie with me, too! Going to Cincinnati would certainly destroy any possibilities of that idyll. There wasn't a chance in a hundred that I could get custody of Donnie, and I refused to give him up.

In early summer Bob had another bad lung attack and returned to the New Jersey hospital. The more I saw of him, the more I loved him. No man has ever been so comforting, so understanding, so completely kind. We never quarreled and it was almost unbelievable to me that life with anyone could be so serene. He was feeling much better the latter part of July when a message arrived from his father that his mother had had a stroke and for him to catch the first train for Chicago.

I'll never know whether it was the unnerving message concerning his mother, the ungodly humidity in New York that week, or a combination of both that brought on his terrible lung attack as we were waiting for his train. Suddenly he turned pale, then he began coughing and choking, gasping for breath. At first I tried to comfort him, then I ran for help to the station master's office. They paged a doctor, but Bob was about unconscious when one arrived. The doctor did something to bring him out of the attack then turned to me and said that Bob should be hospitalized immediately. Bob refused to go to the hospital and furthermore insisted on taking his scheduled train to Chicago. I was completely distraught, and as his train pulled away I had the feeling that I would never see my love again.

Bob arrived in Chicago just barely alive. His mother had improved, and as soon as she realized the state that Bob was in she pleaded with him to go back to his hospital. He was in no condition to make the long trip back to the New Jersey mustard gas specialists, so he remained for weeks in a Chicago hospital. One minute I felt I should be with him and the next minute I felt I might cause more harm than good. Bob's father was kind about calling me occasionally and giving me reports until Bob had improved sufficiently to write me. His letter stabbed me in the heart: he said that because of his health it wasn't fair to ask me to consider marrying him; he asked that I forget him and please not contact him; he also said he would love me until the day he died. Once again something worthwhile had been within my grasp for a moment, only to be snatched away.

Chapter 15

MEN, BOOTLEG HOOCH, MEN, speakeasies, men, jazz trombones, men, insinuating saxophones … that's the method I used to cauterize the wound in my heart. When the United States went dry at one minute after the stroke of midnight on July 15, 1920, New York became a finger-snapping slave to that pagan god called Demon Rum. The Reverend Billy Sunday[23] said goodbye to liquor with: "You were God's worst enemy. You were Hell's best friend … The reign of tears is over. Hell will be forever for rent." What Billy didn't know was that Hell might have been for rent, but you couldn't rent a brownstone house in New York for love or money—they had all been snapped up for speakeasies.

I embarked on a program of dissolving my disappointment in a foggy haze of speakeasies. I was playful and brazen. I made money. Bob hadn't really slipped from my mind, but I refused myself the luxury of dwelling on what the future could have held. I had finally heard from the court in Cincinnati that I wasn't divorced; Phil Cappel was my legal husband. When this information was

---

23 William Ashley Sunday (November 19, 1862 – November 6, 1935) was an American athlete who, after being a popular outfielder in baseball's National League during the 1880s, became the most celebrated and influential American evangelist during the first two decades of the 20th century.

Converting to evangelical Christianity in the 1880s, Sunday left baseball for the Christian ministry. He gradually developed his skills as a pulpit evangelist in the Midwest and then, during the early 20th century, he became the nation's most famous evangelist with his colloquial sermons and frenetic delivery. Sunday held widely reported campaigns in America's largest cities, and he attracted the largest crowds of any evangelist before the advent of electronic sound systems. He also made a great deal of money and was welcomed into the homes of the wealthy and influential. Sunday was a strong supporter of Prohibition, and his preaching likely played a significant role in the adoption of the Eighteenth Amendment in 1919.

received, I discarded it to the wastebasket of my past; I doubted that I'd ever marry again, so what did it matter.

Prior to Prohibition there were certain cocktail bars that could have been strategic locations for picking up "live ones," but, unfortunately, they wouldn't allow unescorted women to hang around. All that changed when the speakeasies came in with a bang; there were very few speaks that didn't encourage attractive, unescorted women to utilize their facilities. The faces behind the sliding-door peepholes were all familiar to me and I had a wallet in my purse crammed with "membership cards" to dozens of hot spots. The newspapers claimed that a certain postwar recession had set in, but there was no recession in my business department.

I had told Tim that I was back in a big way, and had the supply to satisfy the demand—and the demand came hot and heavy. I decided to expand my operations and acquired two other girls to help hold down my apartment. We set up a bar in the living room and the apartment itself became a type of "club." We had our steady customers and the telephone became alive with Tim calling to introduce "regular guys." When I wasn't at home with customers, I was out on the town looking for customers.

In October Bob returned to me. I was in Renard's and it was just before lunch. He walked in dressed in civilian clothes; he had been released from the army. He looked healthy and said he had never felt better in his life. He said he was in New York to marry me. I put on my hat and coat and told Mr. Gold I was leaving his employment, and walked out with Bob.

I told City Hall my name was Helen DeMar, and Bob and I got married. Bigamy? I didn't give it a thought. I wanted Bob, I wanted Donnie … and by God I had them both.

We stayed on in New York until after Christmas. The treatments at the hospital continued and Bob grew progressively stronger and healthier. I broke off all contacts with the "business" crowd and my new way of life centered around Bob, our apartment, and Donnie. Occasionally, Bob and I would go out to speakeasies for an evening, but invariably I'd meet someone I preferred to forget. And it seemed that after such an evening Bob would get sick; it was obvious to me that liquor, combined with smoke-filled rooms, brought on attacks for him. After a while we cut that type of activity from the routine of our day-to-day living.

In January the doctors told Bob that he was strong enough to return to Chicago and the family business. After much discussion we decided that it would be wiser for Bob to go to Chicago alone, find us a place to live, and reacquaint himself with his own business before Donnie and I joined him. Donnie had become a day student, and for the first time since he had started to school he had a real home life.

Donnie and I arrived in Chicago on February 26, my birthday. We were met at the train by an ecstatically happy Bob. When I saw him running toward us, waving his arms, then hugging us both, I knew that I had found the love that I had been searching for since the clay I found Florence Gossett's note in Phil's pocket.

"Did you find us an apartment, Bob?" I asked as we drove southward on Michigan Avenue.

"Yes, I sure did," he replied with a smile.

"Where is it? Tell me about it!"

"It's a surprise. You'll see soon."

It was a surprise. We stopped in front of a handsome building on Drexel Avenue and were ushered into a large reception area, then we glided upward in a brass embellished elevator to the top floor of the six-story building. I noticed, as we stepped off the elevator into a small foyer, that there were only two doors. The door to the right had our name engraved on a tiny brass plaque just below the doorbell. Bob unlocked the door and pushed it open wide; every light in the apartment was on. "Welcome home, Helen and Donnie," he said quietly. Then he took me by one hand and Donnie by the other and we walked into our new home.

Every era has its own high style in interior furnishings and our apartment was 1922; it was heavenly. Decorators from Marshall Field's had worked overtime coordinating the scalloped window blinds with the most valuable rugs ever imported by Bob's firm; the walls and woodwork were painted ivory to blend with the background of the rugs; the accent colors of the rugs—rose, tan, and blue—had been picked up by the glass shades of the Tiffany lamps. The upholstered furniture, considered then to be most modern, was covered in rose-colored mohair and arranged with period pieces I recognized from my visit to Bob's home in Hyde Park.

All was perfection, and every detail including the accessories were keyed to conversations Bob and I had had concerning how we thought a home should look. Then I looked at the mantelpiece and my childhood literally swept over me: there, on the mantel, were pastel-pink bisque figurines from the Levinson home in Indianapolis. Once, when Bob had been very sick and confined to bed for weeks, I had sat in his room and discussed anything and everything I could think of to keep his mind off his pain and discomfort; one thing I told him was about my occasional visits to the Levinsons' home as a little girl and how I loved to sit and look at the figurines on the mantel in Mrs. Levinson's bedroom.

"Bob, those figurines! Where did you get them?"

"In Indianapolis."

"How? How?"

"It was simple. The Levinsons wanted an Oriental rug and I wanted the figurines."

Suddenly I was in Bob's arms and the tears started. Little Donnie didn't know what to make of it all, but he sensed that he was at home and secure with his own family.

For the next two years I lived the type of life I had dreamed about ever since my disillusioning years in Cincinnati. I had everything any woman could want, with the exception of my first-born son. I thought a lot about little Phil, Jr., and wanted to see him, but I was afraid of what could happen to my orderly life if the senior Phil Cappel made a reentrance. I also yearned to see Mama and decided that the time had come to re-establish my contact with her. I called Mama long distance and we both cried so much we didn't do much talking. I told her that I was married and living in Chicago, but because of my still-legal marriage to Phil I couldn't go to Cincinnati to see Phil, Jr. Mama said that little Phil visited her in Cicero occasionally and she was sure he would come to her if she requested it. We arranged to meet in Indianapolis.

How can I describe the meeting? Mama was still beautiful, the same as I had always remembered her. And with her was a young man, my little Phil, now an adult-looking eighteen years old! I had taken Donnie with me. Watching my sons together for the first time since my flight from Cincinnati, I realized that the moment had arrived when I would have to let go of Donnie. Both he and Phil, Jr., begged me to let Donnie return to Cincinnati to visit his father. I didn't have the heart to refuse; but I made Donnie promise that he wouldn't tell anyone where I was living, and I knew he would keep his word. Whether Donnie knew that I had been a whore or not, he loved me and I loved him. Whatever would come to him now, that knowledge would always remain. I wondered if I had been too selfish, for too long, to keep my boys apart.

When the day-long reunion ended I experienced all kinds of emotions. Phil, Jr., had treated me politely and concentrated most of his attention on his brother. No intimate word passed between us. I could have been some distant relative or a friend of the family's. I had to hold back any show of affection. When Mama and my sons caught the train for Cicero, I had a sudden stabbing conviction that my Donnie would never return to me. Their faces blurred through my tears as they waved from the train window. Mama blew me a kiss. I shall always be grateful for that day together. Mama died several years later and the last links with the past were broken.

I returned to my Bob. I had never felt such tenderness before.

In August of 1922 Bob and I were invited to have dinner with Johnny Torrio. Johnny had recently ordered rugs for his own apartment and he and Bob had become friends. After Jim Colosimo's assassination, Johnny had taken over command of everything south of the Chicago River; then he had moved into the suburbs of Cicero, Chicago Heights, Calumet City, and Burnham. He had placed the suburban reins in the hands of his imported-from-New York lieutenant who was known by two names: Scarface Al Brown and Al Capone. I was excited over the prospects of the dinner; not everybody was invited to dine with the notorious Torrio, and I particularly wanted to meet Capone. His name seemed to be in the newspapers constantly. I had met Nick, Johnny's brother, and various other cronies of the Torrio set, but I hadn't met Capone.

Bob was late getting home that evening and I was completely dressed when he arrived. I had given a great deal of thought to what I would wear before deciding on black chiffon. As soon as I saw Bob I knew he wasn't feeling well. He admitted he felt worse than he had in months.

"I know, I know, Bob, and I don't think we should go," I pleaded. Bob was precious to me, and his health was something I didn't tamper with.

"Helen, Torrio's rugs will be the biggest commission I've had in months. He wants us there. We've got to go."

"Torrio knows ... about your condition. Just call up and say we can't come. It's no insult to him to tell him you're sick." I had already decided that we weren't going.

"You've been looking forward to this party," he said.

"That's beside the point. We aren't going." For the first and only time we came close to an argument. In the end I lost—or won, according to the point of view—and we went to the dinner.

I was seated at Torrio's right and to my right was Al Capone. I had assumed, hoped, really, that other wives would be present, but the only other woman at the table was the singer from Colosimo's I knew only as Gladys. She was on Torrio's left and from bits of conversation I overheard between them, I got the impression they were more than chums. Bob was seated across the vast round table talking to Nick Torrio[24] and a man from Big Bill Thompson's office. Capone and I were left to our own conversational devices.

"So you're the famous Al Capone," I said.

"I'm Al Capone. I don't know about the 'famous' part."

"I understand you're also Mr. Brown. Isn't it confusing to have two names?" I thought I was rattling on like a fool but I couldn't stop myself.

"Haven't you ever had two names ... Helen?" he asked.

"As a matter of fact, I have had. But the first name is always Helen."

"My first name is always Al." We looked at each other and both broke into peals of laughter. When Al laughed, he laughed from

---

24 Johnny Torrio's brother and right-hand man.

the stomach. After that the ice was broken and our talk flowed like the champagne.

"I've heard you came here from New York, Helen," he said.

"Yes, I did. Bob and I were married there, but he's from Chicago originally."

"How long did you live in New York?"

"A couple of years."

"I'm from New York myself."

"I know you are," I said.

"What did you do in New York—before you got married?"

"That's not fair, Al, I haven't asked you what you did in New York, have I?"

"No ... but you know what I did," he said with a smile.

"I have an idea you know what I did, too," I said softly. That broke him up and he bellowed with laughter.

"What's so funny between you two?" asked Bob from across the table.

"Your wife has a sense of humor, Bob. You're a lucky guy," said Capone.

I'll always remember Al as a warm human being. I've heard and read volumes of gruesome stories about him and I don't doubt that many of them were true. In all probability he'll go down in the books as the gangster of our time. Be all that as it may, I know only that Al was sweet. As far as I'm concerned, he had a heart as big as the South Side of Chicago.

The waiter brought the menus and Capone and I discussed what sounded good. "What appeals to you, Helen?" he asked.

"Chicken ala King. It's my favorite."

"I'll remember."

"Do that, Al."

As the coffee was being served I became aware that Bob was very sick. I could see that he was choking and trying to hold back from a fit of coughing. I was glad the dinner was almost over.

Johnny Torrio turned to me and said, "Do you like jazz music, Helen?"

"Yes, very much."

"Have you heard King Oliver's band?"

"No, not that I recall," I answered.

"You'd recall it if you had heard him," he said. Then Torrio announced to the whole table, "We're going to Lincoln Gardens to hear King Oliver." I looked at Bob and saw that he was in no condition to go anywhere.

"Johnny," I said, "the dinner has been grand, but I'm afraid we're going to have to go home."

"Why?" Torrio asked.

What the hell, I thought, I'll tell him. "Bob isn't feeling well. We shouldn't have come tonight." At that moment Bob went into a coughing spell. It took a few moments for him to regain his breath.

"I really don't feel like going, Johnny," Bob said, "but don't let that keep you from going." By this time everyone had risen from the table.

"Bob, do you care if Helen goes with us?" asked Torrio.

"Thanks loads, Johnny," I injected, "but I'd better go home with Bob."

Bob had gotten his coughing under control and smiled at me. "Go with them, Helen. You'd enjoy it. I'll be all right." Then he winked at me. "You'll be in the safest hands in the city of Chicago."

We got Bob into a cab and as it pulled away, Johnny Torrio said to his brother Nick, "Will you see Gladys home, Nick?" It was a command, a dismissal. I looked at Gladys and her face was expressionless.

"Aren't you going?" I said to Nick and Gladys who were standing next to the two bodyguards who were seated close to us during the dinner.

"No, I have an appointment," said Nick. Gladys remained silent.

"Are you going, Al?" Torrio asked Capone.

"Yes, I believe I will," stated Capone. Torrio looked surprised, but said nothing. I learned later it was most unusual for Torrio and Capone to go together to any crowded place. One of the bodyguards went for the car and presently the black, steel-enforced limousine pulled up at the curb. The second bodyguard opened the door for us and Capone got in first, then me, then Torrio. The door was closed and the bodyguard got into the front beside the first guard who served as driver.

Lincoln Gardens was at Thirty-first and Cottage Grove Avenue. The canvas awning extended out to the street. The guard jumped out and stood facing the crowd of people waiting to get into the dance hall. The driver got out and ran around the car and opened the door. Torrio alighted first and as I got out he took my right arm; then Capone got out and took my left arm. A man whom I had never seen nodded to the two guards, walked around the automobile and got into the driver's seat and took the car away. Then we proceeded into Lincoln Gardens—with one guard ahead of us, one guard behind us. The hushed rumble of voices floated throughout the crowd. The royalty of Chicago had arrived at the gala.

A group of people occupying one of the dance hall's few tables was given the bum's rush and the table was set up with clean linen, glasses, and ice before we reached it. An aisle appeared right through the mob of people and every eye was on us. I heard the thunder of whispers: "Torrio! Capone! Johnny! Al! Scarface! Who's she? Look at her dress!"

I was glad I had decided to wear the black chiffon and the headache band with the white plume—it was something new, something avant-garde. The drapes of the short dress were edged with glistening bugle beads. It was my debut, and I was dressed for it.

Soon the novelty of our presence wore off and all attention was directed back to King Oliver's Creole Jazz Band. There were six colored male players, and a woman who really pounded the keyboard. The music was frenzied, wild, primitiveness honed to the sharpest edges of sound. The band went into a number called "Eccentric" and the crowd went mad. Then came "Panama" and on the heels of it came "High Society". It was unbelievable music; I wanted to shake, I wanted to shimmy, I wanted to jazz it around. "Come on, Johnny, dance with me," I cried to Torrio.

He was laughing, the music had gotten to him, too. "I can't dance, Helen," he shouted through the sounds coming from the trombone and the cornet. The musicians dived into "Tiger Rag" and I was uncontrollable. I had to dance. "Try it, Johnny, try it!"

Then we were on the dance floor. The crowd applauded when they saw Johnny Torrio really letting loose.

"Twelfth Street Rag", "Wang Wang Blues", and then as a relaxer the low-down, sex-starved, sex-fed blues from "Storyville". Torrio and I were panting when the slow music started and we sat down across from Al Capone whose face was glued to the bandstand and frozen into a soft smile. He grinned and puffed his cigar. Torrio squeezed my hand as he whispered, "I like you, Helen, I've liked you since the first moment I saw you at Jim's over two years ago." His eyes burned into mine, and I stared into the depths of his pupils.

"Don't like me too much, Johnny. I can like you, but I can't like you too much." He hung onto my hand as the cornetist made sounds come from his horn that were heavy with sorrow, with joy, with love, with hate.

"Johnny, who is that colored boy playing the horn?" Torrio snapped his fingers at an attendant waiter and whispered my question to him, then Johnny turned to me and said. "His name's Armstrong—Louis Armstrong. Joe Oliver brought him up from New Orleans. This is his first night here."

"Well, he's damn good, I'll tell you," I said emphatically. When the blues were over the crowd chanted and stormed, "Armstrong! More! Let him play! Let him play!" Armstrong smiled with huge white teeth, bowed, and the sweat streamed down his face as he made his music cry.

Capone smiled and flipped the ashes from his cigar and I gently pushed Johnny Torrio's leg away from mine.

Bob's attacks grew more frequent, more violent. We closed the apartment in Chicago and returned to New York. He remained at the hospital in New Jersey for several months and I saw him only on weekends. I did everything in my power to keep his spirits high, but the doctors knew it was no use and I knew it, too. Finally, they suggested that I take him back to Chicago. I realized then that the end was near. We went home to Chicago.

It was near Christmas when Bob insisted on going by himself into the Chicago Loop; when he returned he sat down beside me on the sofa and said, "My darling, here is something for you. If

anything happens to me this will help you get along for a while."
He handed me a large envelope containing twenty-five thousand
dollars. "I only wish it were more, but it is all I have. This is your
home, Helen, your real home, and the rent on this apartment is
paid for three years." Never have I felt such love within me for
anyone as I did for Bob; I prayed to God to take my health, my
strength, my vitality and transfer it to Bob's body. I would gladly
have perished in order to have kept him alive. On February
8, 1923, he died, just after midnight, with my arms wrapped
around him.

213   De Jonghe Restaurant.

Chapter 16

I WAS UNFORTUNATE in that the term "call girl" wasn't popularized until after my peak. The label of call girl has a certain amount of style, and I have referred to myself as such in various portions of this book, even though I have never been one to sit around and wait for the phone to ring (although it did, plenty). I was certainly not just a streetwalker, and the term harlot is too archaic for me. Hooker? That's a hell of a word! And I can't stand prostitute. I have always considered myself a "good time party girl."

I tried every way in the world to keep myself busy after Bob died. I tried reading, sewing, and going to lectures, but it was no use. I had been in love with him and the memory of his love was driving me insane. After a few months of miserable mourning, I got back into the swing of things, job-wise and business-wise. First, I found myself a selling job at Friend's Store just a few doors south of State and Madison Streets. I really sold. I was on salary plus commission and I rarely let a customer get off without a purchase. Many a customer has bought a cheap fur coat from me on the hottest day in August, just to flee the premises for a breath of air. I was definitely high-pressure.

Soon after I started at Friend's Store, a couple of the other salesgirls asked me if I'd like to go out with them and some of their men friends after work that evening. I told them that my husband had passed away shortly before and I hadn't been out since, and that I'd love to go.

We went to the Gold Room of De Jonghe's and the hooch flowed like ice water. A colored piano player started beating out a hot rendition of "I'll Say She Does" and one of the men bet me ten dollars I wouldn't do the shimmy; before he could bat an eyelash I was doing it like Sister Kate[25]. Then another guy yelled he'd give me twenty more to "take it off" and with that I jumped up on the bar and took off every damned bit of it. The other salesgirls were, I think, a trifle shocked, but the men enjoyed it; in fact, every one of them called me for a date and before I knew it I was back in "business." I was also out of widow's weeds.

My buddy at Friend's Store was a guy named Sol. He was the floor man and was a very important person as far as the salesgirls were concerned, since he was the one who controlled the time cards. Shortly after I got back in circulation I told Sol that I "went out a lot" and would probably be late frequently for punching in at nine A.M. Sol got the drift and told me not to worry about it, and he also told me that his favorite luxury was a certain brand of twenty-five-cent cigars. I got the drift, too. We worked out a friendly arrangement: if I wasn't there by nine, Sol would simply punch my card for me. If for one reason or another I was not coming in at all, I would phone Sol prior to nine and he wouldn't bother with the card—then it was just a plain day off from work. I'm sure that the top management of the store knew of my agreement with Sol, but they never mentioned it to me, probably because I sold

---

25 "I Wish I Could Shimmy Like My Sister Kate"; often simply "Sister Kate," is an up-tempo jazz dance song, written by Clarence Williams (who purchased the rights) and Armand Piron, and published in 1919. It is variously believed to be based on a bawdy tune by Louis Armstrong (about Kate Townsend, a murdered brothel madam) or transcribed from a version performed by Anna Jones and Fats Waller.

The lyrics of the song are narrated first-person by Kate's sister, who sings about Kate's impressive dancing skill and her wish to be able to emulate it. She laments that she's not quite "up to date," but believes that dancing like "Sister Kate" will rectify this, and she will be able to impress "all the boys in the neighborhood" like her sister.

Over the years this song has been performed and recorded by many artists, including Frances Faye and Rusty Warren, a 1959 version by Shel Silverstein, The Olympics in 1960 (released as "Shimmy Like Kate"), the Red Onion Band, and a beat version by The Remo Four in 1964. It was recorded live by The Beatles in 1962, and appears on *Live! at the Star Club* in Hamburg, Germany; 1962. The song arrived in the 1960s and 1970s folk scene thanks to Dave Van Ronk (recording it twice on *In the Tradition* and on *Dave Van Ronk and the Ragtime Jug Stompers*) and Jim Kweskin, who made it part of a "Sister Kate's Night Out" medley on his *Relax Your Mind* album with Mel Lyman and Fritz Richmond. In 1967, the Nitty Gritty Dirt Band included it on their eponymous *The Nitty Gritty Dirt Band* (album).

almost twice as much merchandise as any of the other salesgirls.

The week after I started at Friend's, and quite by accident, I met another man who was helpful to me during the "Chicago period" of my professional career. He was a young lawyer whom I shall refer to as George. We met at lunch one day in Henrici's Restaurant; the place was crowded and he asked me if I'd like to share his table. By the time lunch was over George and I understood each other; he was just starting his practice and needed clients, and I knew that some day I might need legal counsel. I left the restaurant with his business card and I've never been without one since. George is still very much a part of the Chicago scene.

No amount of money on earth would have persuaded me to have taken a man to my Drexel Blvd. apartment where I had lived with Bob. As a result I had set up a completely equipped, large separate apartment at Forty-sixth and Cottage Grove Avenue. I had a cook on tap and girls on tap. The place was like a club or speak; I catered to big dinners and gambling parties with girls available if they were desired. If a dinner wasn't too big, I would many times prepare the food myself. The place was used mostly by union leaders for their private entertaining.

I guess it was the amount of available room I had in the Cottage Grove apartment that prompted me to help Linda Ann. One night I was leaving Peacock Alley of the Congress Hotel and about a half block from the hotel I saw a lovely-looking red-haired girl leaning against a building. Her clothes were expensively cut. She was weeping. I asked her what the matter was, but she wouldn't answer. Finally I asked her if she was on the needle. She immediately stopped crying and looked at me. She seemed to be examining the clothes I had on. Then she asked, "Do you know about such things?"

"Sure," I answered.

"How?" she asked.

"Because I'm a hustler, and I know," I replied.

"You don't look like one."

"Thanks for the compliment. Now tell me what's wrong."

"I'm … I'm sick."

"What do you mean?"

She turned her face toward the wall before answering, "It must be a … a venereal disease."

"Have you been checked?"

"No."

"Then how do you know?" I asked.

"I've heard. I'm sure it is." She seemed ready to faint.

"Are you on the street?" I asked.

"No … No, I'm not. I have a … a boy friend."

"Then he gave it to you?" I accused more than questioned. She didn't answer and I continued, "Have you told him?"

"No!"

"Want to go to a hospital?"

"Oh, no!" she cried.

My mind worked quickly and I said, "I'll take you home with me and I'll get a doctor—a personal, confidential friend—to check you, but first you must swear to me you aren't on dope. Are you on dope?"

"No, I swear it!"

"All right," I said as I turned and hailed a cab, "I don't want anyone around me connected in any way with that stuff."

The doctor's examination bore out Linda Ann's suspicion and he started immediate treatment of her disease. In the pre-penicillin days a case of VD was nothing to be sneezed at—nowadays, of course, it's easier to cure than a common cold, but not so way back then. I gave Linda Ann one of the back bedrooms and laid down a set of hard and fast rules for her. She was to keep to her room if a party was going on in the apartment; she was to follow the doctor's orders explicitly; she was to clean the toilet with antiseptic every time she used it; and she was to make sure that all her dishes were sterilized after every use. I had never been plagued with a malady of that type, and I certainly didn't want to contract it from Linda Ann.

After four or five days Linda Ann was in better health and better spirits, but the doctor said that she should remain in bed for several weeks. She was really a very charming and educated girl from the deep South and although she was wary of telling me too much about herself, I could sense that she was from a nice family. One evening I was sitting in her room talking to her and I asked her who the "boy friend" was who caused her this trouble. She didn't answer the question for several minutes, then she finally told me. I had met the man—he was among the hierarchy of the Capone combine.

"I really think you should tell him, Linda Ann," I said, "He's probably worried to death about you—and wondering where in the hell you disappeared to." Linda Ann had given me the key to her small apartment the second day she was at my place and I had gone there and brought all of her clothes to her.

"I don't know, Helen, I just don't know," she said in a faint voice. "I'm in love with him … and what would he think if he knew that I had … "

"You did get it from him, didn't you?" I asked.

"He's the only one I could have gotten it from. I haven't been with another man in over a year."

"Well, if he doesn't know he has it, he's a regular walking Typhoid Mary!" I exclaimed. "I'll find him for you and tell him; he'll need a doctor—and quick."

"All right, Helen—if you think so," she said.

I made a few phone calls and finally got in touch with the man in question at the Midland Club. The club was just off LaSalle Street on Adams and was quite a hangout for some of the syndicate people. I didn't tell him what it was all about on the telephone; I merely asked him if he could meet me at Colosimo's that evening. I told him it was important.

At seven-thirty that night he was waiting for me. He was a man I didn't know very well and I'm sure he was wondering what on earth I wanted to see him about.

He arose from his table and came toward me as I walked through the restaurant. "You're Helen, aren't you?" he asked.

"Yes, I haven't seen you in several years, Jack," I answered. We sat down at the table and he ordered me a drink.

"What is it you wanted to see me about, Helen?"

"I have a new boarder at my house, Jack. Her name is Linda Ann." He almost leaped from his chair.

"Thank God! I was afraid something had happened to her," he cried.

"Something has happened to her," I said. "And unless she's lying, you've got a ripe dose of clap yourself."

He was silent for a moment, then he stated flatly, "She has it."

"You can bet your sweet life she has it," I said with a tinge of temper in my voice. "I think it's unforgivable for any man who has that to knowingly give it to a girl."

"I swear I didn't know I had it the last time I was with her, Helen. Does she have a doctor?"

"Yes, she has a doctor. And evidently it was caught in time, but she's plenty sick."

"Can I see her?"

"Yes."

He went back to the apartment with me and Linda Ann almost died when he walked in. She turned her face to the wall. He knelt by her bed and asked forgiveness and soon there were tears and embraces. She was crying, he was crying, and I was crying as I slipped out of the room. In the end it turned out beautifully: they both took their treatments and were cured about the same time; they got married and even took a "honeymoon" trip to Europe. I always think of them as my lovebirds.

Linda Ann was with me for two months, and it was during that time that I had quite an experience. I had worked late at Friend's Store and was walking down State Street carrying a large box with a new suit in it. I dropped the box and a man picked it up for me. Interesting, because it was unintentional. I thanked him and he asked me if I'd like to have dinner with him. I had no plans for the evening and told him I'd love to join him. He hailed a cab and we went to the Edgewater Beach Hotel. During the long ride north, and throughout dinner, I was impressed with him. He was a wonderful conversationalist and extremely handsome—he appeared to be between forty and forty-five years old. Suddenly the thought struck me that perhaps he was a detective! I was immediately on guard and was very careful of what I said.

As we were riding back toward the Loop he asked if he could come to my apartment. I told him that was impossible; he pressed on and on and wanted to know if there wasn't some place we could go and I told him yes, that I knew of a place but it was very expensive and he said that the price of the place was of no concern to him. He waited in the cab while I called Linda Ann; I explained the situation to her and told her I thought something was fishy, so for her not to tell him that it was my own place and for her to charge him a hundred dollars for the room.

When Linda Ann met us at the door of the apartment and said, "A hundred dollars, please," he didn't blink an eye. We left about one-thirty a.m., and he dropped me at the Drexel Boulevard building where I told him I "roomed."

As I got out of the taxi he said, "I don't even know your last name, Helen."

"DeMar," I said, "Helen DeMar." It was a name I had used at various times when I didn't want my true identity known. There was something extremely peculiar about the man, but I couldn't put my finger on it. I regretted having told him that I worked at Friend's. "Goodnight," I said. Then I walked quickly into the building.

A week passed and I had completely forgotten about the man. I was leaving Friend's after work and there, standing on State Street, was my companion of a week before. Sol had left the store with me and as the man said, "I've been waiting for you, Helen," Sol scurried off with a light remark about not forgetting the cigars if I didn't punch in on time the next day.

I was even more wary of the man this time than I had been a week before. We walked slowly up State Street talking in generalities; we turned east on Washington Street and just past the corner was a French millinery shop. The show window displayed a single hat: a purple velvet beret with the entire breast of an egret and scores of egret strands on it. I gasped when I saw it. It was the most sensational hat I had ever seen. It was priced at three hundred dollars.

"Look at that hat!" I cried. "I've never seen anything to slightly compare with it since I worked at a fancy millinery store in New York."

"Do you want it?" he asked.

"Want it ... what do you mean?"

"If you like that hat, I'll buy it for you tomorrow," he said.

I couldn't believe my ears, but I assured him that I loved the hat. As we were standing there, staring at the lavish beret, he held a key toward me and said simply, "I've rented an apartment for you at Forty-fifth and Michigan Avenue. There's no furniture in the apartment, but there's twenty-five hundred dollars in the bathroom medicine cabinet for you to use to furnish it." I was stunned momentarily but regained my senses quickly and reached out and took the key from him. Jesus God, I thought, what's going on here?

The next day I wore the fabulous beret (it had been delivered to the store) and went to the apartment. It was on a high floor in a tall building. The apartment was small, but beautiful. There was a sun parlor with a sweeping view of Lake Michigan. And sure enough, the bathroom medicine cabinet was stocked with money. Within ten days the apartment was completely furnished.

My "keeper" was evidently married because he only came to the apartment on Sunday afternoons and evenings. This simplified things for me because, with three apartments, I had to do some tight scheduling not to get my addresses and dates crossed! This arrangement lasted for five or six months. Early one Sunday he called (luckily, I was already there) and said he was bringing a gentleman friend to the apartment with him for dinner. I fixed a nice dinner and served it in the sun parlor. After dinner my "keeper" had to go out to replenish our liquor supply, and while he was gone the dinner guest asked some very suspicious questions concerning the apartment and its furnishings. He wanted to know if all the furniture was new. I told him yes, then I added that I had purchased it with money that my late husband had left me.

The men left after midnight and I jumped in a cab and dashed over to my Drexel Boulevard place. I found the card of the young lawyer I had met at Henrici's and called his home number. Finally the phone was answered, and I recognized his voice. I told him who I was and he remembered me. I apologized for calling him so late and he said it didn't matter. I told him all the details of how I had met this man, about the hat, about the apartment, everything. I wound up by telling him about the dinner guest and his suspicious questioning of me.

"Helen, don't you know where this man works?"

"No. In fact, George, I don't even know his last name. He told me it was Smith, but I'm sure he was lying, just as I was—I told him my last name was DeMar."

"Has he ever mentioned the type of work he does?"

"No, but I'm sure it has something to do with finances. He could be a banker or a stock broker."

"Can you be at my office at eight o'clock in the morning?"

"Yes."

"Okay. Where are you now?"

"At my own apartment."

"Don't go back to the place at Forty-fifth and Michigan tonight."

"I don't intend to," I said.

"I'll see you at eight sharp," he said as he hung up.

It was a Thursday morning. I walked into George's office exactly at eight o'clock and he was asleep with his feet on the desk. His eyes opened and he yawned. George had been working all night.

"Do you have two hundred and fifty dollars, Helen?"

"Yes."

"I need it to pay for all the information I got last night." I opened my purse and gave him the money.

"Your sweetheart is in real trouble, Helen."

"Oh?"

"He's a bank cashier—he's been taking home samples. As a matter of fact, he has taken home over a hundred thousand dollars in samples." George yawned again.

"Jesus," I said.

"They are ready to move in on him any time. Your dinner guest last night was a federal agent who has been on the case."

"Jesus," I reiterated.

"Can you get everything out of that apartment on Michigan Avenue by Monday morning?"

"Everything?" I asked.

"Everything. Store it, sell it, give it away. Only you've got to get everything out of there. It's the only tangible evidence of your connection with this man."

"Okay."

"If I were you, I'd rather not have any of that furniture in my possession—but, of course, that is a decision you'll have to make."

"What do you suggest I do with it?"

"Give it all to the Salvation Army. Call them from here and tell them that if they get their truck over there within an hour they can have the whole apartment full of new furniture."

"Will I be involved, George?"

"I don't think so, Helen. After all, you knew nothing about it."

I picked up the phone and called the Salvation Army. They assured me they'd meet me at the apartment in one hour with their salvage truck and their crew of movers. I turned toward the door.

"Thanks, George."

"Think nothing of it, Helen. Call me again sometime."

"I will. The very next time I shack up with a bank embezzler."

I couldn't help smiling at my one strange contact with the Salvation Army. I wanted to send a little card: "With the compliments of a hustler and a thief."

Chapter 17

THREE OTHER MEN are particularly outstanding in my memories of Chicago, and I think of them as following on the heels of one another, so I'll call them Snap, Crackle, and Pop.

I really can't recall Mr. Snap's name, which is unusual inasmuch as when our affair ended I was left with a clever "souvenir" to remember him by. Snap was a piano player, and for some reason I have a weakness for musicians.

It began one winter evening at a little speakeasy called Friar's Inn in the basement at Van Buren and Wabash Avenue. I stopped there after work for a drink and was invited to join a group of merry-makers. The next night my phone rang and a man's voice asked if I had been at Friar's the night before. When I told him yes, he said that he had been "smitten" with me and had inquired around as to who I was. He went on to say that he was the piano player with the orchestra at Friar's and wanted me to drop by the next evening. Well, I've never been one to ignore piano players who are "smitten" with me, so, of course, I went. Mr. Snap was rather attractive and for a month or so he squired me around the Chicago and suburban speakeasies. Never once during the whole month did he suggest that we spend the night together. I had begun to consider our relationship as a platonic interlude until one evening he stammered and stuttered and asked if I would spend the night with him. I assured him that it could be easily arranged.

The next morning he presented me with his plan: He was

going to divorce his wife and marry me; he had already informed his wife, and she wasn't keen on the prospect in view of the fact that they had a child. But that didn't matter to him, he was crazy about me. This was the first I had heard about the wife and child so I told him to get the hell out. He kept bothering me with phone calls at all hours of the day and night, but I refused to see him.

Some weeks later I was sashaying down Michigan Avenue doing a little "window shopping" and just as I was in front of Blum's Vogue, a car pulled up to the curb and I heard a woman scream, "Take this, you husband-stealing bitch!" Then bang, bang, bang! Bullets were popping all around me. Mrs. Snap was getting her revenge.

Only one bullet hit me, and that was in the leg. Luckily for me, Mrs. Snap was a lousy marksman. Blood was gushing all over the sidewalk and the wound in my calf was burning like hell. I grabbed my leg just above the torn flesh and squeezed hard to stop the flowing faucet of blood. I heard the squeaking of brakes at the curb and thought the Snap woman had probably circled the block and was coming in for a second attack.

"Helen! What in the name of God is wrong?" I looked up to see a police lieutenant bending over me. It was a guy I had known for several years.

"Hi, Dave, need a transfusion?"

"Who shot you, Helen?"

"A jealous wife, Dave, a jealous wife." He picked me up in his arms and carried me to the police car. "Will it get in the newspapers, Dave?" I asked.

"You know better than that, Helen."

I never heard another word from Mr. Snap. Maybe Mrs. Snap shot him, too. If so, I wonder if his scar is as big as mine?

Now, for Mr. Crackle. There was a shooting associated with him also. Crackle was a railroad official from Dallas. I met him in front of De Jonghe's. I was just sort of wandering by and he was just sort of lounging at the entrance. He whispered softly as I passed, "Alone?"

"Yes," I whispered back. Well, the first thing you know, we're in the Cold Room at De Jonghe's just laughing and passing the time of day like old friends. He had never been to Chicago before and was interested in hearing about the people and spots he had read about. After about a half hour of shooting the breeze, I said to him, "Why just talk about the nightlife in Chicago? Let's go on a tour and you can see the city in action."

"Do you think it would be safe?" The anxiousness in his voice was overshadowed by the anticipation.

"Safe as a babe in arms, honey," I answered. "Nothing is going to happen to you when you're with me."

"I can't afford to involve myself in any 'trouble,'" he said.

"Don't you worry about 'trouble' Sweetie," I intoned. "And I can't afford to spend a fortune tonight, either … "

"How much would a big night on the town cost?" he asked.

"Whatever you want to spend, my dear," I answered. Then I continued, "I, personally, want fifty dollars for myself. That would include a big breakfast at my apartment."

"You mean … ?" he asked in a hoarse voice.

"Exactly, my dear," I laughed.

"Well … " he said, and it was settled.

We had dinner there at De Jonghe's, then went to Colosimo's. From there we went to a place called "The Blue Bird" on South Halsted; I asked the cabbie to wait for us and we went inside. The place was packed with people and the cigarette smoke was so thick it hung like a San Francisco fog. We had a couple of drinks and talked for a moment with the Italian proprietor before getting back into the cab and proceeding to an intimate little spot on South Racine. It was a wonderful speak, not well enough known to the general public to be jammed to the gills with tourists and sightseers. The bar was in front and in the rear were several small drinking alcoves; heavy draperies could be pulled across the front opening of each alcove to give complete privacy. The only furnishings in each unit were two chairs, a loveseat, and a table on which flickered a solitary candle. The alcoves were designed to accommodate four people comfortably, or two people amorously.

Mr. Crackle and I were seated in one of the alcoves and we left the draperies open so we'd have a direct view of the bar. We had several drinks of good bonded liquor. I asked Mr. Crackle how he liked this Irish section of Chicago; I told him that this was Spike O'Donnell's[26] territory. Just then a big rhubarb started brewing at the bar between one of the customers and the bartender. I recognized the customer as being a notorious hijacker from Detroit. There were threats, curses, and then ... bang! The bartender had pulled out a pistol and shot the customer. The customer toppled neatly off the bar stool—he just sort of tipped straight back and lay prone on the floor. Then quick as a flash two men heaved up the body as someone opened the front door and they literally threw the body out onto the sidewalk.

"Jesus!" screamed Mr. Crackle. "Did you see that?"

"See what?" I asked. My voice was steady.

"That shooting!"

"What are you talking about, Cutie Pie? I didn't see anything —and I didn't hear anything—and neither did you. Now remember, you didn't hear or see anything. Close the damned drapes and let's sit on the loveseat."

Well, Mr. Crackle was shaking so hard I was afraid the loveseat was going to become unglued, but I suppose it was constructed to withstand any contingency. The police arrived within ten minutes, and, when questioned, I assured them that my drinking companion and I hadn't seen anything nor heard anything but the panting of our own breaths.

After the police left, the bartender resumed his duties and I pressed the bell. The bartender came and inquired what we wanted, as if nothing had happened. I told him to bring us another round of drinks, and to please call us a cab.

"Now, Mr. Crackle," I said to my companion, "you're really going to see something!" Our next stop was at the Entertainers' Café at Thirty-fifth and Indiana Avenue—it was the most famous black-and-tan club west of New York City. As we got out of the taxi, a long purple Pierce Arrow automobile pulled up behind us. I recognized the car and told Mr. Crackle to watch who got out of it. A negro man alighted and helped out a magnificently dressed blonde white woman.

---

26 Edward O'Donnell (1890 – 1962) known as Spike O'Donnell was a member of the Southside O'Donnell gang and not the larger more notorious West Side/O'Donnell Mob.

"That's Cleve Pierce, the biggest negro pimp in town. He has over thirty of the most beautiful white women in Chicago working for him," I said.

Mr. Crackle couldn't believe his eyes. "Who is that woman he's with ... some movie star?"

"No, but she's good-looking enough to be," I laughed. "That's Cleve's favorite—she works only the biggest hotels such as the Palmer House. That mink coat she has on is supposed to have cost over twelve thousand dollars."

There was standing room only in the café, but Izzy Shore, the proprietor, was a special friend of mine and came over and told us he'd see that we got a table. Soon we were seated at the side of the dance floor. Carl Dickerson's band was really hitting out the hot tunes of the day and the white men were doing the Charleston with the high yellow girls. Hustlers—black, tan, and white—were circulating freely. About one o'clock a.m. the rest of the colored pimps began arriving with their women. It was frantic.

At three a.m. we decided it was time to leave, and on the way out I asked Izzy for a box of his best cigars—I knew Sol would have to punch me in at the store next morning.

Mr. Crackle was a true Southern gentleman, so I fixed him hot biscuits for breakfast. As he left the apartment he told me that he'd seen more the night before than he had seen in Dallas in ten years. I told him I was sorry it had been only a week night—that Chicago had a lot more action on Saturday nights.

The last episode of this little trilogy concerned a gentleman I think of as Mr. Pop. If ever there was a son of a bitch, it was Charlie Pop. I hated him so much I decided to cook his damned goose by marrying him. Can you think of a better way to get even with someone? Oh, Charlie was slick all right. He had me fooled for a few hours until I was tipped off.

Charlie looked like an aging movie star; he had that smoothed-back hair heavily laced with gray. His manicured fingernails were as spellbinding as his pin-striped suit. The whole business started out so genteel-like right at the corner of Monroe and Michigan Avenue. Charlie and I saw each other at the same time; then I gave him the boom-boom look—that straight-into-the-eyes stare.

The next step was to saunter slowly down Michigan, pausing here and there to admire the merchandise in display windows—truly a never-fail technique. Charlie was tagging along, about one display window behind me. This, I thought, is a "live one" and he looks like he's just rolling in the long green! I stopped in front of an exclusive dress shop and gave my undivided attention to a black-and-white evening gown.

"That's such a lovely gown," he stated.

"Yes, it is nice," I agreed.

"I can tell you like fine clothes," he continued.

"Indeed I do; I'm in the ready-to-wear business."

"I'm surprised that you work ... and I think you're just kidding me. You aren't dressed like a working girl." I was absolutely bundled in a new, big-collared sable cape.

"My late husband left me well provided, but I love to work. I'm at Friend's Store on South State." I had found it was always disarming to name exactly where I was employed; it gave the impression I had nothing to hide.

"My name is Charles Pop," he said suavely. He swept off his hat to expose his magnificent hair, probably knowing that the five-thirty p.m. sun would strike it at just the correct angle.

"I'm Helen Worley."

"My dear Mrs. Worley, I know you might think I'm rude to be so bold as to ask you to dine with me, but I'd so enjoy your company at dinner. Would you care to join me?"

"Why, Mr. Pop, I do think that would be lovely ... and fun." I moved slightly to let the five-thirty sun hit my white teeth at just the correct angle as I smiled enchantingly. Or at least what I had been told was enchantingly.

"Where would you like to eat?" he cooed like a bulldog.

"Why, I think Henries would be nice," I replied. Henries was definitely not a pick-up spot; it had a certain amount of class and I thought that by suggesting it, he would think that I was not a rounder. I certainly didn't want to be considered a rounder.

"Henries would be a good place ... but I have a suggestion. Have you ever been to Colosimo's? The food there is superb."

"I've heard of it," I said demurely.

"Let's go there. I'm sure you'd like it."

As we walked in the door of Colosimo's, I gave the headwaiter the signal. It meant: "You don't know me, no one working here knows me. Get the word around." My dinner (chicken ala king) was good as always, and not a single soul on the staff gave a hint of recognition to me. As we were eating, Charlie leaned over and patted my hand and pushed a crumpled bill into my palm. I glanced down and saw a hundred-dollar bill; I slipped it into my purse. As we were having a liqueur with our dessert, he pulled the same deal: another one-hundred-dollar bill. Wow, I thought, I've really found a live one.

Gladys, the singer who was with Torrio the first night I met Capone, was wandering around the dining room singing request songs. Charles Pop beckoned her to our table. "What song would you like to hear, my dear?" he asked me.

"I'll just let the young lady sing her favorite," I said, smiling at Gladys. Gladys sang, "Ah, Sweet Mystery of Life", a song she had done at my request at least fifty times. When she finished she winked and indicated she wanted to see me privately. Charlie thanked her and handed her a hundred-dollar bill as a tip. I excused myself and met Gladys in the ladies room.

"Do you know who that is?" Gladys demanded.

"He said his name is Charles Pop," I answered, perplexed.

"Yeah, that's his name, and he's the biggest bastard that ever drew breath!" she cried.

"What do you mean?" I asked.

"I mean he's got the sneakiest, lowest, filthiest hobby I've ever heard of. He gives girls money, then gets them arrested for accepting money under false pretenses. That's how he gets his kicks—by getting girls arrested. He even had three of them sent down to the women's reformatory!"

"He gave me two hundred dollars during dinner," I said.

"Yeah? Well, I'm not surprised. Did you see that tip he gave me—one hundred bucks for one damned song! He really throws money around; and it's dangerous money. Watch out for him, Helen. God, I wish this town could get rid of him!"

"Maybe I can clear him out," I said.

"How?"

"I'll think of a way."

"Well, good luck, and watch out for him. He's a mean devil." With that she was gone. After a moment I heard her singing again. By that time I had a plan in mind. Women's Reformatory! Why, that lousy snake!

Charlie took me home after we lingered at our table sipping brandy. I let him know at Colosimo's, and in the taxi, that I was falling for him. I gave the flirtation everything I had. As we stood in the foyer of the Drexel Boulevard building, I opened the door to my apartment and let him get a good look at the Oriental rugs and the Tiffany lamps, but I didn't ask him to enter.

"Aren't you going to invite me in, Helen … for a nightcap?" He had his face close to mine.

"You've hurt me, Charlie. Really hurt me." I spoke softly.

"What do you mean?"

I opened my purse and removed his money; I pressed it into his hand. "I would have gotten up and left, but I didn't want to create a scene. And, besides, I was so magnetized by you, Charlie, I couldn't force myself to leave. You insulted me, Charlie. I'm not that kind of a girl. Money doesn't interest me."

Charlie was nonplussed. "I'm sorry, my dear. Will you forgive me?" He kept staring into the apartment. I was glad all the Tiffany lamps were lighted.

"My husband left me very well provided, Charlie."

He looked again at the living room rug and said, "Yes, I can see that."

"I thought there could be something fine between us, Charlie, until … that money." Charlie looked into the apartment again, then ran his eyes over my figure. I could see the wheels turning in his mind; this was really going to be a deal for Charlie. All that and money, too.

"Forgive me, my darling girl," he said as he embraced me.

"Yes, Charlie, yes. I'd forgive you anything."

"May I come in … please?" he begged.

"Charlie, oh, Charlie, I couldn't trust myself … in an apartment alone with you." I whispered into his ear. "Let's go out to a dark little club and just sit and talk, my dear one."

Charlie asked me to marry him; I accepted tentatively, telling him I would give him his definite answer the next day. We made an appointment to meet the next day in the Loop.

When Charlie and I met he had come from his bank; he had twenty-five hundred dollars to "buy me a little something." We went to Marshall Field's and I bought everything in sight: including a fur neckpiece, four black nightgowns, a half dozen slips, and other assorted luxuries. I wound up buying five-dollar handkerchiefs. I spent the twenty-five hundred dollars quickly. I left Charlie with a mound of packages and excused myself to go to the restroom. I hurried to a telephone and sent myself a telegram.

The telegram was waiting when Charlie and I arrived at my home with all the packages.

"Is something wrong, my dear?" asked Charlie as I gasped over the telegram.

"Yes. My Mama is ill. She's in an Indianapolis hospital. I must go to her immediately." I sobbed a little as I continued, "Just when I have found your love, Charlie, fate is snatching me from you!"

Charlie could see that I was being snatched from him and he didn't like it. He wanted no postponement of this marriage. "Marry me before you go, Helen, my dearest one!"

"Yes, Charlie, yes!"

We were married the following day, and I went directly from City Hall to the depot where Charlie bought me a ticket for Indianapolis. We parted with kisses and words of encouragement.

I got off the train in Gary, Indiana, and called George, the lawyer. "George, I was married today to the biggest bastard on earth. I don't know how much he's worth, but whatever you can get, I'll give you two-thirds of it." George said he thought he could get a court date about any time I wanted it. He wanted to know the grounds for the divorce, and I told him, "physical cruelty." I bought a ticket for Hot Springs and went there and enjoyed the baths for two weeks before returning to Chicago.

Charlie and I moved to his apartment on the Far North Side; he wanted to move into my apartment, but I put him off ("I must get used to you, my dearest, in new surroundings; my own apartment holds too many memories for now"). I would not let him near me ("Please, Charlie, I'm too worried about my Mama for that"). Charlie became nasty and I became short-tempered. It culminated at dinner about five days after my return; I threw a bowl of mashed potatoes at him and he struck me. Now, I was waiting eagerly for the next slap which came two days later.

"You struck me twice, you bastard! I'm getting a divorce!" I screamed. Charlie was amazed to find how fast the process servers could work. I moved back to my apartment and awaited the court date. I called Al Capone and got him on the telephone. "I got married several weeks ago, Al," I said.

"I heard about it, Helen."

"He's a horrible man."

"Why did you marry him?"

"To repay him. You know about those girls he sent up?"

"Yeah."

"I doubt if he'll send more of them up."

"Oh?"

"I'm divorcing him day after tomorrow. Al, will you do me a favor? It'll only take about a half hour."

"I don't promise favors unless I know what they are."

"Well, this is very simple. I want you to escort me into the court—with those bodyguards. I just want you to seat me in court and then leave."

Capone began laughing softly, then he bellowed into the telephone. I just hung on until he finished. "Helen, you're a damned card. Are you trying to scare old Pop to death?"

"Will you do it, Al?"

"Sure, I'll do it. What time?"

"Ten o'clock. Thursday."

"My car will pick you up at nine-thirty at your apartment."

"The one on Drexel Boulevard," I said.

"Okay."

It was exactly ten o'clock when we walked into the court. George, my lawyer, was seated at a table by himself. My dear husband, Charlie, was at another table with two lawyers. I marched into court on the arm of Al Capone. In his right hand Al carried his big gray Borsalino hat. The two "gentlemen" behind us kept their black hats pulled low over their eyes. I took the chair beside George; Al held it for me. Then I whispered to him and pointed in the direction of Charlie Pop. Al turned and looked at Charlie. Charlie's face had turned as white as the streaks in his beautiful hair. Then Al patted my hand, whispered, "You're a card, Helen," and left the court room followed closely by the boys in black. That's all there was to it.

Charlie had a quiet conference with his lawyer. The whole divorce took only a few minutes. Charlie was a dear not to interfere. We got thirty -thousand dollars: twenty for George, ten for me. I've never laid eyes on Charlie Pop since that morning. I think he left town.

Chapter 18

1925 BROUGHT CHANGES to the underworld setup of Chicago. Early in the year Johnny Torrio was shot down in front of his apartment on Clyde Avenue, but he lived through the riddling of bullets. Everyone knew that Hymie Weiss[27], who succeeded the assassinated Deanie O'Banion[28] as ruler of the North Side, ordered the shooting. Torrio was luckier than the Terrible Gennas—Angelo, Mike, and Tony—who didn't live when they got theirs.

Johnny was tired, frightened, and sick of the whole thing. I was having a drink with him one night when he said, "Helen, I'm quitting. I've had it. I'm giving the whole package to Al and I'm going to Italy, maybe somewhere close to Naples, where I can enjoy the sunshine and not hold my breath waiting to be pumped full of hot lead." Johnny was serious and he did exactly what he said he was planning to do. That is when Al Capone became the emperor of Chicago.

---

27 Henry Earl J. Wojciechowski, also known as Hymie Weiss (January 25, 1898 – October 11, 1926), was an American mob boss who became a leader of the Prohibition-era North Side Gang and a bitter rival of Al Capone.

He was Catholic, despite the "Jewish-sounding" moniker (he carried a rosary and a Bible). As a teenager, Weiss became a petty criminal. He befriended an Irish-American teen named Dean O'Banion. With Weiss and George "Bugs" Moran, O'Banion established the North Side Gang, a criminal organization that eventually controlled bootlegging and other illicit activities in the northern part of Chicago.

28 Deanie O'Banion (July 8, 1892 – November 10, 1924) was an American mobster who was the main rival of Johnny Torrio and Al Capone during the brutal Chicago bootlegging wars of the 1920s. The newspapers of his day made him better known as Dion O'Banion, although he never went by that first name. He led the North Side Gang until 1924, when he was murdered.

< **Al Capone.**

It was late in the summer of that year when Capone called me for help. I had arrived home from a date with a nice guy from New York at two am. I had asked the old sweetie in for a drink, but I think he was scared of me. He made an excuse about having to get up early and left in the cab he had kept waiting. I was getting ready for bed when the phone rang.

Without any pissing around, Capone asked, "Do you know who this is?"

I said, "It sounds like Mr. Brown."

"You're right. Are you alone?"

"Yes."

"Good. Meet me at the Midnight Frolics in forty minutes. I'll send a cab around for you."

Al was just entering the Midnight Frolics with two bodyguards as my cab pulled up. He saw me and waited at the door. I remember thinking that he looked much better in his flat-brimmed straw hat than he did in his usual wide-brimmed Borsalino.

Al had a face made for smiling. Big laugh crinkles formed at the sides of his eyes and a dimple showed on the left side of his mouth as he said, "You're a sport to come out so late, Helen."

"The hour means nothing to me, Al."

"I thought you were here when you called, Al," I said as we entered the nightclub.

"No, I was at the Four Deuces. There's a big private party going on there tonight. They've taken over the whole place."

"Including the top floor?" I asked with a smile. That was the floor where they kept the girls.

"Yes. The top floor, too. Big deal." We went back to his favorite corner table and he sat with his back to the two sheltering walls, facing the main portion of the club. "Helen, I hate to ask you to do this, but I need help from someone I can rely on." He paused as a glass of champagne was poured for me and a glass of plain water was poured for him. Then he continued, "Have you ever heard of our place—the cheap whorehouse—at Adams and Green Streets?"

I nodded to indicate that I had heard of it; I knew nothing about it, but I had heard of it.

He paused again to light a cigar. "Well, something crooked is going on out there and I need somebody to check up on the place for me. Will you do it?"

"You know I'll do it, Al."

"Somebody is robbing me blind, and I don't like it," he said softly.

"If this 'somebody' is caught, what happens to them?" I asked. I certainly didn't want to get involved in "fingering" anybody for Capone.

"They lose their job. Nothing more." Then he realized what my concern was about, and he laughed, "You've been reading too many stories about me, Helen. Nothing like that will happen."

He gave me a set of keys and told me what he wanted done. The regular "madam" was off tonight and one of the girls was pinch-hitting; I was to take over the madam's spot and keep a record of how many men came in from the time I got there until eleven a.m. the next morning. Al knew I had a job at Friend's, so he told me to go on to work directly from the whorehouse and take the night's receipts with me. He said he'd see me at Colosimo's the next evening after I got off from work, and we'd discuss the records and receipts then.

"Do you know Mike Fisher, Helen?" I nodded, and he said, "Mike is tending bar on the first floor; I'll call him that you are coming, so go in and go upstairs and take over the joint. Oh, yes, the price is a dollar and twenty cents; a buck for the room, a dime for a towel, and a dime for protection." Then he laughed again. "If your records get messed up, just count the towels."

"Any time limit involved?" I asked.

"There sure is—ten minutes! If any of the jokers want a second throw, get another dollar and twenty cents. If anybody causes trouble, just holler down for Mike. Okay?"

"Okay."

By three-thirty I had taken my station in a big overstuffed chair at the head of the stairs over the speakeasy. There was a rickety table next to the chair and on the table was a cigar box with bills and change in it. On the other side of the chair was an orange crate stacked with white, clean, ragged towels. I counted all the money in the cigar box and recorded it, and the time, on a piece of paper. Then I settled back and presided over my domain.

The hallway was lit by two low-watt, bare bulbs dangling on cords from the ceiling. There were three straight-back chairs forming a "waiting room." The "working rooms" were small cubicles partitioned off with beaverboard; I peeped into an empty one and saw only a sheet-covered cot, a stool, and a tin can with cigarette butts in it. There were two clothes hooks screwed to the partition. No clothes hangers and no other appointments. The "door" to the cubicle consisted of a heavy, soiled piece of twill nailed at the top and hanging straight to the floor. I didn't have time for much more investigation because the early morning rush started.

The place was open around the clock. There were three eight-hour shifts of nine girls each shift. There was very little time to actually talk to the girls; not that they wanted to talk. When they weren't busy they wanted to lie on their cots and sleep, or they would occasionally get up and wander aimlessly around smoking cigarettes. The majority of them wore sleazy slips; lazier ones wandered around with nothing on. None of them were attractive; they were either fat or skinny, flat-chested or pendulous-bosomed. It seemed to me that they were all damned lucky to have full-time employment.

It was extremely busy from four a.m. until eight. Most of the speakeasies closed at four and the guys headed our way. It was interesting to notice the contrast between that crowd and the group that arrived after seven. The earlier crowd sat on the floor until a girl was available—they didn't care which one. It was hard to get them out after their ten minutes were up; I had to enlist Mike's aid several times. When Mike went off duty a huge, ugly boy of about twenty-two took over as a real bouncer, and he threw any troublemakers out into the street.

The set that arrived about seven a.m. were getting off a night shift or on the way to work; many of them spoke no English. On the other hand, some of them were clean-cut looking guys on the way to laboring, or in some cases, white-collar jobs. They were the men who had little money, but a great craving for sex. Most of these men asked for a certain girl and waited until she was available. Three chairs were not enough to seat the waiting crowd and the men would sit patiently on the floor. Whereas the speakeasy crowd had been loud and boisterous, this after-seven group would sit in silence, keying their ears to the sounds coming from the cubicle. They obviously savored, and were stimulated by, the sounds. Ten minutes in a cubicle was totally adequate for them. Jesus God, what a dump!

Somehow I got through the next day at the store. Sol had punched me in at nine, and I arrived at eleven-thirty. After work I went to Colosimo's and Al was waiting for me. He arose as I walked toward his table. He smiled as he said, "For some reason you look older and wiser today."

"I think you owe me a drink. I want a straight shot with a glass of water," I said.

"I really did hate to ask you to do it, Helen. But I want to find out about that place and I knew that you could do it."

"It's some place, all right."

"Did you learn something you didn't know?"

"No."

"Did Mike have to help you?"

"Yes."

I had put exactly the amount of money that was in the cigar box back in the box for the daytime madam's use; I showed Al my record of how much had been there. Then in an envelope I had the money that had been taken in between three-thirty and eleven a.m. I had the extra twenty cents (dime for a towel, dime for protection) collection in a separate envelope. It looked like quite a bundle; I had them tied together with a string. While I sipped my drink he counted the money twice.

"Are you sure you took in this much, Helen?"

"You don't think I'd add to it with my own money, do you?"

"There's over two hundred dollars here. You were there less than seven hours, and it was a week night. I've never collected over a hundred and fifty from that place for an entire eight-hour shift."

"The light dawns, Mr. Capone," I said with a smile. "Madam does all right for sitting in an easy chair and doling out towels."

Al looked around Colosimo's and saw two men sitting toward the front. He motioned for them to come back to our table. "I want to tell Ollie and Ralph about this," he said.

We were joined by two men who were very much a part of the syndicate. Capone related what had happened and they thought it was the funniest thing they had ever heard.

"You know, Al, I've heard you say many times that nobody is really on the legit," laughed Ralph.

"That bitch has been taking us for years; fifty, maybe even more a night. We'll get rid of her quick!"

"Now, Al, you know what you told me!" I injected.

"She'll be fired, honey, fired. But she's going to have a hell of a time finding another job in Chicago, I can tell you that."

I felt we had to be fair to the madam, so I said, "I'm not keen on that place, but I think for the sake of research you should try another night. It could be that last night was something special. Want me to do it again tonight?"

They pondered it over and decided it would be well to have another night's tally before getting rid of someone who had been with them for many years.

"Well, I'd better get home and get some sleep if I'm going to be battling drunken maniacs later."

Capone reached in his pocket and pulled out a fifty-dollar bill. Then he reached in and got another twenty. "Here, Helen, I sincerely appreciate your help. And don't forget to buy a couple of boxes of cigars for the floor man at your store."

He ordered me a cab and I went home and had two scrambled eggs.

At midnight Al called and said he had been thinking about it and he thought that the next night would do just as well since he had forgotten to return the keys to the place to me. "Get yourself a good night's sleep and earn your money at your store tomorrow. Then when you get off work I want you to join me for dinner at the Blackstone Hotel. I'll leave word with the headwaiter to bring you to my table. I'll be with a beautiful woman. I think I've found just the one for the Blackstone … see what you think." (Several weeks before Al had asked me if I knew someone special to handle the

Blackstone for him, but I couldn't think of anyone available who had the class to really put it over.

Cousin Adele was the only one who came to mind! "I'll have the keys to the Adams and Green place with me and I'll give them to you, but don't mention anything about that business at dinner."

Al was right. The woman was a humdinger. She looked like a sensationally formed, exquisitely dressed society woman from Lake Forest. As a matter of fact, she still does. I saw her not too long ago at the Imperial House in Chicago and she's still marvelous-looking. I understand she has retired to an elegant, glass-walled apartment house on Lake Shore Drive and does nothing but collect art and go to benefits. The dinner that night at the Blackstone Hotel was lovely; the entire conversation orbited around the opera, new books, and miscellaneous non-business subjects. No wonder the dame made herself a fortune.

The next night's receipts at Adams and Green Street proved that the night madam was coining the intake and she was literally kicked out on her ass. And once again, Sol had punched me in at nine and I didn't arrive until noon. I handed him two boxes of twenty-five-cent cigars and I said, "Never say you haven't received a gift from Capone, Sol."

Chapter 19

PERHAPS it was the two nights at the Adams and Green Street place, or maybe a hankering to have a house of my own that prompted me to become a real live madam. With the exception of the world-famous house run by Vickie Shaw[29], practically all the houses in Chicago were controlled by one combine or another; and I certainly didn't want to be in competition with those forces. I knew that in order to make my place really pay off, I'd have to be away from the Chicago area.

It was Capone himself who suggested a likely location: Superior, Wisconsin. Al said that town was booming because of the ore boat trade, and it was not controlled by any syndicate; he didn't think I would have trouble "moving in." On the other hand, he didn't want me to leave Chicago, and offered me the management of several of his places. I didn't want to compromise my friendly relationship with Al by becoming an employee of his.

I disposed of my furniture, with the exception of a few choice pieces from the Drexel Boulevard apartment, which went into storage, and I left for Duluth, Minnesota. Duluth was just across the bay from Superior and was connected to it by the Interstate Bridge. I checked into the St. Louis Hotel at Duluth, registered as Miss Helen Cappel, and quickly sized up the two towns. Duluth seemed buttoned up, but Superior was filled with speakeasies and cheap whorehouses. What could be a moneymaker, particularly

---

29 Vickie Shaw was one of the famous Chicago madams, along with the Everleigh Sisters, who ran independent brothels. Ms. Shaw ran her 'house' until her retirement in 1949.

Helen and friend behind the bar at the Sun Flower Inn.

Sun Flower Inn c. 1940s.

1928 article about Eddie Mack a.k.a. John Jerge.

JERGE SLAYER STILL ELUDES N. Y. POLICE

Brunette Believed Decoy for Gang Killers — Witnesses Are Questioned.

From the New York Bureau of the Buffalo Evening News.

NEW YORK, June 19.—The life of Edwin J. Jerge, formerly of Buffalo, N. Y., better known by his alias, Edward Carter, shot to death at Broadway and 36th street Sunday afternoon by one of four men in a sedan, was opened up wide by the police yesterday but today they had not found the girl companion who vanished after Jerge was killed, had not discovered any trace of the murderer or his companions, and had failed to establish any reasonable motive for the crime.

The entire detective force of New York was assigned to the case early in the morning at the lineup at police headquarters when Inspector John D. Coughlin, who declared himself incensed over the boldness of the murderer and his companions in committing a crime so openly, ordered his men to take no rest until they had brought him some tangible progress in solving the homicide.

Miss Sheerin Questioned.

He then summoned detectives on the Broadway run to his office for a secret conference. The men later admitted that their task was to interrogate all their acquaintances in the theater district.

Doris Sheerin, the girl who owns the coupe in which Jerge was killed as he waited for a red traffic signal to change and while hundreds of strollers passed, was questioned by District Attorney Banton during the day, as were three men. He refused to give their names, saying it might defeat "the ends of justice," but as a matter of fact they were the two pedestrians and the restaurant chef who witnessed the murder. The three men spoke freely to reporters after the murder, and their names are known. Miss Sheerin has been absolved from any connection with the crime. She is an actress, now giving at 45 West 51st street.

Chicago Theory Discarded.

An attempt to link Jerge with a Chicago gang and to link that gang with the murder for an alleged doublecross collapsed last night dismally. Jerge was arrested in 1916 with two other members of the Dopey Benn gang, which was supposed to have been allied with the Chicago Capone mob in the robbery of the Washington National City bank in Chicago. It was common talk then that Jerge betrayed Finn and Beckman and these two threatened revenge. They were released from prison three years ago and soon after were killed by a Long Island railroad train in Long Island city. It seems curious that their comrades would wait three years to murder Jerge, who had strutted up and down Broadway fearlessly and openly a frank target for anyone who wanted to shoot him down. That gang is extinct.

Member of Buffalo Family.

Jerge, it developed yesterday, is the right name of the man who was known as Carter, Atwater, Kayton, Mack, Palmer, Sackett, and George. He is a member of a family in Buffalo of good repute. His father and brother hold what police described as "important" positions there. Jerge came to New York in 1914, was arrested for picking pockets, served five months, and was next heard of with Finn and Beckman in 1916. He disappeared again until

EDWIN J. JERGE

MUST SPEND LIFE IN JAIL

Californian Runs Afoul of Baumes Law.

James W. Fisher, 40, California, must serve the remainder of his life in Auburn prison as a result of his conviction as a fourth offender, Tuesday morning by a jury before Justice James E. Norton, in Supreme court.

According to Jerome Cantor, assistant district attorney, Fisher thrice has been convicted of felony. He was fined on a charge of stealing an automobile owned by Mrs. Mary M. Gethoefer, 255 Jersey street. He was arrested a day later while trying to sell the automobile. He said he was hired to sell the machine on commission.

Police records were said to show Fisher has served time in prisons in California, Massachusetts and New York on larceny charges.

YOUNGEST DRY AGENT KILLED NEAR MALONE

Warren C. Frahm's Car Ditched, Chasing Rum Runners.

Warren C. Frahm, who is believed to have been the youngest dry agent in the prohibition service, was killed at 4 o'clock Tuesday morning while pursuing two automobile loads of bootleggers on a highway near Malone.

Frahm in one car and another agent in a second car were keeping a vigil on the roads leading to the border. They con...

NEW TRIAL IS DENIED TO WILMONT WAGNER

Court Rules No Additional Evidence Shown in Counsel's Plea for Trooper's Slayer.

Wilmont Leroy Wagner, Canadian farmhand, scheduled to die in the electric chair at Sing Sing prison Thursday night for the slaying of a state trooper, Tuesday was denied a new trial by Justice George E. Pierce in Supreme court.

Rogers Curtin, representing Thomas F. Rogers, who defended Wagner at the trial, Monday afternoon applied to Justice Pierce for a new trial on the ground of newly discovered evidence. Justice Pierce ruled Tuesday that nothing to indicate new evidence had been discovered had been presented to him.

Two affidavits were presented Tuesday by Mr. Curtin in which the condemned man alleged his sister, Mrs. Grace Miller, had been friendly with Allegany county officials during the trial. Wagner also alleged that Justice Charles H. Brown, who presided at the trial, was prejudiced against him. The court delayed decision until Tuesday morning because Mr. Curtin said he wished to present additional affidavits. When he failed to appear with them Tuesday, Justice Pierce announced his decision.

Wagner was convicted of first degree murder for the killing of State Trooper Robert Roy, who came to the farmhouse to arrest the youth for failing to pay for a small quantity of gasoline he had obtained from a filling station. Wagner also was indicted for the killing of State Trooper Arnold T. Rasmussen, who accompanied Roy. He was not tried on the latter indictment.

TWO BOYS HIT BY AUTOS

One, Only 4, Is Taken to City Hospital; Other, 10, to Columbus.

Two children Tuesday were reported injured when struck by automobiles. Edward F. Snyder, 4, of 171 Waverly street, is in the City hospital being treated for injuries suffered when he was hit by a car driven by Miss Margaret Reilly, 145 Hastings street. The accident occurred near ... street. The chi... Alva ...

Interior of Colosimo's Restaurant.

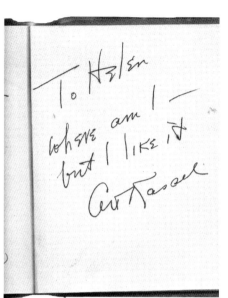

Sign in from musician
Al Kassel

Autographed picture of Al Kassel

Paul Poberezny, founder of the Experimental Aircraft Association.

Helen, behind the bar at the Sun Flower Inn c. 1940s.

Helen, behind the bar at the Sun Flower Inn c. 1940s with patrons.

Phil Cappel, Jr. Helen's oldest son.

Joseph McCarthy. He worked at the Sun Flower Inn when he attended nearby Marquette University. He later became the notorious right-wing senator from Wisconsin who led the House Un-American Committee Hearings. Though faded in this image, the picture is signed to Helen.

Patrons at the Sun Flower Inn.

A night at the Sun Flower Inn. Helen is behind bar in print shirt.

Enjoying cocktails at the Sun Flower Inn.

Party time at the Sun Flower Inn.

Party time at the Sun Flower Inn.

Sun Flower Inn patron admiring the infamous nude painting.

in Superior, was a flossy house with some class to it. I found a vacant house at 510 John Street that had the right location and remodeling possibilities, rented it on the spot, and then went out and found a crew of carpenters and told them to get to work on the modernizing I wanted done.

I arrived back at the St. Louis Hotel about five o'clock in the afternoon. It had been a productive day. In addition to finding the house and getting the carpenters started, sarouk-style carpeting had been selected for the entire house and elegant furniture — reproductions in the French provincial style—had been ordered for the upstairs bedrooms. To top off the shopping, I had bought two hostess gowns, two suits, an afternoon dress, three hats, and assorted accessories. All told I had let loose of almost five thousand dollars—in cash.

There were no bellboys in the lobby, so I stumbled up two flights of stairs balancing my pyramid of packages. As I juggled the boxes, trying to dig my key from the far recesses of my purse, my door swung open and I was face-to-face with a man I had never seen before. Startled, my first reaction was that it was the wrong room; then I saw my sable wrap hanging at the foot of the bed and I knew that it was my room. Robbery? Well, I thought, if this is robbery here is the best-looking robber I've ever seen. "Who are you, the homecoming committee?" I asked sarcastically.

"Please step into the room, Miss Cappel," the man said softly. His voice held a certain authoritativeness, and I didn't dare refuse. He stepped aside and I saw a second man seated in the room's only chair.

"I've never cared for my boy friends arriving in pairs," I said in a weak attempt at a joke. The second man arose from the chair and indicated that I was to sit there. Then they both stood facing me.

"We're from the police chief's office, Miss Cappel." Relief poured over me like a reviving shower. I had been almost certain it was a holdup.

"The police? Why would the police break into my room?"

"We didn't break into your room. We merely described you to the desk clerk and he handed us a key to Miss Cappel's room."

"We didn't even ask for the key," said the plainclothesman who had met me at the door. A half-smile formed at the tips of his lips.

"Isn't that entering without a warrant?" I asked.

"Not in this particular hotel," said the policeman and broke into a grin. I turned and scanned my eyes over the room's furnishings and my luggage. "We haven't opened a thing," said the man.

"The police chief wants to see you, Miss Cappel," injected the second man.

"What does the police chief want to see me about?" I asked.

"He'll tell you."

Soon I was in the office of the Chief of Police of Duluth. As I entered he fired a question at me. "Can you ride a horse, young woman?"

"Why, yes," I answered. "I can ride horses. But I haven't been on one in years. Why?"

"Have you been to South Dakota recently?"

"I've never been to South Dakota. What's this all about?"

He kept ignoring my questions. "You've been spending lots of money today, haven't you?" he asked.

By this time I had seated myself in a chair that had been pushed up by one of the silent plainclothesmen. "Listen, chief," I said, "the money is mine. If I want to spend it, what difference does it make to you?"

Then he told me. A bank in South Dakota had been robbed by a lone, "attractive," woman; she had fled with the loot on horseback and was last seen in the vicinity of the Black Hills. He wanted to know if I was that woman—if I had come out of my Black Hills hideout for a money-spending fling in Duluth.

The whole story struck me as hilarious. I laughed until tears came to my eyes. The plainclothesman thought it was funny, too, but the chief could see no humor in it.

"What character reference can you give me, Miss Cappel?" the Chief asked. "I want to be sure you aren't the Black Hills lady."

"Chief," I said, "I'd never go into the Black Hills ... I'd be afraid I'd never get out!" Character reference—boy, that was hard to come up with. Mama had told me when I saw her in Indianapolis that one of her brothers was now the mayor of Noblesville, and I told the chief to call my uncle.

The long-distance phone call must have been interesting, and I would have liked to have heard what my uncle said, because the chief kept looking at me as he listened to the voice in the phone. Finally, he hung up and said, "You may go, Miss Cappel." My curiosity got the best of me and I asked the Chief what my uncle had said.

"He said that he's heard you've had several husbands, and that you must have just cleaned out some poor guy. He doubts that you'd rob a bank." As I turned to leave, the chief said, "If you're still here in the winter, come by and I'll give you tickets for the ski tournament."

One of the plainclothesmen drove me back to the hotel. He asked me if I was going to remain in Duluth. I told him I was going to stay in Superior and he wanted to know what I was going to do there. I told him I intended to run the "flossiest house in Superior." He became very interested.

"You'll make a killing. This area needs a real fancy place," he said.

"In order to have a fancy place, I'll need some fancy women. Who are the two most beautiful girls around here?" I asked him.

He answered without hesitating, "Fabiola and Mona—I don't know their last names."

"Do you know where to contact them?"

"Sure. They're in different houses."

"Would you tell them to see me at my hotel?"

"When?"

"Any time before nine a.m. in the morning. I've got to be in Superior before eleven."

He looked at me and winked, wickedly. "What do I get for doing you the favor?"

"A free night on the house," I replied.

"Does that include the madam's services?"

"No. I've retired."

It was just prior to daybreak when there was a knock at the door. I was so drowsy with sleep, I could hardly pull on my robe, turn on the light, and fumble with the lock. I opened the door and stared at two of the most beautiful females I had ever seen. The tall black-haired one said simply, "I'm Mona." Then the shorter, light brunette said, "I'm Fabiola." It took me a moment to wake up enough to realize why they were there. I must have looked puzzled because Mona said, "You sent for us." Then I remembered the plainclothesman and my request to him.

I told them the set-up I was developing: a place with class. I told them my rules: no drugs allowed; a moderate amount of alcohol. I told them my price: five dollars for me every time a room was utilized—whatever they could get above that price was their own; plus room and board free of charge. I also told them I wanted the place to have a reputation for style. They would have to keep themselves groomed and well-dressed when not actively engaged in business. They accepted my deal and I accepted them as "my girls."

I told them that I expected to open two weeks from the following Saturday and I wanted them to go into seclusion for three days before opening. I thought it would give the boys something to talk about to think that Mona and Fabiola were "preparing themselves" for a wing-ding. They agreed and we parted until "opening day." I felt I was very lucky. Mona and Fabiola were real surprises; with their looks they could easily have been big-time call girls from New York or Chicago.

The next morning I had another streak of luck. I found Annie, a colored maid, who was to be my faithful friend and confidante for the next two years.

The remodeling was so successful I was amazed myself. The house was small, but an efficient little gem. On the first floor there was a large entrance hall, a reception room, and a private bedroom, sitting room, and bath for me with a connecting door to the modernized kitchen. Off the kitchen was a small maid's room. Upstairs, there was only a hallway, a bath, and two large bedrooms: one for Mona, one for Fabiola. I decorated the bedrooms around the girls: red and pinks for the black-haired Mona and muted greens and olives for the fabulous Fabiola. When the rooms were furnished with Berkey & Gay furniture, I knew that the men in

Superior would go crazy over the effect. It was like Prairie Avenue in Chicago!

Two days prior to the opening I had an absolute stroke of genius. It was a Wednesday; the place was opening the following Saturday night. The house was completed except for the finishing touches and I had moved my luggage and hat boxes in. I was gently unpacking a stupendous dress I had purchased just before leaving Chicago. It was all white and well above the knees in front; a floating panel hung clear to the floor in back; it was covered with crystal beads; the big droopy sleeves were edged with beige fox. As a wham-bam companion piece I had found a white hat in the Cleopatra-Theda Bara style—really rather Arabic —that had a beige-satin snake sort of thing coiled around it. I held up the dress, wondering when I could knock hell out of Superior with it, when my inspiration struck!

I whizzed over to Duluth where I found just what I wanted in an automobile dealer's showroom: a white Stutz Bearcat with an open top. For forty dollars, the dealer said I could borrow it for an hour on Saturday afternoon. For another ten dollars I acquired his twenty-year-old son who promised to drive it for me, and wear a white coat and white hat to boot. Next I went to the bank and got two hundred one-dollar bills. The props were assembled for my little tableau!

The timing was excellent. At five-fifteen on Saturday afternoon, Tower Street in Superior was absolutely alive with ore boat sailors on shore leave. Slowly, ever so slowly, my driver—all in white—drove me down Tower Street (the main drag) in the all-white Stutz Bearcat. But I was the star of the production in my white-beaded, white-fur trimmed dress and the white snaky hat. I stood beside the driver and gently, ever so gently, threw away the dollar bills.

I don't mind saying that the pedestrians went wild. Children, dogs, sailors, and elderly men literally ran after the car screaming and/or barking with joy. I didn't do much else except to hoot a few times: "Have a drink on Helen at 510 John Street!" I just sort of yelled it in a lady-like manner to match the understated, virginal setting of my little public relations stunt. As we passed the Androy Hotel, where ever so many men were clustered, I sort of raised my arms above my head and gave a little Gilda Gray[30] shake-shake. Effective, really—and understated. By five-forty, everyone in Superior had heard of Helen. I've often thought that I missed my calling by not going into advertising. I'm sure I could have been big at BBD&O[31].

By the time I got back to 510 John Street, the crowd started arriving. Annie, the maid, and I got them into a semblance of a line that ran out the entrance hall, across the porch, down the steps and half-way down the block. We insisted that they couldn't have drinks until they crossed the threshold of the entrance hall. We had terrific moonshine and some splendid bonded stuff that had been rustled up by a local contact of Art Miller's, a well-known hijacker of the local scene. We got a dollar a shot for the booze. I put Annie in charge of pouring and collecting for the drinks. I had my hands full making change and collecting the five dollars a head every time a new guy went upstairs to replace the one coming down the stairs. As they started up the steps I'd tell them, "Five bucks for the room—payable here and now! What you get upstairs you pay for at the time. Go right into whichever room has the open door."

Poor Mona and Fabiola—they didn't even have time for dinner or a midnight snack. We closed up shop about six a.m. and all sat down for a hearty breakfast of ham and eggs. As the girls were wanly sipping coffee, I slipped into my room to count the income. Annie had taken in a hundred and ninety-four dollars for drinks and I had two hundred and eighty in the room-rental shoebox. I

---

30 Gilda Gray (born Marianna Michalska, October 24, 1901 – December 22, 1959) was an American actress and dancer who popularized a dance called the "shimmy" which became fashionable in 1920s films and theater productions.

Although the shimmy is said to have been introduced to American audiences by Gray in New York in 1919, the term was widely used before, and the shimmy was already a well-known dance move. Gray appropriated it as her own, saying that she had accidentally invented the shimmy while dancing at her father-in-law's saloon and "shaking her chemise" (or her "shimee," as her Polish accent rendered it).

31 BBDO is a worldwide advertising agency network, with its headquarters in New York City. The agency began in 1891 with George Batten's Batten Company, and later in 1928, through a merger of BDO (Barton, Durstine & Osborn) and Batten Co. the agency became BBDO. They're still in business today.

did a little figuring and decided the girls turned about twenty-eight tricks each. Not bad for gals from Superior, Wisconsin.

I decided that when a business person makes back her advertising outlay, the first day in business, she has little to complain about. My only complaint was that I hadn't had time to change from my white-beaded dress. The beautiful thing had been ruined and the entire downstairs floor was covered with beads. Some of the more exuberant clients had passed the time, while waiting to get upstairs, pulling beads off my dress and shooting them at each other like spitballs. Ah, well, they did have fun, and a dress of that particular type had limited use because it is too chic not to be recognized upon second wearing. A stylish madam can't afford to be seen in the same outfit too many times. People think you can't afford something new, and that's bad for business. So I took it off and wadded it up, then I opened the door to the kitchen and shouted to Annie, "Here's something you can wear the next time you get married," and I passed it across the room like a football.

"Lawsy, Lawd, Miz Helen!" she cried with glee. I was so delighted by her big smile I threw her the snaky hat, too. Annie spent the rest of the morning picking beads off the floor and furniture. She was determined to replace every one of them.

As the novelty of my damask wallpaper and my presence wore off, our household duties grew more routine. The standing-in-line business was only on Saturday nights. Other nights became clubby and like family. Mona, I learned when we finally had time to "visit," was French Canadian and musically inclined. She loved to play the piano, so I promptly acquired one for the reception parlor. It was so restful to lounge around the reception room with our regular patrons and listen to Mona play little ditties and sing cute little French songs. Then she'd bound up to her red room with a customer and be back tripping over the piano keys before you could say "Jack Robinson." Fabiola, on the other hand, was a wonderful conversationalist, and men liked to talk to her almost as much as they liked escorting her up to the green room. She remained in her room much longer than Mona, but I didn't scold her unless we were rushed. After all, not everybody's hobby is playing the piano.

Everything in Superior was lovely. I paid off the local officials very heavily and they caused me no trouble. The plainclothesman who had recommended the girls to me came by and collected his reward: first in the red room and then in the green. The next time he came by I made him give me five bucks to go upstairs. I don't know which room he went to but he was gone so long I rather suspected it was the green one.

I had a clientele worked up in no time. My choice of location was ideal; John Street really jumped. Practically every other house was a speakeasy. At the corner of Fifth and John, just two doors from me, was Superior's most famous speakeasy, Jack's.

Jack was an ex-prizefighter and everybody was crazy about him. He directed many a big crowd of men to my place. One evening several guys sent down by Jack were just clearing out and I was seated in my special chair in the reception room when a handsome young man walked in. He was Latin-looking, with fiery eyes and black hair. I got up to greet him—as I did for all customers—and he grabbed me and kissed me.

I pushed him away and said angrily, "I'm not one of the girls here!" Then I looked at him again, smiled, and said, "It's a pity because you are rather nice. Just have a seat and one of the girls will be down in a minute." I examined his suit; it was expensive and beautifully tailored. I hadn't seen men's clothing of that quality since I had left Chicago. "Are you from Superior?" I asked.

"No, just passing through," he said. He offered no more information, so I changed the subject.

"Would you like a drink?"

"Yes, thank you."

I got a bottle of Old McBrayer Bonded from the cabinet and when he saw it he said, "You drink good liquor here." I poured him a drink.

"Yeah, we get it from good sources."

"Oh, who?" he asked.

"From Art Miller," I said.

"Do you know him?" he asked.

'No."

At that moment Fabiola came into the room. As they started up the stairs he turned and gave me ten dollars. They went up to the green room and about three minutes later Fabiola came running back down to the reception room. Her face was drained of blood and she whispered to me excitedly, "Helen, that guy has a gun—I'm afraid of him."

"Don't be silly, Fabiola. He's not going to shoot you. If he has a gun, it's because of something else—not you. Now get back upstairs!"

At that moment the man came into the reception room, laughing. "She's afraid of me. She saw my gun." Then he turned toward Fabiola and tossed a ten-dollar bill at her. "Forget it, honey, run on upstairs by yourself, will you?"

I sat back down in my chair and he sat down in a chair next to mine and said, "I'm much more interested in you than what's upstairs."

"How nice. But I told you I'm not one of the girls."

Just then a crowd of local men entered and following on their heels were Mona and Fabiola. Mona started playing the piano and the stranger-with-the-gun leaned over toward me and said, "Isn't there someplace you and I can talk—away from all this noise?"

There was something magnetic about him. He was the sexiest-looking man I had ever seen. I was surprised when I heard myself saying, "Yes." I went to the kitchen and told Annie to take the place over. Then I took the stranger to my private sitting room. It was small; there was only space for my chaise longue and a big easy chair. He sat down in the chair and I heard the front door open and a batch of new voices.

"I'm sorry, but I've got to run out to the reception room for a minute," I said.

A big party had arrived. They wanted only talk, drink, and food. This wasn't unusual; not all of our patrons wanted to go upstairs. I sent Annie back to the kitchen and I got drinks for them. As I was fixing the drinks I peeked into the sitting room and saw my black-haired stranger was sound asleep in the easy chair. He remained asleep in the chair for four hours while I hostessed the party. Finally the crowd left and I returned to the sitting room. As I opened the door he bounded up in his chair with a frightened look on his face. Then he realized where he was, smiled at me, and looked at his watch.

"I've been here four hours!" he cried, unbelievingly.

"You sure have," I said.

"I must go. What do I owe you?"

"Don't be silly. You don't owe me a thing."

"I think I like you, Helen."

"Well, I like you, too. What's your name?"

"Art Miller," he said.

Alcohol runner, hijacker, crook, pimp—these were the things that were Art Miller. Yet after we had talked for an hour I was in love with him. My life had been saturated with men, yet I had only been in love twice before. There is no explaining what it was or why, only I went for Art like I had gone for Phil and for Bob. And he went for me, too.

As we sat there talking, he confessed the real reason he had come by that evening was to peddle some new girls he had acquired. A pimp. I had always loathed pimps; now I was in love with one. He was thirty-two, I was forty-one. I told him about my life, my children. He told me things I couldn't believe. With my experience, I thought I was beyond being shocked, but he shocked me! I knew he wasn't for me; but I wanted him. I went to the door and called Annie; I told her not to disturb me—for her to run the house for the rest of the night.

Art left about three a.m. At four a.m. he called me on the telephone "just to talk a minute"; at noon the next day he called again "just to say hello." The following morning he called me at four a.m. again and said he'd be there in an hour. He arrived just after five.

"Get ready, Helen, we're going on a three-day trip."

"A trip? What do you mean?"

"I want you to meet my mother and father—they live way up in Minnesota."

I called the girls to the reception room and told them to take themselves a rest for a few days. Then I told Annie to close the house until I got back. Within half an hour Art and I were on the way. The first eighty miles were nothing but brush country, but the last one hundred and twenty miles were beautiful scenery.

Art's mother and father were simple country people and their pride in Art was obvious. They, of course, didn't know what he did; they only thought he was a business success. When he introduced me to them he presented me as his wife, and I don't think I've ever been so ashamed and embarrassed. Finally, we got to the bedroom we were to share and I cried, "Art! Why did you tell them we were married?"

"Because I want to sleep with you while we're here, and besides I'm going to marry you on the way back to Superior."

We remained with his parents for several days. The day we left we got married in some obscure town in Minnesota.

Why I married him is unexplainable, even to me; but we gave each other happiness for over a year. He went his route and I went mine. I didn't inquire into his activities, and he didn't complain about mine. Sometimes we'd see each other for several nights in a row, then he'd be gone for weeks at a time. He was still an alcohol runner and a hijacker, but I believe he was truthful when he told me he had stopped the pimping business.

Chapter 20

ONE AFTERNOON Mona and Fabiola returned from a shopping trip to Duluth, filled with excitement.

"Helen, Helen," Mona called as they entered the house. "Where are you?"

"Here, in the kitchen," I replied.

They came scampering in like two beautiful kids.

"Helen, there's a huge convention going on in Appleton. Let's go down and spend the night!"

Fabiola took up the reins, "We could drive down in your car. It would be so much fun!"

"I'll bet we could really make some money!" Mona stated emphatically.

The idea had appeal. "When would you want to go?' I asked.

"Now! Let's leave now!" cried Fabiola.

"It's too late in the afternoon—Appleton is a long way. Let's leave very early in the morning. Okay?"

"Oh, let's go now, Helen."

"I don't want to. I'm expecting a call from Art tonight," I said.

"Oh, Helen," Fabiola said with a hint of reproach in her voice. Fabiola thought it was inconceivable that I had married Art Miller. She thought that being a pimp was bad enough—but a gun, too, made him impossible. "Art won't care."

"I know he won't care, but it happens that I want to talk to him." Fabiola opened her mouth to say something but I stopped her before she formed the words. "Now, Fabiola, if you and I are going to remain good friends, I don't want you to say another word about Art. Understand?"

"All right. I was only going to say that he is good-looking."

"I know what you were going to say. But let's leave it unsaid, okay?"

"Okay."

"We'll leave early in the morning for Appleton."

I had bought a new Ford just two weeks before and the long drive to Appleton was fun. We all wore our best clothes and when we stopped for lunch at a small-town hotel dining room, the admiring glances from the men—and the women—assured us that we wouldn't be overlooked in the convention crowd in Appleton. During the last leg of the trip, Mona sang her little French songs and Fabiola and I joined in the choruses. Anyone would have thought we were three ladies on the way to chaperone a Girl Scout Jamboree.

We arrived in Appleton late in the afternoon. The big convention parade was just over and the streets were swarming with people. We checked into a local hotel and I made a couple of inquiries. All inquiries pointed in the same direction: about three miles out of town to a place called "Blazing Stump."

"Blazing Stump" was run by a woman known as Old Ma Gooley. It was a converted farmhouse in the fork of the road, and the name of the place—I learned later—came from the fact that every so often sheets of flame would shoot out of an old abandoned well in the yard. It was a natural phenomenon and was quite a curiosity piece around Appleton. I, personally, didn't think that the blazing well was anything to compare with the pissing phenomenon that was Old Ma Gooley—she was grotesque.

We entered the farmhouse and found the place absolutely jammed with men. A pale, limpid, distracted-looking guy was standing behind a beat-up bar, dishing out the rottenest moonshine I had ever tasted. He was Ma Gooley's son. Ma herself was planted at the foot of the stairway.

Ma Gooley was the ugliest apparition of a woman I had ever seen—clumps of fat all squashed together like mounds of modeling clay. Her main interest in life appeared to be a sheaf of paper she clutched in her hand and the world's biggest wrist watch that was strapped to her arm. The watch was the size of an alarm clock. She would consult the paper, peer at the watch, and then shout upstairs in a raucous voice, "Get more money in room number six!" Or room number one, four, or whatever it might be. This woman had a keen interest in business.

I walked over to Ma Gooley and asked her how much the rooms were. She stared at me with beady eyes, but didn't utter an answer. I told her I had two real fast girls with me and maybe we could help her out of her peak-evening rush. She snapped a question at me. "Where are you from?"

"Superior." Then she turned her beady eyes on Mona and Fabiola. By this time the girls had a complete circle of men around them.

"The boys like your girls," hissed Ma Gooley through her puffy lips.

"Boys always like those girls," I said.

"You hustle, too?" she asked me, appraising my figure.

"No."

"Will you help me keep time?" she asked.

"That depends on how much your rooms are."

"Hot and cold running water—but they won't have time for that tonight. One dollar for ten minutes. They can stay as long as they want. All I want is one dollar for every ten minutes or fraction thereof they stay in one of my rooms."

"You've got yourself a deal, Ma." I signalled to the girls and they flew up the stairs. There was a slight squabble among the men about who was going to be first with the girls. I helped settle it, and the remainder of the fans lined up to wait their jolly turns.

As the night wore on I felt like a timekeeper at a track meet. Ma Gooley caved in about two a.m. and I took over the watch and score card. After an hour or so of screaming "Get more money in room six," I had to wet my whistle with a bit of Son Gooley's rot-gut. After a few shots of that stuff, I became lightheaded and rather giddy in my approach to the patrons. I pretended I was a coach at a ball game, and every time there was an opening available I'd slap a new "player" on the rump and tell him to get in there and fight for the home team. This helped pass the time and kept my mind off my aching feet. Mona and Fabiola, I thought, were damned lucky not to have to stand up for ten hours in high-heeled shoes.

At four-thirty a.m. Mona called me upstairs and confessed she was at about the end of her trick rope. I told her we couldn't possibly leave until daylight—we might get highwayed or rolled because we had made a real bundle of cash. Fabiola must have been a girl who enjoyed her work, because she didn't give one peep of complaint.

At seven-thirty we pulled up stakes and went back to our hotel room. The girls had made well over five hundred dollars each, by charging what the traffic would bear, and they gave me two hundred dollars apiece. I never laid eyes on old Ma Gooley after that, but I heard she carried on up until fairly recent times. Just like old firemen, old madams never die ... they just keep putting out other people's fires.

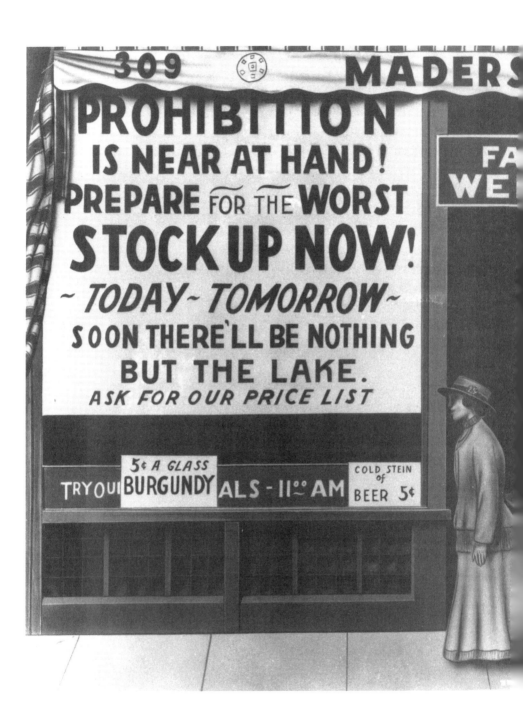

Chapter 21

I NEVER INQUIRED of Art Miller just what his alcohol running and hijacking operation entailed. Every time I found myself visualizing such an operation—particularly the hijacking—I put it out of my mind. Art became edgy and nervous and I saw him less and less. When he was with me he wanted only to be in my private sitting room or bedroom with the doors locked. He was continually checking and rechecking the doors and windows to be sure they were securely fastened. I asked him if the police were after him and he said "no."

It was Fabiola who told me what was wrong with Art; she had had a drunk customer who spilled the beans. Art had encroached on another hijacker's territory and the enraged competitor had sworn to get even. I decided not to let Art know I knew.

Art was on the verge of a mental breakdown. He finally told me the story Fabiola had gleaned months before. He also told me that he had missed an assassin's bullet on at least three different occasions.

His business had collapsed—he had been erratic in supplying his customers with booze and they had switched their trade to the revenge-bent competitor. Art was broke and frightened out of his mind. I planned his escape from his personal hell: he was to take my Ford and drive to his parents' home in Minnesota and stay out of sight for a few weeks until I could dispose of the John Street house, which I had bought about six months after I moved in. Then I would join him and we could drive to California and create a new and better life for ourselves.

I had over twenty thousand dollars in cash hidden in a tin box under the floorboards of my sitting room, directly beneath the big easy chair. I had saved this money for a bright future; it had become a symbol to me. I had spent money right and left the past seven years, but I was determined that this nest egg would never be wasted on frivolities. Here was my chance to do something worthwhile with it, so I pried up the floorboards and gave Art seventeen thousand dollars to take to Minnesota for safekeeping. I knew that as soon as Art disappeared from sight the man who wanted total revenge would start in on me—and setting fire to 510 John Street might be his first step. I didn't want my money to burn up.

It was after midnight when we slipped out the kitchen door and across the small back yard to the old stable that had been converted to a garage. I stuffed the paper bag full of money under the front seat, then I kissed Art goodbye. Art backed out of the garage and drove down the alley in darkness. I saw the headlights flash on as he pulled out into the main street. I said a silent prayer. No matter what he was, or had been, I loved him.

It was almost ten o'clock the next morning before the police informed me of the "accident." The car had careened off the side of a hill, they said. I knew better. Art had been unconscious when they found him, pinned under the steering wheel.

"Yes, he is alive and conscious. No serious injuries. We have him in jail. No, Mrs. Miller, we didn't find a paper bag full of your money under the front seat, but we did find a paper bag full of dope under the front seat." During Prohibition, alcohol running and hijacking booze were accepted evils, but dope was a different matter entirely. "We've been wanting the man who's been trafficking drugs into Wisconsin, now we have him." The competitor had gotten his revenge.

Before I could get to the jail to see him, my Art Miller ripped up a mattress cover, fashioned the strips of muslin into a rope, threw his hastily-made rope over an overhead heating pipe and hanged himself.

The stark fact that I was losing elasticity and wasn't able to bounce back after a personal disaster became apparent to me after Art's suicide. I turned the operation of the house over to Annie and I kept to my room. The mock gaiety of alcoholic laughter and false flattery became distasteful to me. I knew that the things which many customers came to my house to get, other than pure sex, were missing from the menu. There was no longer a vivacious Helen to talk with, no longer a sympathetic Helen's ear to pour a sad story into. Helen had lost her zest for life. The machinery of my establishment had lost its supercharger.

I kept thinking that tomorrow I'll throw off my gloom and the four of us—Annie, Mona, Fabiola, and I—will sit down, have a big laugh, and think of some spicy new addition to add to the house's repertoire. I thought that maybe a lively professional piano player with a rickety-tickety style might be what was needed. I would say to myself, "Stop thinking of what might have been. Get on with living." But each day I'd put off the discarding of my despondency until tomorrow—and tomorrow never came.

I wasn't really too surprised when Fabiola, with a show of tears, said she had decided to leave me. She was going to a house across town; not a good place at all. My gloom had gotten to Fabiola and she wanted to get away from me.

After Fabiola left I found another girl to occupy the green room. She was pretty to look at, but had an ugly disposition. When it became obvious that she was on the verge of alcoholism, I told her to take off. Then Mona, Annie, and I sat down at the kitchen table and I told them I had decided to close the house permanently. I told them I wanted to go home—to me Chicago was home—and see Al, Ralph, Ollie, Gladys and the rest of the gang. Even if I had to go back to Friend's Store or manage Capone's Adams and Green Street place, I was determined to return to the swim of things.

Once again the choice furnishings went into storage and everything else went to Annie. I offered Mona anything she wanted, but Mona had no desire to be tied down with the millstones of possessions. I sold the house the last week of August, 1927, then went over to Duluth and caught the evening train for Chicago.

I didn't really feel like eating, but I thought maybe a good sandwich and a glass of milk would make me feel better, so I went to the dining car. Shortly after I was seated, the dining car steward seated a middle-aged gentleman across from me. We made idle conversation and he introduced himself. He was a steel broker from Milwaukee. He asked where I was going and I told him "Chicago." Then he asked if I was from Chicago, and I felt too tired to beat around the bush, so I told him exactly who I was, what I had been doing in Superior, and what I intended to do in Chicago.

"May I call you Helen?" he asked politely.

"Of course. Everybody does," I answered.

"Why don't you stop off in Milwaukee and look the town over? It might be a better spot for you than Chicago."

"I don't know a thing about Milwaukee. I don't know one soul there," I said.

"You know me, Helen. I live there. I could make some contacts for you."

"Is the town controlled by combines?" I asked.

"Not really. There are various elements around, but they're all small-time. Nothing like Chicago. You'd have no trouble on that score."

"Is the town alive?" I asked.

"Very much so. Why don't you spend a day there and see for yourself? I know someone who'd be pleased to show you around."

What did I have to lose? "All right, my new friend," I said, "I'll get off the train with you."

The steel broker gave me his card with his office address, which was on the twelfth floor of the First National Wisconsin Bank Building. He also gave me the name of a girl who lived in the Cass-Wayne Apartments; he told me he'd call her the first thing the next morning and she'd be expecting me to drop by and visit with her. She was the one who'd show me around.

I checked into the Pfister Hotel and for the first time in many months I had a night's untroubled sleep.

BUTTERFLY THEATRE, Milwaukee, Wis.
Most Luxurious, Exclusive, Refined
Photo-Play House in America.
Absolutely Fireproof—Perfect Ventilation.
Change of Program Daily.
Complete Change of Air Every 3 Minutes.

Chapter 22

MILWAUKEE IN THE LATE 1920s was a town of unblushing, brawny vice rammed through with scents of European cooking, cheap perfume, and workers' sweat. The rumbling, guttural accents of Germans, Dutchmen, and Poles mingled with the silky Italian tones and were kneaded with bubbly sounds of sex to produce a symphony all its own. The city's gentry tried to mislead themselves into thinking of Milwaukee as fragile and culturally dainty, but it was as strong as an American buffalo. Maybe that's why, to me, the initial symbol of Milwaukee was the delicate-looking, welded-metal giant butterfly of the old Butterfly Theatre on Wisconsin Avenue; that butterfly may have looked fragile, but it couldn't have been knocked down with a sledge hammer.

That was Milwaukee way back then—and I liked the place from the very first day.

The afternoon following my arrival I went to see the woman at the Cass-Wayne apartments. I rang her bell and she came to the door and whispered hurriedly, "I'm being raided, wait out on the street for me!" I ran down the stairs and thunderbolted up the street to the corner. Presently three policemen came from the building, got into their car and drove off. Cautiously, I ventured back to the apartment and rang the bell once more.

"I'm sorry, my dear, that I couldn't invite you in a while ago, but I thought you'd probably prefer to remain outside under the circumstances." She gave a nervous little laugh.

"I've never heard of a raid where no one was taken in," I said.

< A postcard for the Butterfly Theatre, Milwaukee.

"Maybe I shouldn't have used the word 'raid.' It was more of a routine call. There's not too much to worry about in Milwaukee," she stated.

My steel broker friend had called her that morning, and she was prepared for my visit. We got her car out of a nearby garage and she spent several hours driving me around the town, explaining the ins and outs of the city.

It would have been impossible to have counted the speakeasies and bordellos she pointed out. There were at least three hundred speaks in the Third Ward alone. The South Side—Mineral Street, National Avenue, First Avenue and Second Avenue—was loaded with them. We returned from that area over the Sixth Street viaduct and turned up St. Paul Avenue. Between Sixth and Twenty-Seventh Streets there were thirty-five more speakeasies. There was something about that particular shitty street that appealed to me and I looked closely at all the buildings. "What's that place there?" I asked, pointing to an unkempt building.

"That's 1806—it's been pinched several times. It's a terrific location, but it's hotter than a goddamed firecracker," she answered.

We drove slowly up the street and I told her I was interested in 1806. She suggested that we go in if I wanted to see the inside. She turned the car around and we parked in front of the place, but on the opposite side of the street. After we knocked and waited a full minute, a young man opened the door and admitted us. There were about six or eight customers at the bar, and I told the bartender—a scared-looking little man—to give everyone a round of drinks on me.

I had never seen a place so fucking rundown. Many times speakeasies looked much better inside than they did outside, but this one looked even worse. I had expected the sagging little porch on the front exterior to be a cover-up for a smart-looking interior. Not so, the walls and ceilings were cracked, with great hunks of broken plaster hanging down like cobwebs; the floor was sagging, and squeaked when someone walked across it. The main room was about twenty by twenty-five feet. What fun it would be to fix this place up, I thought!

I called to the young man who admitted us and he came over. "Are you the bottle man?" I asked.

"Yeah."

"What's your name?"

"Gus," he answered.

"Well, Gus," I said, "I like your place."

"I'm glad," he stated in a bored voice. He obviously thought I was being sarcastic.

"I'm not kidding. I like it. Do you want to sell it?"

He pepped up immediately. "Sure," he said.

"How much do you want for it?" I asked.

"Three hundred bucks—for the door key. I don't own the building. I rent the place."

"What if the owners wouldn't rent to me?' I asked.

Gus thought for a split second before replying, "Then you'd get half your money back."

"Who owns the place?" I asked.

"Schlitz Realty," he said flatly. "A subsidiary of Schlitz Brewery."

"You've got yourself a deal, Gus," I said as I opened my purse and pulled out three one-hundred-dollar bills. "Give me a receipt, please." Gus gave me a receipt and the key and before I knew what was happening he put on his cap, said goodbye and left.

I turned to the customers, and to the bartender who couldn't believe the transaction had been pulled off so quickly, and said, "Have a drink on the house, boys, then clear out. This place will be closed temporarily. When you see it in a few weeks, you won't recognize it."

As soon as they finished their drinks, we all left together. I handed the bartender ten dollars and told him his services wouldn't be needed in the future. Then I slammed the door and locked it, dropped the key in my purse, and turned to my lady companion saying, "This has been an interesting tour."

The next day I met with a man from the Schlitz Realty and he okayed my lease. I was once more in business and my despondency had completely vanished. It seemed the most natural thing in the world to be settling in Milwaukee.

For two weeks following the signing of the lease, I did nothing but peek behind Milwaukee's closed doors. I'd go to speakeasies in the afternoon, in the evening, and at night. I found out exactly what competition I faced—and I also found the best maker of moonshine that ever scampered around finding empty bottles. His name was Louis, and he was my supplier for almost six years. I also found a source for Old McBrayer Bonded; and momentarily I thought of Art Miller, only to put him out of my mind and concentrate on the problems at hand.

Most of the speakeasies had girls upstairs. They would flock around the bar trying hard to look like customers, but I'm sure they didn't fool anybody. There were claptrap speakeasies, ordinary speakeasies, and fancy speakeasies. I was tired of fancy speaks and fancy women after the two years in Superior and, besides, my cash reserve was too low to open a fancy place. I had sold the house at 510 John Street at a ridiculously low price to dispose of it quickly and had put my small chunk of money into "gilt-edged securities" (two years later the "gilt" was the only part of the securities worth a damn!) I decided the wisest move would be to open an ordinary, unpretentious speakeasy and serve good food. The food in most of the speaks was so lousy that I felt something decent to eat would be a drawing card.

After my two weeks' tour of the Milwaukee operations, I hired cleaning women, repairmen, and painters and dug into 1806 St. Paul Avenue with a vengeance. It was no structural remodeling, only a clean-up campaign, but it took more ready cash. The building itself wasn't large, only thirty by sixty-five feet. Behind the main barroom was a dining room and a kitchen. Upstairs there were four rooms and a bath. There was no central heating; a big coal stove in the barroom was my "furnace."

Exactly nine days after the cleaning women and I started scouring, scraping, and clawing at the dirt, I opened the door on my first customers. The food menu was simplicity itself: ham and eggs, raw-fried potatoes, and hot biscuits. That menu, coupled with the best moonshine ever distilled and Old McBrayer Bonded, made me a quick success as a restaurateur.

I opened at nine a.m. every day and closed at nine p.m. From observations made during my tour of the other speaks, I knew the Moral Squad went into operation at nine p.m. By clearing everyone out at that time I was almost assured of immunity from police harassments.

Within a few short weeks, I had a seventy-to-a-hundred-dollars-a-day business going—without "girls." But just as a leopard can't change his spots, I couldn't bear to see the extra bedrooms upstairs going to waste, so I was a pushover when one of my best customers said, "Helen, you need a girl upstairs, and I've got just the one for you." Soon my little stairway was creaking and groaning with the pitter-patter of hot feet.

Seven weeks had passed since my opening and the only policeman I had seen was the beat officer. Then one afternoon about four p.m. two plainclothesmen came in and asked me what I was running. I told them I had a restaurant, a speakeasy serving moonshine and bonded stuff, and a girl upstairs. Then I said, "How much do you want a week?"

"We aren't going to arrest you," one of them said. "As a matter of fact, we've been on this job for three weeks and you're the first person who has told us the truth."

"Why not?" I asked. "I don't mind paying off either—I paid off at the last place I had."

"Where was that?" the second man asked.

"Superior."

"Would you tell our boss, the chief, just what you told us?" asked the first plainclothesman.

"Sure, I have nothing to hide. I'm not doing anything that thirty-four others on this same street aren't doing."

"Can you come down to the station in the morning?"

"Yes."

Early the next day I put on my smartest black-and-white outfit, told the girl upstairs to mind the store, and went to the police station to meet the chief. He wanted to know my background, where I had worked—everything. I even told him about the Duluth chief calling my uncle.

After we chatted awhile I said, "Now, Chief, you know who I am, what I am, and what I'm running. The question in my mind is 'how much'?"

"How much?" he asked, puzzled.

"How much is the payoff to the police? I'm used to it; I've always paid off," I said.

He looked me directly in the eye and said sternly, "Helen, there is no payoff to Milwaukee policemen."

The chief was right; in all my forty years in Milwaukee, I've never known of a policeman accepting a payoff. The Milwaukee Police Department is probably the cleanest in the country.

Evidently my interview with the chief was terminated, so I arose to go.

"I'll probably be seeing you again, Helen. Unofficially, I hope."

"I hope so, too, Chief," I said. "Unofficially."

"The best way for it to be 'unofficial' is for you not to get caught," he said with a smile.

"Don't get caught, eh?" I asked.

"The best advice anyone in Milwaukee can give you," he said as we shook hands.

Chapter 23

I'VE ALWAYS BELIEVED in mental telepathy. No matter how much people who don't believe in such things argue against it, I'm still a believer.

It was late in the fall of 1927. Only a couple of men were sitting around the bar that afternoon and we were talking about Capone. I was fighting mad because they were running him down. They claimed it was a shame that Al hadn't gotten bumped off the year before when his headquarters had been raked by machine gun fire from eight touring cars. "Who do you think engineered that job, Helen?"

"I don't 'think'—I know who engineered it," I answered.

"You know, for sure?" one of them asked.

"Everybody who knows Al well has a pretty good opinion of who was behind it," I stated.

"Who?"

"Hymie Weiss—and, of course, Bugs Moran[32] and Schemer Drucci[33]."

"Do you think that's why ... eh, Hymie Weiss got cut down a couple of weeks later?"

---

32 Adelard Cunin (August 21, 1893 – February 25, 1957), better known as George 'Bugs' Moran, was a Chicago Prohibition-era gangster. He was incarcerated three times before turning 21. On February 14, 1929, in an event that has become known as the Saint Valentine's Day Massacre, seven members of his gang were gunned down in a warehouse, supposedly on the orders of Moran's rival Al Capone.

33 Vincent Drucci, also known as "The Schemer" (born Vincenzo D'Ambrosio; 1898 – April 4, 1927), was a Sicilian-American mobster during Chicago's Prohibition era who was a member of the North Side Gang, Al Capone's best-known rivals. A friend of Dean O'Banion, Drucci succeeded him by becoming co-leader. He is the only U.S. organized crime boss to have been killed by a policeman.

"Sure that's why. Listen, you guys, Capone is a peace-loving man. I know for a fucking fact that he had begged and pleaded with Hymie to cut out the shit so everyone could live and let live. Al is far from being the cold-blooded animal he's cracked up to be. Weiss brought about his own downfall."

I went on to tell them how I had heard that Al spent over ten thousand dollars saving the eyesight of an innocent woman who happened to be on the street and was struck with flying glass when the bunch of North Side assassins riddled the windows of Capone's place.

"Al couldn't sleep at night if he thought that some harm had come to a completely innocent person because of his business differences. He's that way. I've been in the car with him when he's had the driver stop so he could hand a fifty-dollar bill to some old beggar woman. Don't you believe all the rot that's put out about him!"

Just at that moment the telephone rang, and it was Al. I was elated. "Long time no see, Helen. I've heard you have a nice place up there," he said.

"This is fantastic, Al! I was just thinking and talking about you with two of my customers." I looked at the two guys and they had turned chalk-white. "Why don't you come up some time and see for yourself?"

He laughed. "I'm afraid that if I left town I couldn't get back in!"

"You're kidding."

"Not completely. We're in the midst of hot elections down here. That's why I called—I'm having a big blast, a party ... want to come?"

"I sure do. When and where is it?"

"Keep it quiet. Next Monday night. At the Hawthorne. It'll start early. I want all the guests to arrive before dark ... " he gave a short laugh, "so we can see who's entering the place."

"It's a date. What time?"

"About four-thirty or a quarter of five. Not after five."

"See you then, Al."

I knew there were unseen eyes on me as I entered the

Hawthorne Hotel. Some men I had never met before greeted me and escorted me up to a lavish suite where a great buffet table was laid with glistening china and silver.

Al was talking with a group of people and as soon as he saw me he excused himself and came directly to me. He took both my hands and said softly, "Great to see you again, Helen." He smiled his gentle smile, and his dark eyes told me he was truly glad I was there.

He dropped my right hand and I reached up and laid my index finger against the scar on the left side of his face. "How's my beautiful Scarface Al Brown?"

"Couldn't be better," he said.

Al was sensitive about that scar, and only the people he really liked could get away with mentioning it without angering him.

"I want you to meet everybody—but remember, it's a secret who's here. Never tell."

Nothing on earth could make me break my word, but one thing I can tell you: many of the great people not only of Chicago but of America were there. You name the field—politics, society, the stage, the arena—they were all there.

Waiters circulated throughout the sumptuous suites with trays of champagne goblets and highball glasses. There was no homemade stuff there; it was the finest bonded booze available anywhere in the world. I had just started down the buffet line when Al came over and whispered in my ear, "Somewhere among the spaghetti and ravioli you'll find a bowl of chicken ala king."

I looked at him and smiled. "So ... you remembered?"

"Didn't I tell you I would?"

A dance orchestra began playing soon after the buffet started and the opening number was "Ah, Sweet Mystery of Life". Maybe it was a coincidence that that particular song was first, but it almost brought tears to my eyes.

Al was busy being the host and I didn't get to talk to him again until after midnight. "Al, I want some sort of tricky arrangement worked out for storing the hooch at my bar. The cops seem to be getting on to all the conventional hiding places. Know a good 'engineer' who could design something for me?"

"I sure do," he said.

"Would you have him call me in Milwaukee?"

"Okay. When do you want him to call?"

"In about a week."

"Can you stay in Chicago that long?"

"I'm going to New York for a few days," I said.

"New York?"

"Yes, I'm going there to see Tex Guinan[34] and Belle Livingstone[35]. I've heard so much about their places, I want to see them in action. I've been tucked away in the back woods for a few years, you know!"

"Have you ever been to Helen Morgan's[36]?" he asked.

"No."

"I was there a couple of months ago—she's worth hearing. Very good. You'll have to go there."

---

34 Mary Louise Cecilia "Texas" Guinan (January 12, 1884 – November 5, 1933) was an American actress, producer and entrepreneur. Born in Texas to Irish immigrant parents, she decided at an early age to become an entertainer. After becoming a star on the New York stage, the repercussions of her involvement in a weight loss scam motivated her to switch careers to the film business. Spending several years in California appearing in numerous productions, she eventually formed her own company.

What she is most remembered for are the speakeasy clubs she managed during Prohibition. Her clubs catered to the rich and famous, as well as to aspiring talent. After being arrested and indicted during a law enforcement sweep of speakeasy clubs, she was acquitted during her trial.

35 Isabel Graham (1878 – February 8, 1957) was born in rural Kansas and found abandoned while an infant. Named Isabel Graham, she moved with her foster parents to Chicago.

She adopted Belle Livingstone as a stage name. While in a show in New York, a publicist let it be known that Belle's measurements matched those of the Gibson Girl, a pinup drawing idolized in the 1890s. Her photograph was published nationwide as the "ideal woman." A New York writer said she had "poetic legs." She knew Teddy Roosevelt, Diamond Jim Brady, Isadora Duncan and Lily Langtry. She performed in a Broadway show that traveled to London in the early 1900s, then ran her own "salon" in Paris. For her hourglass curves, a journalist called her "the most dangerous woman in Europe." A self-described bohemian, Belle claimed to have had many affairs with prominent European men. She married three more times, to an Italian count, an English engineer and a wealthy Cleveland man.

In 1927, at age 52, after a long, comfortable life in Paris but with little money, Belle returned to New York. Friends took her to a speakeasy hosted by Texas Guinan. Belle hatched an idea for a "super-speakeasy" for New York's upper crust, with a $200 annual membership.

36 Helen Morgan (August 2, 1900 – October 9, 1941) was an American singer and actress who worked in films and on the stage. A quintessential torch singer, she made a big splash in the Chicago club scene in the 1920s. She starred as Julie LaVerne in the original Broadway production of Hammerstein and Kern's musical *Show Boat* in 1927, as well as in the 1932 Broadway revival of the musical, and appeared in two film adaptations, a part-talkie made in 1929 (prologue only) and a full-sound version made in 1936, becoming firmly associated with the role.

"Thought you didn't get out of town?"

"I was in New York for two days, and both nights I sat in a back corner of Morgan's place and sipped her terrible happy juice and not one soul recognized me."

Two nights later I was in Helen Morgan's. The spotlight cut through the drifts of cigarette smoke and illuminated her as she sat on top of the piano and sang. When she finished "Why Was I Born?" I understood why Al insisted that I see her. She was an authority on lives like ours—Capone's and mine.

After I arrived back in Milwaukee, Al's "engineer-designer" gave me a call and we set a date to begin. He drove up from Chicago and arrived about six a.m. I kept the bar closed all day while he devised a hidden container for my bootleg hooch.

The main reservoir was a long metal tank about fifteen inches wide which fit into the ceiling above the kitchen. The floor boards above the kitchen, and directly under the bed in my second-story bedroom, were neatly cut away and hinged to make a trap door. The metal tank, which the "engineer-designer" had fabricated in his shop in Chicago, fit neatly between the floor-ceiling joists. A narrow copper tube ran from the tank down inside the wall and its outlet was the metal latch plate on the door jamb between the dining room and kitchen. To activate the spigot, I had a hollow tube-key which I would stick in the little hole in the metal plate and booze would start flowing out. The metal tank held twenty gallons and was, of course, filled from my bedroom. I'd push the bed aside, pull back the rug, open the trap door, unscrew the cap, then Louie would pour in his delightful moonshine.

As my "engineer" friend was leaving he gave me several tips. "Have you ever been raided, Helen?" he asked.

"No," I answered.

"Well, you probably will be eventually. There are two things to remember: don't keep more than two quarts of booze out at any one time. If the raiders are at the door, pour the stuff down the sink, turn on the water for a couple of seconds, and keep the cops occupied for the length of time it takes you to count seventy."

"What do you mean about counting to seventy?" I asked.

"The latest trick that the cops pull is to go directly to the trap under the sink. Everybody pours their booze in the sink when they are being raided but what they don't know is that it takes over a minute for the stuff to clear the trap. If the coppers dash in with plumbing tools and find it in the trap, you've had it. See?"

"I got ya, Buster," I said.

"You needn't worry about the tank. Unless they are tipped off where it is, they'll never find it. The trap is the main thing; be sure and count to seventy."

From that time till repeal I had many raids, but they never found a shred of evidence. Many times I've yakked to the cops about any and everything while my goddamed mind was ticking off 67-68-69-70!

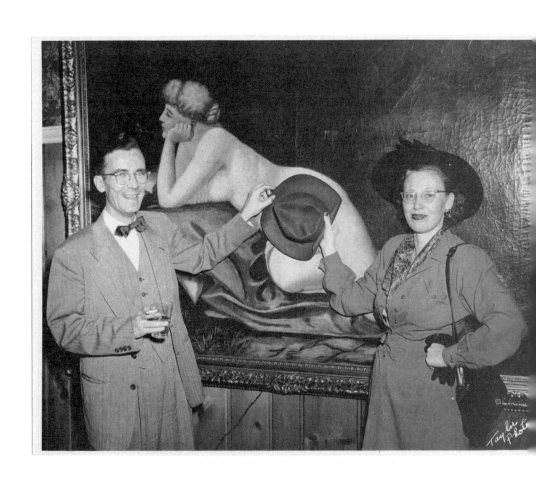

Chapter 24

THE MOST NOTABLE PURCHASE I made after I opened my speak was a massive oil painting. The painting had been the focal point of a famous speakeasy located in Milwaukee's Old Grove Hotel. The speakeasy had been padlocked by the government and all furnishings were to be sold at auction. When I heard this news, I decided to try and buy the fucking painting; I couldn't believe that many people would want it, and I assumed that I could get it cheaply. I was wrong.

Many people were interested in the picture and the bidding was heavy and heated. There were at least six or eight people determined to have it, and the bidding got into the hundreds of dollars. The raises were only five and ten dollars each time so it took quite a while for the price to get to five hundred and eighty dollars, which was my bid when the auctioneer slammed down his hammer and yelled, "Sold to the young woman in the pink hat!"

The audience was small and informal and the auctioneer asked, "Now young lady, since you own the painting of a voluptuous nude damsel reclining on a cushion and perusing a book of Greek classics, why don't you tell us why you were so determined to own this grrr-eat oil masterpiece."

"It's really no mystery, sir," I joked. "That happens to be a goddamed portrait of me when I was hustling in the Yukon. And that's no Greek classic I'm reading—it's the Sears & Roebuck catalog!" The house practically came down with laughter and ever since that day in 1928 that has always been my version of the history of the painting.

The picture was hung immediately in my bar and was never removed except for cleaning and a bit of restoration when I remodeled the place in 1940. It was at that time that I replaced the narrow frame with the elaborate six-inch-wide gold leaf frame which it now has. Of my few remaining possessions, it is my most prized souvenir.

Soon after I bought the picture, I regretted having done it because I needed the money. I had invested all my remaining cash in a get-rich-quick stock deal and quickly lost every penny I owned except my "gilt-edged securities," which I refused to touch. I needed to make more money than the speakeasy was bringing in, so I turned to the employment that many females think of when they want to build up their income—fucking!

A man I'll call Dom got me actively engaged in selling sex once again.

Dom ran a large-scale operation from his cigar store headquarters in the Edison-Juneau Avenues area. One day Dom was in my place and I was lamenting the fact that I felt obliged to close every evening at nine even though I needed to make more dough.

"Why don't you continue making money after nine?" asked Dom in his broken English.

"What do you mean?" I returned.

"You know about my girls? They make big money. They're good-looking. You're good-looking. Why don't you be one of my girls?"

I told him I'd give it a fling and soon I was making about eighty dollars between nine p.m. and three a.m. No "madam stuff" at Dom's; I was right on the line—and it was fatiguing, to say the least.

During this period of working at Dom's place, I had rented a small cottage on Highland Avenue as a get-away-from-it-all home for myself. I had furnished it with my best furniture from the various storage warehouses in Chicago and Superior. It was my retreat from the world of booze and sex, and I enjoyed being there for the few hours after work was over at Dom's and before I opened my speak on St. Paul Avenue at nine a.m.

After three a.m., a few of us girls would always stop at a little speakeasy at 31 East Juneau Avenue for a pepper-upper (we could use one after turning twenty to twenty-five tricks each) before going home. I mean, we'd be damned fucked out.

The bartender at 31 East Juneau was a cute kid they called Guy; he was only twenty-three. Much too young for me, I thought, although I enjoyed talking to him. Guy would mix the drinks for all the other girls first; then he would mix mine, hand it to me with a smile, plant himself squarely in front of me on the opposite side of the bar and say, "Now for the best part of my day." A woman has to be in her forties before she can appreciate this type of flattery from a twenty-three-year-old boy. We would talk until the other customers screamed for more booze.

Neither Guy nor I ever mentioned my extracurricular activities or Dom's establishment where I had just come from. The conversation was always light, witty, and general. Guy's chit-chat became something that I looked forward to each night. At this point my feelings for him were really quite maternal, and I was surprised one night when he asked, "Helen, a few of us are all playing hooky from our jobs Halloween Night, and are going out to Sharpshooter's Park for a little fun, would you like to come with me?"

"I'd love to," I answered quickly. After all, I thought, all work and no play makes Helen a dull lay.

As far as I recall, the exceptional thing about Sharpshooter's Park was the dance orchestra and, in particular, the piano player. He was an extraordinary musician and we all commented on him. We learned his name was Tony Sarnow, and I decided that if I ever got to the point where I could afford an entertainer at my place, I would try to get Tony.

There were three couples of us at the park. About two-thirty or three a.m. the merriment wore a little thin and Guy took me home. He didn't believe me when I told him I lived alone, so I asked him to come in and see for himself. I wasn't at all surprised when he announced that he was spending the night; in fact, I was pleased—after all, I hadn't been fucked all evening and one misses it.

The next morning at eight-thirty I left Guy a note telling him I had to go to the bar and asking him to call me during the day. I was tired, which was nothing new for me, and I was hung over, but somehow I made it through the morning. He called about three in the afternoon. He told me he was still at my place and he felt great. I told him I felt lousy. He suggested that I close the bar and come home—it sounded like a goddamed inspired suggestion.

I must admit that I was surprised to find that he had moved into my house. His clothing and all his possessions were neatly stashed away in various rooms of my place. "Do you mind?" he asked airily.

"I'm not sure," I answered noncommittally.

"You don't like living alone, do you?"

"Not particularly," I answered.

"Well, now you don't live alone any more."

That settled that.

I was too tired to go back to the bar or to Dom's. About ten p.m. the phone rang and it was Dom. He wanted to know why I hadn't shown up the night before and why wasn't I on the way there now? He claimed customers were asking for me. Before I had a chance to make up a plausible excuse, Guy grabbed the phone and said, "This is Guy Cromell. Helen and I have paired up. Don't call her anymore!" He slammed down the phone and that was the end of Dom.

Guy continued at 31 East Juneau for about a month, then he quit and became my bartender. A long time afterwards—in April of 1929—a plainclothesman tipped me off that the city was going to put the heat on speakeasy owners and the only evidence they had on me was that Guy and I were living together illegally. He said it could be used against me and he suggested that Guy and I either break up or get married. That very evening, I noticed that my cottage was being watched by the police, so Guy and I spent two weeks at various apartment hotels. We decided it was stupid to go on that way, so we drove to Waukegan and were married. It wasn't the keenest of romances, but it was expeditious.

The glamor that was missing from the marriage ceremony itself was forgotten when we bought our wedding gift for each other. It was a sporty, black-and-green Hudson roadster. Jesus God, it was a real piss-elegant deal! Six weeks after our wedding we took off in the car for a belated "honeymoon" to the Speedway Races in Indianapolis.

After the races, I asked Guy to drive with me to Cicero and Noblesville. Being in Indiana brought back memories I had long assumed were dead. I knew I shouldn't go back to those little towns, but I was bedeviled by a magnet that kept pulling me to them.

Guy had heard only sketches of my early life, but he sensed the trauma that I was subjecting myself to as we drove slowly down the narrow streets. He asked me no questions and I gave him only directions on which way to turn.

As we drove slowly past Leona's house, I knew that behind those vines on the front porch was a swing, and in that swing I could see a young Phil Cappel and a young Helen Worley— laughing, pouting, teasing. Then I could hear the words that were dancing around in that young girl's mind: I am here with Phil Cappel, the only man I'll ever really and truly love. From that house—the house that had been Leona's and maybe still was— came the sound of a piano being played, and I remembered the nights that Leona had played the piano as Phil and I courted on the porch, and I couldn't contain the pressure that had built up within me. I covered my face with my hands and my body shook with dry sobbing.

"Why are you doing this to yourself?" asked Guy gently. "Don't you know it's too late, Helen?"

Of course it was too late. Young Helen Worley had died a long time ago in Cincinnati. I forced myself back to the Helen of today and wiped my eyes. I reached for Guy's arm.

"Good girl," he said. "Now buck up and let's set a speed record to Chicago." Guy made a U-turn in the middle of the main street, stepped on the goddamed gas pedal, and the black-and-green Hudson barreled toward the big city.

Hours and hours later, the twinkling lights of Chicago's South

Side signaled a welcome to me. We drove north on Michigan Avenue and as we approached the Congress Hotel I told Guy I wanted to stop there for the night. As we entered Peacock Alley, the music of Paul Whiteman's band filled the air, and I knew that of all the places I had revisited that day, this was where I could be without having my fucking soul torn to shreds. Guy had been right when he said it was much too late.

Sun Flower Inn piano player Tony Sarnow.

Helen dear
    We've had lots of fun
    In this Inn named for "Sun"
    But the joy of our hour
    Was when they added the
                    "Flower"
                Irene E. Wright.

To Helen
    If All the People in this
World Were Like you I Don't
think Any One Would Ever
Be Blue
                Joe Taylor
                Milwaukee Braves
Helen I certainly go with Joe
"This "Right"

Chapter 25

"OH, NO YOU DON'T," I said to the steady customer at the bar. "No more girls for me. That last one was more trouble than she was worth!"

"This gal needs the work, Helen. She supports her mother and father and a seven-year-old daughter, and they are all about to lose their home. Come on, Helen, give her a break. She's really a very nice girl."

The next day the man brought her by to see me. I liked her. She wasn't the usual type of hustler. There was something warm and human about her. She wasn't beautiful, but she was attractive. She told me her hard-to-remember-and-pronounce name, and I informed her I was going to call her Lee. I told her that her board and laundry would be free, but I wanted one dollar every time she turned a trick in her upstairs bedroom. The very week that Lee started at my place a Trans-Atlantic ocean liner captain from New England ascended the narrow stairs with her. Later, as he was leaving the bar, he turned to me and said, "Some day I'm going to return here and marry that girl." Yeah, like shit you will, I thought!

Well, anyhow, Lee really pulled in the customers; she must have had a marvelous flair for her work because it didn't take her too long to pay off a forty-two-hundred-dollar mortgage on her family's home. And, at a buck a trick from her, I made a pretty penny also.

It was while Lee was at her peak as my little upstairs

moneymaker that I was having a conversation with my favorite customer, Art Shires[37]—"The Great Shires" we always called him. As one of the big names in baseball, Art had been with the Chicago White Sox, then with Washington and Boston. At the time he started coming to my place, he had joined the Milwaukee Brewers preparing for a tornado-like, barnstorming tour of the Midwest. "If you'll get rid of the girl upstairs, Helen, I'll bring you a lot of business," said Art.

"Now, Art, you know that I think the world of Lee. I couldn't possibly put her out!"

"I know, I know, but it's not good for our standing in the city to hang around places that have 'girls available.' A lot of the guys on the team actually won't come here because of that one thing. This place is fun, Helen, and you have the best food in town. There's no reason for you to run a cat house!"

"This is no cat house!" I cried instantly.

"Of course it isn't, but you know what I mean," Art said.

It was just a few weeks after my talk with Art Shires when there was a rap on the door and I peeked out and saw the sea captain who had been so taken with Lee that first week she had moved in. He gave me a smile as I let him into the barroom and the first thing he said was, "Is Lee still here?" I assured him that she was and he went upstairs and stayed all afternoon. It was late in the evening that the two of them came downstairs and told me they were going to get married! She even had her suitcase already packed. So, just like the hero of a costume novel, the sea captain married my little hustler and moved both her and her young daughter to a serene village in New England. I was so touched I actually cried when they kissed me goodbye. It was July 5, 1931. I got on the telephone and called Art Shires and told him the upstairs was empty.

---

37 Charles Arthur Shires (August 13, 1906 – July 13, 1967) was an American professional baseball player. He played in Major League Baseball as a first baseman for the Chicago White Sox, Washington Senators and Boston Braves. In a four-year major league career, Shires played in 290 games, accumulating 71 hits in 298 at bats for a .291 career batting average along with 11 home runs, 119 runs batted in, an on-base percentage of .347, and a .988 fielding percentage.

Shires was a colorful personality with a penchant for self-praise, earning himself the nickname "Art The Great."

"You keep the upstairs empty and I'll put your place on the map, Helen," Art said.

"Okay, it's a deal," I said. After I hung up the phone I sort of wished I hadn't been so hasty. It was sort of lonesome around there, not hearing the old bed squeaking at the joints. You know, it was a rather warm and comforting sound. Sort of a boost to lagging spirits on rainy nights!

Art kept his part of the deal and I kept mine. He started bringing fellow ballplayers, newspaper writers, visiting celebrities, and well-known local people there. The popularity of the place seemed to blossom almost overnight.

Toward the end of August the barnstorming team was assembled, ready for their tour. Art called one evening and said they wanted to have a big party and a real "feed bag" and what did I think about having it at my place. I told him it was a brilliant idea, and that I would take care of everything but the invitations—I told him to invite anyone he liked but to use a little discretion because I wanted to be sure of who was there—speakeasy operators had to be careful who was admitted through their doors.

The morning of the party I got up before daylight and started baking hams, slicing cold cuts, and boiling potatoes for potato salad. When those chores were accomplished, I drove to Port Washington to get fresh perch. When I told the man at the fish market that I wanted fifteen pounds of perch he exclaimed, "Have you any idea, lady, of how many perch there are in fifteen pounds?" I told him I did indeed, and on second thought he had better make it twenty pounds. Then he wanted to know if I was having a fish fry, and I admitted that it was going to be "something like a fish fry."

The guests started arriving early. I imagine there were about thirty men in all. Among the guests were several old names that baseball fanciers will recognize: Bubbles Hargrave[38], Bernie

---

38 Eugene Franklin "Bubbles" Hargrave (July 15, 1892 – February 23, 1969) was an American catcher in Major League Baseball who played for the Chicago Cubs, Cincinnati Reds, and New York Yankees. He won the National League batting title in 1926 while playing for Cincinnati. He was nicknamed "Bubbles" because he stuttered when saying "B" sounds. Bubbles' younger brother, Pinky Hargrave, was also a major league catcher.

Neis[39], Jack Rothrock[40], and Gordon Slade[41]. The party lasted until five a.m. and "Helen's Place" was put on the map.

"Better wear your bullet-proof vest!" shouted a customer as I lugged gallon after gallon of moonshine from the bar and stashed it into my Hudson roadster. "The North Side Chicago mob will rub you out when they find out you're encroaching on their territory!"

Besides being a speakeasy operator, a barkeep, an ex-madame, a party-giver extraordinaire, and a housewife, I had become an alcohol runner. One of my customers, a Milwaukee attorney, had brought the vice president of a major Chicago newspaper to my place, and the gentleman was overwhelmed by the quality of Louie's hooch. I told him that, for a price, the hooch was available in practically unlimited quantities. So we set up a business arrangement: I would buy the stuff from Louie for only six dollars a gallon (price undisclosed, of course) and sell it to Mr. Publisher for twelve. The only hitch was that I had to deliver it to his fancy home in Winnetka, Illinois. This particular Winnetkan either had great thirst or many friends—or maybe he was running the stuff even farther down the line—he used fifteen gallons a week!

At first I was rather leery of getting into hot water until my "protection" was worked out satisfactorily. Mr. Publisher apparently knew the right people, because my roadster was

---

39 Bernard Edmund Neis (September 26, 1895 – November 29, 1972) was an American professional baseball outfielder. He played in Major League Baseball (MLB) for the Brooklyn Robins, Boston Braves, Cleveland Indians, and Chicago White Sox between 1920 and 1927. He later managed in the minor leagues in 1932 and 1933.

40 Jack Houston Rothrock (March 14, 1905 – February 2, 1980) was a utility player in Major League Baseball who played for four different teams between the 1925 and 1937 seasons. Listed at 5 ft 11 in (1.80 m), 165 lb., Rothrock was a switch-hitter who threw right-handed. He was born in Long Beach, California.

Rothrock was a line drive hitter and aggressive baserunner. He entered the majors in 1925 with the Boston Red Sox, playing for them through the 1932 midseason before joining the Chicago White Sox (1932), St. Louis Cardinals (1934–1935) and Philadelphia Athletics (1935, 1937). In 1927 was considered in the American League MVP vote, then in 1928 played all nine positions, plus pinch-hitting and pinch-running duties. He became just the second American League player ever to play all nine positions in one season.

41 Gordon Leigh Slade (October 9, 1904 – January 2, 1974), nicknamed Oskie, was an American professional baseball shortstop. He played six seasons in Major League Baseball (MLB) from 1930 to 1935 for the Brooklyn Robins/Dodgers, St. Louis Cardinals, and Cincinnati Reds. As a member of the Brooklyn Dodgers in 1932, Slade was thrown out of a game for arguing by National League umpire Charlie Moran.

always met in Deerfield, Illinois, by a police car. We'd quickly transfer the moonshine to the police car and take off in a cloud of dust for Winnetka, which was about ten miles away. We'd pull into Mr. Publisher's swank driveway and stop the car on a giant revolving disc which automatically spun the car around and faced it out the driveway. To me, this was the most memorable thing of the whole rum-running because I've never seen one of those turntable contraptions anywhere else except at apartment buildings.

Quick as little beavers the cops and I would heave the booze from the police car and tote it into Mr. Publisher's rumpus room which opened off the front of the house. The door was always unlocked for us and my one hundred and eighty dollars was always under a blue and white Ming vase. No sweat, really, and there was never any contact with my newspaper man. Actually, I only saw him the first night I met him at my bar, but our "dealings" lasted until Prohibition was repealed. The policemen claimed they were "taken care of," so after the first try I never again offered them a tip as they returned me to Deerfield and my parked Hudson. I've always had the feeling that Louie's smooth stuff wound up at Chicago's most elegant athletic clubs.

Guy and I had two close calls with the law. Had it not been for a tip-off, they would have gotten us the first time for sure.

Guy had been deer hunting for several days and had gotten home late in the afternoon. After he cleaned up and had dinner he announced that he had to have a haircut. He called the Astor Barber Shop and his favorite barber told him they were going to be open until nine p.m. and for Guy to come on down.

At eight-thirty the phone rang and a voice squealed, "Helen?"

"Yeah, this is Helen."

"This is 'Kink' on Clybourn Street. The Feds just got me. Cleaned me out. Heard 'em mention your place. Hurry, Helen!"

There were only about six customers in my place. I slammed down the phone and shouted, "Get your glasses over here! A raid!"

They quickly lined up their glasses and I poured the remnants of their booze down the drain and threw the glasses into a bucketful of soapy water. Then I poured out the pitcher of moonshine and hurriedly turned the water tap on for a couple of seconds. I raced around to the front of the bar and told everybody not to utter a word. I was trying to count to seventy when the pounding started on the door. I opened the door and ten federal agents came dashing in. I had seen two of the men before and knew them as a Mr. Kenshaft and Mr. Kimmerlein. I stayed clear of the rear of the bar—had I gone back there they could have booked me as the keeper of the place even without finding the evidence.

Mr. Kenshaft stayed by my side as the others searched the place from top to bottom. They even tore up a loose section of an old stairway in the back of the building. But they found nothing; they weren't smart enough to compete with Al Capone's designer-engineer.

"What are you trying to do, Kenshaft, wreck my home? There's nothing here," I said.

"Yeah? I'll bet this place is loaded with moon. Where do you keep it, Helen?"

"Why, Mister Kenshaft, what a leading question," I jeered.

"Where's your husband?" he demanded.

"At the barber shop."

"Call him and tell him to get home."

Unfortunately, a barber who didn't know Guy answered the phone. I told him who I was and that my husband was there. I asked him to please tell Guy to get home at once because we were being raided. The barber thought it was humorous and relayed the message in a loud voice which was heard by every patron of the shop. Guy related later that one gentleman who was having a shave, and whose face was covered by a wet towel, reared up in his chair and asked the barber what he had said and the barber repeated it with a grin. The man behind the towel was none other than Mr. Cunningham[42], the Federal Chief of the Milwaukee District!

Guy raced home, and was taken to the station by the raiding officers on suspicion of selling moonshine. I called our attorney, Tom Leahy, and he asked that I be in his office at eight-thirty the

---

42   W. Frank Cunningham, Deputy Prohibition Administrator for Eastern Wisconsin. Newspapers of the time and later researchers note that Cunningham was less than zealous in his enforcement of the Volstead Act.

following morning. We bailed Guy out and when the case came up in federal court, it was dismissed for lack of evidence.

The second incident happened on a bitter, blustery March night. Snow had piled up two feet deep and the street was lined with stalled, abandoned cars. There had been no customers in the place the entire evening and we were getting ready to go upstairs when there was a loud knock on the door. I peeked out and saw a man standing on the front porch with a girl in his arms; a second man was coming up the walk also carrying a girl. "Look," I said to Guy and he peeked out, too.

"It's about time some customers showed up," Guy said.

"I don't like their looks, and I've never seen them before, don't let them in, Guy."

"Don't be silly," said Guy as he opened the door for the foursome.

They appeared to have been drinking for some time and were well on the way to flying high. They guzzled our moon for about an hour, yet I still had a funny feeling about them. Finally I turned to one of them and said, "You look sorta familiar to me, yet I can't figure out where I've seen you."

"Probably right here in the neighborhood," he said. "I work for Dan Rome's Plumbing Company."

"I thought I knew all the people at Rome's," I said.

"Well, I'm sure you've seen me around." He fished in his pocket and pulled out a card which had his name, Harry Monroe, and the plumbing company's name and address printed on it.

Perhaps that should have been enough assurance to me, but I was still leery of them. I went behind the bar and, without anyone noticing, I poured a quart of moonshine down the drain. When the foursome paid their tab and announced that they were leaving, they asked to buy a quart of moon to take with them.

"The jug's empty, folks," I said. "Sorry."

"There's an extra quart back there, Helen," said Guy.

"Nope, it's all gone."

Guy came behind the bar and stared at our empty pitcher and at the empty quart. "Well, for the name of … "

"It's all gone, Guy."

He grabbed the pitcher and I knew he was headed for the secret spigot. I put my hand on Guy's arm and squeezed firmly. "See, the jug's completely empty!" I gave his arm three quick squeezes. He hated to back down, but he told the people we were out of moon.

As soon as the two couples left, he turned to me angrily, "Did you pour out a whole quart of moon?"

"I did."

"What in hell is wrong with you? We could have gotten ten or fifteen bucks from that crew of drunks!"

"Maybe it was foolish, but I had a feeling … "

"You and your feelings!" he stormed. "Didn't you see that guy's card? He works down in the 1100 block at Rome's."

"I'm sorry, Guy, I guess it was a stupid thing to do, but … "

Guy ranted on while we undressed and went to bed. He was still sputtering when he fell asleep. At five a.m. the phone rang and rang. I stumbled downstairs and answered it. It was a friend of ours who operated a speakeasy on Canal Street.

"Helen, did you have two men and two girls at your place tonight?"

"Yeah, why?"

"Did they see any moonshine there?"

"They saw plenty—in fact, they drank a whole jug of it. Why?"

"Well, they came on to my place. They were all blasted and one of the girls mumbled something about seeing you. Those two men are federal undercover agents."

"Damn it, I thought so! I had a feeling about them!"

"One of my other customers who works at the courthouse recognized them. They're Harry Monroe and 'Squirt' Merkle. This other guy—the one at the courthouse—has seen 'em put the finger on several of the National Avenue operators."

"The one called Harry had a business card with Dan Rome's Plumbing Company on it," I said.

"I don't know about that, Helen. All I know is what I'm telling you. You'd better get ready for something because they're sure as hell feds."

At eight o'clock the next morning Guy was at Dan Rome's door when Mr. Rome arrived to open his shop for the day. Dan Rome said that Harry Monroe had worked for him about two or three years before, but was now with the government. Guy told him about being shown the business card by Monroe, and Rome was blazing mad. Mr. Rome claimed to have heard rumors of Monroe doing that before, and he was sick and tired of that character going around to speakeasies buying moon and getting evidence on Rome's credentials. As Guy left him, Dan Rome was on his way to see Mr. Cunningham, the district chief. We heard later that Harry Monroe got booted out of his job, but the prospects of such revenge were little consolation at the moment.

We also learned later the way "Squirt" Merkle got his nickname. He'd sometimes keep moonshine in his mouth and go to the washroom and spit it into an empty flask. The flask's contents would be used as evidence when the operators were pinched.

As soon as Guy got home we went directly to our attorney's office and told him everything that had happened. He told us we could expect a raid within ten days and for us to go home and clean house. "Don't even have a bottle of soda water around," he said.

I called Louie, our distiller, and told him to get over quick and drain the reservoir. Louie carted all the moonshine away with him, and I poured out the beer. Then Guy and I just sat tight for days.

Attorney Tom Leahy was right—nine days later, at midnight, the raid came. And what a raid! I'll bet there were twenty-five men. They tapped, they poked, they knocked on walls and cupboards, they went over the place with a magnifying glass, but they didn't find the reservoir tank. And, of course, there hadn't been a drop of alcohol in the place for days, so the whole building smelled as refined as the WCTU headquarters. When they finally cleared out, my "feeling" told me it was the last raid I'd have to endure for some time. So the very next day I called Louie and told him to "fill 'er up!"

Guy had been hunting while we were temporarily out of business, and had bagged a large quantity of wild ducks. We decided to have a duck dinner for about ten guests, and needed a supply of beer. The evening before the party I drove over to

Random Lake to a place that made terrific beer. I got a whole barrelful and it took two men to lift it into the car for me. On the way home, I happened to think of our fellow speakeasy operator on Canal Street who had warned me about Harry Monroe and "Squirt" Merkle, and thought it would be a nice gesture if I went by, bought a few drinks and thanked him for tipping us off.

I had just gotten seated at the bar and ordered a drink when a watchman at the front door hollered, "Raid! Four police cars out front!"

Jesus God, I thought fleetingly. I've just gotten out of my own mess and they'll catch me here. Then I thought about the barrel of beer in the car! Caught running beer! I shot off that bar stool with a propelling energy I never knew I possessed and streaked into the ladies' room. There was only one small high window above the john. A prim-looking dame with pulled-back hair and pince-nez was seated on the can as straight-backed as if she were sipping tea at a D.A.R.[43] meeting.

"Well," she said haughtily, "can't one have some privacy?"

"Sister, in about ten seconds you'll think you're pissing in the middle of Grand Central Station. Get off the can!" I demanded.

"I will not. You wait your turn—outsider."

I didn't waste more time conversing with her. I put a foot on one of her legs and one on the other and bounded up in her lap. Then I put a foot on her left shoulder and a foot on her right shoulder. She screamed like a stuck pig, but it didn't deter me as I threw open the window. With one foot on her head, I gave myself a push and sailed through the window and fell to the ground. Then I ran like fury to the car.

Driving home, I wondered if the leisurely-minded bitch had gotten herself unstuck from the hole in the john seat, or if the cops had had to pull her out.

No matter what anyone says, the Prohibition era was fun, a real gasser. And many of us hated to see it fading into limbo. Old Andrew J. Volstead probably never envisioned the joy he would kick up when he pushed his famous Prohibition Enforcement Act through Congress in 1919. Maybe President Wilson knew it

---

43 D.A.R. is the abbreviation for Daughters of the American Revolution.

would be a blithering blast. Could that be why the act was passed even with the presidential veto on it? Whatever the cause and the effect, the U.S. Prohibition laws became invalid with the ratification of the Twenty-First Amendment to the Constitution in 1933. With repeal came the type of letdown one feels after a big fucking party is over. Gone were the thrills of going to a speakeasy; in their place came the resignments of visiting a neighborhood "tavern."

Each state set up its laws governing the taverns. Licenses to sell liquor were granted to those individuals who had the okay of the police department and the license committee. Guy and I received our license with no trouble. The new laws were highly organized, highly efficient, but they took a lot of fun out of drinking. The purring thirties replaced the roaring twenties, and "Helen's Place" turned into a tavern—but not exactly a "neighborhood tavern."

Chapter 26

WHILE MANY SMALL BUSINESSES around us were failing, being sucked into the pits of the Depression, our own enterprise seemed to be going nowhere but up. It seemed crazy, but of course we were selling the anesthesia people wanted to help ease the shock of their own losses. Millions of men were out of work—I believe the estimate was fourteen million. Commodity prices fell to a new low and national income was about half of what it had been before the maniacal October days of 1929. Calvin Coolidge and Herbert Hoover were in wide unpopularity, and the election year of 1932 was a snap for Franklin D. Roosevelt.

It was during this staggering period that Guy became a playboy of sorts. We had many customers who made big money off the Depression and this was the crowd that appealed most to Guy. He became their constant fishing and hunting companion, and nothing was too expensive for him to buy if he really wanted it.

Guy and I were really riding high on the crest of the Depression, and yet Guy became angry with me when he found out I had been slipping money to the college boys who would occasionally come to the newly named "Sun Flower Inn." "What gives between you and that Marquette University crowd?" he demanded.

"Not a damned thing," I said. "It so happens that those kids are having tough sledding trying to stay in school. A buck means a hell of a lot to them, and it doesn't mean a fucking thing to me. Why shouldn't I pass a couple of dollars to them if I want to?"

< Patrons at the Sun Flower Inn.

"Don't forget that half of the money around here is mine!" he said sarcastically.

I was livid with fury, but I held my tongue. Of course, Guy was right—I guess. He was my husband. But I was the one who got up at the crack of dawn every weekday morning to start preparing food for the seventy-five men who ate lunch with us at noon. I had had my regular lunch customers for several years, then when the Huntzinger Construction Company had acquired the contract for building a giant Swift's packing plant in our area, at least forty or fifty of the foremen and supervisors would pour into the place for their mid-day meal.

It was, as a matter of fact, Mr. Huntzinger himself who named my bar the Sun Flower Inn; the small front yard was spiked with hundreds of the tall, yellow weed-flowers. I had intended clearing the sunflowers out, but there wasn't time to do it because I was the one who did all the grocery shopping, food preparation, serving of meals, clearing of tables, and washing dishes. When all that was over, I'd get on my hands and knees and scrub the floors. There was considerable work involved in making the money that we made.

Guy did what he considered his portion of the work. He'd get out of bed about ten-thirty a.m., have a leisurely breakfast, open the bar and work it until after my kitchen chores were done. At that time he'd turn the bar over to me, put on one of his one-hundred-and-fifty-dollar suits, top it off with a forty-dollar hat, and meander downtown for a hair clipping and a manicure. Then he'd come home for dinner and work the bar late in the evening, when the big shots started arriving.

The amount of hard work that fell in my direction wasn't what bothered me; it was Guy's complaint about my giving money to the college boys that burned me to a crisp. I have some sort of a bug about education; I want people to be educated, and in the depths of the Depression there were damned few kids in the higher-educational establishments. Maybe it harked back to the feeling that events had been rough on my own kids during their early years (now that they were grown our contact had been re-established without drama or trauma; those boys were hard workers and had gained good educations for themselves and had acquired good jobs). Without belaboring the point of my own boys, I couldn't sit by and see those Marquette students drop out of school because of lack of funds.

I was loaded with dough and even to this day I think I put it to good use in the early thirties. I've paid many a tuition bill for boys who are now doctors, lawyers, and Indian chiefs. And I'm not trying to put myself in the do-gooder category either. I just want all those people who say "Helen threw her money away" to be aware that it didn't all go for frivolities.

I decided to hell with Guy—I was determined to help those college kids any way I could and that's when Joe entered my life. He came around one day asking if I had any work that he could do; he said he was at Marquette and really needed the money. I liked him from the outset. He was nice-looking, quiet, extremely well-mannered, and pleasant to be around; I judged him to be a couple of years older than most of the students. Anyway, I gave Joe a job for all day on Saturdays and any afternoons he didn't have classes.

He had been helping me do odd jobs around the place for several months and had gotten my little front yard looking halfway decent by working on it for two consecutive Saturdays. It was late in the afternoon and he came in from the yard looking tired. "Joe, you've certainly done wonders with that yard. You'll be back next Saturday, too, won't you?"

"What did you say, Helen?" he asked absently.

"I asked if you'd be back next Saturday?"

He looked down at the floor and didn't answer for a moment .Then he looked me square in the eye and said evenly, "I'm afraid I won't be able to work for you any more, Helen."

"Why not, for God's sake?"

"I doubt if I'll be at Marquette much longer," he said despondently.

"What do you mean?"

"I'm thinking of leaving school."

"Leaving school?"

"I'm afraid so."

"Money?"

"Yeah—that and other things."

My mind worked rapidly. "How would you like an icy-cold beer, Joe?" I asked him.

He accepted readily and as he was sipping the beer I asked him how old he was.

"Almost twenty-three," he replied.

"Well, you aren't going to quit school because I'm not going to let you."

Joe laughed. "How can anybody stay in school when they're broke?"

"You have help from home, don't you?"

"Some. A little. I worked in a grocery store in Manawa for over a year and saved every penny. But it's gone."

"How much money do you need, Joe?" I asked him.

"It's not only money. I'm broke, sure, but everything seems to be wrong. I don't really want to be an engineer, Helen." He said it with great intensity. This boy was one of my favorites, plus being a good worker, and I wouldn't have let him quit college for anything in the world. He had great potential and I knew it.

"You'd make a lousy engineer. What you should be is a lawyer."

"A lawyer?"

"The best son-of-a-bitching lawyer in Wisconsin!"

"I've often thought that maybe I'd like law."

"Sure you would. You change to law school as soon as you can—and don't worry about the tuition. Ill help see to that."

"I wouldn't take money from you, Helen," he said.

"You're right you won't take money from me—free. But you'll earn it. I need help here. Real bad. If you'll clean this place for me every morning and every evening I'll help pay your tuition. I don't want any lazy, half-ass cleaning job—I want this place clean! I'm tired of working like a pack-horse."

Joe switched from Marquette's School of Engineering to the School of Law, and he was immediately in much better spirits. I could tell that he had found his niche.

Each morning he'd come over early and sweep and clean the barroom; after classes in the afternoon he'd be back to help me do anything that needed to be done in the dining room. I paid him only a meager wage, but it evidently was enough to help see him through school. Finally, in 1935, he received his law degree, and I couldn't have been prouder if he had been my own son.

The year following his graduation Joe practiced in the little town of Waupaca. Late in 1936 he moved on to Shawano and became a partner in a law firm there. Whenever Joe was in Milwaukee and had time, he always called or came by to see me.

When Joe was elected circuit judge, I was so delighted I couldn't wait to see him to congratulate him, so I called him up long-distance in the middle of the night.

Later, when Joe's name became a national household word I often mused what would have happened to him had he dropped out of school or had continued on as an engineer. No matter how he was praised, nor how he was condemned, the late Joseph R. McCarthy, United States Senator has always held a warm spot in my heart.

When I think back to the year 1937 I can't recall anything good. The so-called marriage between Guy and myself was on the rocks—completely and totally. There had been recriminations, curses, and bitterness on both sides. A numbness had developed in me as I waited for the inevitable to happen; and I almost felt a sigh of relief that Good Friday when he said he wanted his freedom. We had lived at the peak of extravagance, and I could not quarrel with his expensive tastes because I had expensive tastes myself. When the time of parting came and the issue of money was brought up, I found that there was damn little left to argue about. I gave him all of what there was. What the hell, he had given me pleasure and companionship and real loving in the early years of our life together. I still had my own business, and I could afford the gesture. I wished him good luck. He packed all his high-priced clothes and drove off smiling.

That evening I borrowed money from one of the plumbing and heating contractors in the neighborhood to have enough cash to open the bar. The man told me I was a fool to give all my money to Guy—but I said I had been a fool before and I'd be a fool again, so fuck it!

Another great sadness came to me in the autumn of that same

year. I received a telegram from Phil, Jr., that stated crisply that his father was dead and gave the time and location of the funeral. I knew that nothing could be accomplished by exposing sorrow that would undoubtedly be taken as affectation and as an affront to the remaining members of Phil's family—and to my own sons—yet I felt compelled to go to Cincinnati. My sorrow was transformed into self-torment when I arrived there and found that Phil had committed suicide. Then I heard that Phil had come to Chicago in 1923 searching for me and had learned of my way of life and had returned to Cincinnati to spend the next fourteen years in loneliness. How sad and strange it all was—and how differently it might have turned out. I didn't ask what had happened to Florence Gossett. It no longer mattered.

As a contrast with 1937, 1938 was a wonderful year. It started off with my meeting a lady who has had considerable influence on me. I was in Gimbels Store, hurrying to get past the hundreds of shoppers on the first floor when I reached a blockade. I was frankly annoyed. I wanted only to get past the group of people clustered around an aisle booth. A demonstrator, I thought, showing some asinine, goddamed new can opener! I looked at the woman seated at the center of the raised dais and our eyes seemed to cling for a split second. She was in the middle of a sales spiel, but as she looked at me she said, "I feel the presence of a Pisces—a strong, angry Pisces." I noticed how handsome this woman was, then I saw a plaque which said, "Marguerite Carter[44]—Unitologist." I didn't know what a unitologist was.

"When is your birthday?" she asked me, ignoring the other people.

"February 26," I answered.

"I thought so."

That comment alone was enough to keep me glued to the spot. I stayed and listened to Mrs. Carter and found that the term "unitology" is synonymous with astrology—a subject which I

[44] Marguerite Carter (January 31, 1899 – November 22, 1988) was an American astrologer and columnist. Her full-page ads, prominently featuring her photograph, appeared in all the newsstand astrology magazines for decades. Many clients proudly mention that in the family archives is a hand-drawn, typewritten chart and interpretation by the noted columnist.

knew little about, but one which I found fascinating. Mrs. Carter explained her theories of how planetary influences affect human affairs.

After her selling speech was over—she was making personal appearances in department stores all over the country promoting her horoscopic services—Mrs. Carter and I talked at length. I learned that she was one of the best-known persons in her field and from her headquarters in Indianapolis she had a tremendous business of doing both personalized and general horoscopes besides writing syndicated newspaper and magazine columns. In any case, Marguerite Carter and I became friends and I have great respect for her. I have seen her many times since that first encounter. When people ask me if I'm a "firm believer," I can only answer that at the times when I have not consulted the cyclic patterns of my planetary influences before making major decisions, I have always regretted not doing so.

At the first meeting Mrs. Carter gave me some unsolicited business advice and as a result I invested in the stock market and my finances soared, so I did something I had wanted to do for ten years: I hired Tony Sarnow, the pianist who had impressed me so much the night Guy took me to Sharpshooters' Park in 1928. The customers were crazy about Tony. Not only could he play a mean piano, he had a seething, exuberant Italian personality that amused the gentlemen and wowed the ladies. He was a sensation and pulled customers into my place by the hundreds. Tony had two bad faults: he owned a beat-up, horrible-looking old Essex automobile and he drank too much. I decided to do something about both of these flaws and I started with the Essex, since I thought that problem could be solved more easily.

"Now, Tony, let's have a heart-to-heart talk about that car of yours," I said engagingly.

"What about my car, Helen?" he asked.

"Well, it's a junk heap—that's what," I said.

"It drives good."

"I don't care how it drives, I want you to get rid of it. It's bad for business to have that pile of manure parked out front with all the customers' Cadillacs!"

"I can't afford a new car, I have expenses at home which are more important," he said quietly.

I knew that Tony supported his elderly mother and several other members of his family.

"Don't you worry about that—I want you to have a decent-looking car."

Within thirty minutes we were at the Buick dealer's showroom and I had purchased Tony a snazzy new Buick coupe. He kept complaining about accepting it, and I told him to either accept it or quit working for me. I told him it made me sick to my stomach to look out the front window and see that old Essex. Tony agreed that the new Buick did look better, but he went on to say that it probably wouldn't drive any better. In any case, he accepted the new car after much quibbling. That was one problem out of the way.

The liquor problem wasn't so easy to solve—in fact, it was never completely solved because Tony was an alcoholic. But I was able to keep it in line as much as possible.

"Stop that drinking, Tony!" I demanded. It was about midnight and he was absolutely stinking tight. The customers were buying drinks for him and he was pouring them down his throat like ice water and playing hell out of the piano. He ignored my command as I knew he would. I reached under the bar and pulled out a giant, wooden shillelagh that I had acquired and whammed it down on top of the bar with all my might. The impact echoed and reechoed through the barroom like a crash of thunder.

Everyone jumped and there was complete silence. Tony stopped playing the piano and looked at me with a stunned expression.

"Knock off the drinking, you goddamed shit ass!" I yelled.

Tony looked at me searchingly, then he hung his head and said, "Aw, Helen, you're just a little fallen star from heaven."

The customers went wild with laughter, and that routine became a nightly procedure for us. The customers ate it up but it had a purpose as far as I was concerned—no one was to buy a drink for Tony after my "gavel" struck the bar. If I noticed him sneaking another drink, I'd strike the bar with the club again.

Tony always referred to me as his "little fallen star from heaven" and it never failed to get a laugh. Not only did the customers go for the shillelagh bit, they wanted to hear more of my foul language.

Today one hears much about "corporate images" but it hasn't been too many years ago that the general public rarely heard the term. My "corporate image" evolved itself during this period with various tidbits of four-letter words and risqué talk. This type of talk became the main feature of my bar; it was what the old customers came to hear and what the new customers came to investigate. The clincher for my reputation in the field of ha-ha came with an entry I claimed to have made in a condensed milk slogan contest. I really did enter the slogan in the contest, but I didn't win. Why I didn't win I'll never know because the slogan swept the continent in a matter of days. Here it is:

No shit to pitch,
No tits to switch,
Just punch a hole
in the son-of-a-bitch
It's Carnation Milk!

No longer was the Sun Flower Inn referred to as the Sun Flower Inn, even though the brass plaque on the front door still proclaimed it as such. My bar became known as "Dirty Helen's"—and that name, too, raged across the country like wildfire; fanned no doubt by the enthusiasm of thousands of salesmen and servicemen who made it their home away from home. Dirty Helen's became a spot that couldn't be ignored on a Milwaukee nightlife tour. It became "the place to go" after dinner at Mader's, Fazio's Spaghetti House, The Casino, Karl Ratsch's, the fabulous Eugene's, John Ernst's, or any other of Milwaukee's great restaurants.

I'll never as long as I live forget that Friday, September 1, 1939, when the newspaper headlines screamed "WAR! BOMB WARSAW!" The Poles were attacked by Nazi planes and troops and Hitler ordered his people to "Remember always that you are representatives of the National Socialist great Germany. Long live our people and our Reich!" The radio reiterated that Great Britain and France were determined to fulfill their obligation to Poland despite Adolph Hitler's Reichstag speech.

The United States was on a powder keg and we knew it; maybe that's why the national American Legion Convention held in Milwaukee in the fall of 1941 was such bedlam. People realized their restraint and their pent-up anxieties in a wild, final burst of whoop-dee-do overshadowed by the knowledge that soon all would be different. More than one hundred thousand visitors poured into the city. Every available room was taken. The streets were packed with buses and cars, and all the highways leading into the city were snarled in traffic jams. All of us—the city's barkeeps—kept open around the clock. The people who were there at five a.m. were just as merry as the ones who arrived at five p.m.

After the first day of trying to serve the customers I knew I'd have to have help. I phoned the Bartenders' Union and told them to send over a first-class bartender. Within a couple of hours they had sent over nine different bartenders, and I had shipped them all right back. Where the union had picked them up I'll never know. They were all grubby-looking, unshaven, or had dirty fingernails. If there's anything I can't stand it's people with unkempt appearance.

The business agent of the union was becoming impatient with me, too, so when he closed his office at five-thirty he came straight to the Sun Flower Inn. "What's the deal, Helen? Why are you sending all those bartenders back?" he demanded.

"The goddamed deal is that I'm not running a fucking dive. How dare you send those awful-looking men over here? I expect neatness in my bartenders. I want one that looks like ... " at that moment I noticed the young man who was with the business agent, " ... him!" I pointed at the young man in the business suit. "I'll take him. What's your name, Cutie?"

"Carl."

The business agent interrupted quickly and said, "Don't be ridiculous, Helen! Carl is the secretary of the Union. He can't tend bar."

"You mean to tell me," I shouted, "that the secretary of the Bartenders' Union doesn't know how to tend bar?"

"It's not that he doesn't know how—he isn't one of the workers."

"What do you do at that office—play?"

"Now, Helen, you know what I mean!"

"What I mean is, I want a bartender who looks like Carl!" I turned to Carl and said, "I'll give you five bucks an hour."

"Five bucks an hour?" asked Carl.

"Yep," I answered.

"You've got yourself a bartender, Lady."

"Then take off that coat and wrap this fucking white apron around your waist, because you're employed." I turned to the business manager and said, "Either drink up or stop taking up valuable floor space."

He gave me a big smile. "You beat all I've ever seen, Helen. I've heard you were some bitch."

"That's the sweetest thing I've heard today. Hey, Carl, fix my friend here a drink—on the house."

Late that evening a large party of out-of-towners entered with their host, Freddy Lange. Freddy was the playboy president of the Crucible Steel Company and a dear friend and customer of mine. Freddy was nuts about polo and among the contingent of convention-goers he had scoured up enough players to make two teams. He insisted that I come out to the polo field the next day and watch them.

"Listen, Freddy, don't you think I have enough to do here, with this goddamed mob in town, without driving out in the country to watch grown men romping around on horses knocking a pissy ball around? I'm busy, kid."

"Aw, please, Helen," he begged. Finally I said I would come out for a little while.

Early the next morning I called a florist and told him I wanted a horseshoe of roses "just like they hang around the Kentucky Derby winners' necks." He told me it would be expensive and I told him to forget that part of it and start wiring his fucking roses together.

At three-thirty the next afternoon I put a case of bourbon and a case of scotch in the waiting taxicab. I stopped by the dime store for paper cups, then went to the florist to get my "horseshoe of roses." The thing was so goddamed big we couldn't get it in the cab (it cost seventy-five bucks). I wound up transferring my happy juice to the florist's wagon and making him drive me to the polo field.

Freddy came galloping up in his clever white outfit and before he could figure out what was going on, the florist and I flung the drape of roses around the horse's neck and the various bored photographers who had been sent out by their papers went wild snapping pictures.

"Enough of this croquet, kiddos," I yelled. "Let's have a cocktail party!" The florist hauled out the booze and I got the paper cups. The be-suited, sunglassed gals who had been perched on the let-down tops of their convertibles scrambled over as their boy friends jumped from their horses and—Jesus God!—we had the biggest, son-of-a-bitching society party of the entire convention. The Whitefish Bay set had to take a back seat to Dirty Helen the next day in the "social notes."

Poor, high-living Freddy was sent to prison for income tax evasion in April of '46 and he never regained his old zip up to the day he passed on in '56.

The last squeals of delight emanating from the convention had barely faded into the past when Tony Sarnow, too, began to fade. I had stopped harping on the subject of his heavy drinking because it was apparent that the alcoholic stimulus was all that was holding him together. He would begin the evening with an ashen face and it was only after consuming several straight shots of liquor that his complexion took on any sort of color. He continually lost weight and he'd go into coughing fits that wracked his body. I hadn't witnessed such coughing and choking since my days with mustard-gassed Bob. I had known all along that Tony had a supposedly arrested case of tuberculosis and I was sure it had flared up again.

"Tony, I insist you go to a doctor. If you won't go on your own, I'm going to make an appointment and take you there myself. And

I can do it, too!" I screeched at him.

"I've been to a doctor, Helen," said Tony softly.

"Well, what did he say?"

"What I thought he'd say. It's my TB again."

"You mean you come in here every night with active TB!"

"It's not contagious. That stage was passed long ago."

"What about all this cigarette smoke in here? You're killing yourself, Tony. I want you to take a few months off and take a good rest and lots of fresh air."

Tony didn't want to obey me—or his doctor, with whom I had a long talk—but in the end he knew he had to. He was too weak to continue playing his piano night after night. When he took to his bed for an extended rest, he was never able to get up again. His elderly mother did all she could for him, and I went to their home every afternoon—taking him kettles of chicken noodle soup, homemade ice cream, and pies—but Tony had lost his desire to live and death came quickly. Up to the very last day he would always smile at me and say, "There's my little fallen star from heaven."

The funny thing about it is that it was actually Tony who was the fallen star from heaven. People still ask me whatever happened to Tony and when I tell them, they say, "He was a grand person." They just don't know how grand, how kind, how sweet he really was.

I wish this God damn war was over so I could have gin

A Slim Sabin

Chapter 27

THEN CAME that infamous day—December 7, 1941. But the worst was that truly low day, almost exactly five months after Pearl Harbor, when Corregidor fell. Even though I was sixty years old, I felt I had to do something constructive for the war effort; I wanted to get a job building planes, building tanks—anything war-like. I wanted to help fight back.

My best friend during this time was a woman named Marge. She would come to the bar practically every afternoon and she became my confidante. "But, Marge," I cried to her, "Surely there's something I can do!"

"Don't you realize, Helen, that you are doing something? Isn't this place swarming with servicemen every night? Don't you know that when they're here, listening to your line of crap and laughing their heads off, that they aren't thinking about what's in store for them when they get their orders. It's important, dear, really important. People have to laugh—to make their crying easier later."

"I really don't know, Marge."

"Just believe what I tell you. The U.S.O's are fine, and they serve a purpose. But you know, and I know, that there are certain boys who would never in a thousand years go to a U.S.O. if there's anywhere else to go. They're just kids, really, but they like to feel that they've been somewhere racy and off-beat—somewhere like this bar. We both know that the Sun Flower Inn is as safe as their rumpus rooms at home—but they don't know it. And that's what

< Helen's sign-in book. An anonymous sailor in World War II.

makes it interesting for them. You can do more for the war effort right here in this bar than anywhere else in the country."

I thought a lot about what Marge had said and decided she was right. That's when I went all out to do what I could. Let 'em laugh, let 'em yell, let 'em drink, let 'em go to the kitchen and make their own sandwiches. They were my boys and I loved 'em. When they were at Helen's place they were at home. I fought the Japs and the Germans with my own weapons. And like all Americans I suffered losses—including Carl, the bartender, whom I had come to love as a son. I had a premonition, when I saw Carl off for the induction center, that he would never survive the war.

For all those years I had continued to lease my place from the Schlitz Realty Company. The building had needed rejuvenating for a long time but I didn't want to put extensive repairs into property I didn't own, so I bought the building and within ninety days after the purchasing deal closed I started the modernization program that was to last for almost three years. The place was practically torn down and rebuilt.

With wartime restrictions I had one hell of a time finding any insulating materials. Finally I wrote a cute little personal note to Tommy Manville, who was connected in some way with a company that produced the stuff, and told him I thought he was perfectly sexy and goddamed attractive and could easily see how his various wives thought so, too. I added a tiny risqué aside that he and I had much in common and would he be sweet and considerate enough to send me a bit of insulation. Mr. Manville sent me a whole fucking carload of the crap (with no bill, of course) and it took every available inch of space in the barroom to store it while the workmen stripped the walls to the studs.

It was on the very day that the workmen ripped some areas of old rotten siding off the building that Martin Pflug came to my place as the organist. I had had an assortment of piano players after Tony died, but none had been particularly good. Martin had been the dining room organist at Gimbels Department Store for many years and he was horrified, that first night, at the shenanigans pulled off at the Sun Flower Inn. Well, anyway, the day that Martin moved his Hammond into the barroom was a day to remember!

Siding had been ripped away from the building's exterior, and before it could be replaced a snowstorm hit us. The first night Martin played the snowflakes kept blowing through holes in the walls and sliding across the keyboard. There Martin was —wedged between huge stacks of insulation and with snow all over his organ—and I kept requesting "Ah, Sweet Mystery of Life." And, he informed me he didn't cotton to my "vulgarisms" ! I was sure he wouldn't return the next night, but he did—and for practically every night for the next ten or eleven years.

The most difficult part of my remodeling program was acquiring a gas heating plant, so I had to rely on my pot-bellied stove for many months. The stove was opposite the bar and it seemed to amuse people that I never kept much fuel on hand. When I needed some coal briquets I'd call a cab, leave the customers to fend for themselves, and take off for the coal yard. The colored man who waited on me at the coal yard would always make the same comment, "Uh, uh, fox furs, taxi cabs, and coal by the bushel!" When I'd get back to the barroom I'd throw the briquets into the stove, switch in about a half bottle of Old Forester and throw in a match. Truly a never-fail technique for starting a nice fire, and much more reliable than kindling.

It was during the final stages of my remodeling that Howard and Betty entered the scene. Howard was a factory worker at one of the heavy equipment plants and he and his wife, Betty, liked to sally around the bars in the evening. Betty was a former waitress at a place in Chicago called the Red Rooster and had a certain feeling for nightlife. Howard knew a little something about everything and was quite a conversationalist. Only one thing kept him from being a man of the world: money.

There was a tinge of sadness mixed with great elation when Howard's elderly aunt was hit by a train in Waukegan, Illinois. Howard was the beneficiary of her fifty-thousand dollar accident insurance policy. There was even more elation when we learned that the policy had a double indemnity clause! A hundred thousand dollars—and all for our sweet Howard and Betty.

The first check Howard received was for forty-two hundred dollars. He cashed it immediately and came rushing into the bar with a fistful of large denomination bills. "Drinks for everyone, drinks for everyone!" he shouted. "And ring up the change, Helen!" Howard would allow no one to pay for a thing that evening or many more evenings to come. There were big tips for Martin as Howard and Betty danced (I made an exception to the "No Dancing" rule in their case) to their favorite song, "Twelfth Street Rag."

Howard and Betty were terribly patriotic, and formed a sort of U.S.O. of their own with my place as headquarters. They loved servicemen and collected them in droves. Betty thought of herself as Milwaukee's Perle Mesta[45], and no expense was spared in doing for the fighting men. Howard and Betty arrived nightly with scores of soldiers, sailors, and marines and everyone partied and stomped their feet to the "Twelfth Street Rag" until the closing hour. After two a.m. Howard would host a supper party for everyone at the Lake View Restaurant. Gus, who ran the restaurant, was delighted to remain open for us.

It was hey, hey, until the inheritance was depleted—about four months later. "I had fun," stated Betty emphatically as Howard returned to the factory and she found a job as checkout girl at an A & P.

It was through Howard and Betty that I met Pierre. Dear Pierre. While picking up servicemen at the train stations, bus terminals, in front of the "Y," etc., to be their guests at their nightly soirees, Betty would occasionally come across someone who was not directly "in the service," but had enough governmental connections to justify expending patriotism on him. Such a pick-up was Lord Andrae. They were overwhelmed by him, and plucked him off the Greyhound bus from Chicago just for me. He was something: British to the eyebrows; slender as a reed; that

---

45 Perle Reid Mesta (née Skirvin) (October 12, 1889 – March 16, 1975) was an American socialite, political hostess, and United States Ambassador to Luxembourg (1949–53).

Mesta was known as the "hostess with the mostest" for her lavish parties featuring the brightest stars of Washington, D.C., society, including artists, entertainers and many top-level national political figures.

She was the inspiration for Irving Berlin's musical *Call Me Madam*, which starred Ethel Merman as the character based on Mesta in both the Broadway play and the movie.

bushy European hair; black, penetrating eyes; belted-back suit with peaked lapels; just like something out of one of those movies about Singapore.

Prior to my meeting him, Betty informed Lord Andrae that I was the one for him and when he arrived at my place his arms were filled with red roses and a box of cellophane-wrapped Whitman chocolates which he presented with a flourish.

Oh, his background, his breeding. A Peer. A cousin of the British royal family; and the Pretender to the throne of France! And in Milwaukee on a diplomatic, secret war mission. How chic!

I was mad about him. Basically, I knew I was the stuff that Peeresses are made of. I could see myself at the opening of parliament, girdled to the nines in white satin with a train. And a tiara! Jesus God.

Pierre and I were inseparable for weeks. He came nightly to the bar and always always formed a little meue with his lips when I refused to accept payment for the scotch he had consumed. We would hold hands as Martin played "The White Cliffs of Dover" and one tiny tear would form in Pierre's left eye. I held my wagging tongue: no risqué talk in the presence of Lord Andrae. Our love was cool, detached, mature. Lady Andrae! Jesus God! We had discussed the possibilities of our marriage.

When we went out it wasn't to some noisy restaurant or some ridiculous night club, it was to stroll through the park—my arm linked through his. Our strolls were extremely classy; I bought a special outfit just for walking. Sort of a crock-brindle brown tweed suit with a long skirt and some tacky walking shoes (low heels are very bad for one's feet). I even let my black-dyed hair grow out a bit at the roots—to give me that British-rundown-aristocracy look. You can tell how taken I was with his lordship.

Pierre was so fond of fine music it made my heart sing. One Wednesday evening he suggested that we go to the Methodist Church to listen to choir practice (wasn't that a pisser?) and I decided that, surely, Peeresses didn't wear their walking clothes after dark, so I wore a perfectly marvelous black satin dress with my best Isenberg clip just at the foothills of my bosom; as accessories I chose an extremely smart white turban and long white gloves. Over my left glove I snapped on my widest rhinestone bracelet. I'm sure the entire choir knew we were visiting royalty and probably thought I was wearing the crown jewels because every time I moved my arm and my bracelet caught the rays of the overhead lights the choir would practically stop singing. I was sorry I hadn't worn the rhinestone tiara that Marge had just bought me at the Boston Store—that would really have knocked them out! We didn't stay too long because the music wasn't too good; they hardly kept in tune—probably weren't used to an audience at their rehearsals. So Pierre suggested we go back to the Sun Flower Inn and drink my booze.

I believe the credit goes to Martin for puncturing my bubble of happiness. In any case, someone called out their own local gestapo to track down the background of "Lord Andrae." He was indeed British, but hadn't been near Great Britain for twenty-five years, and his "diplomatic mission" in Milwaukee was that of being one of the assistant chefs at a private city club.

When confronted with this information, Pierre confessed that he had perpetrated a hoax but suggested that we get married anyway, because "we could be so happy on your income." I told him that I held no grudges, but to get lost because he bored me. As he was leaving I asked him a question that had been on my mind nightly during our courtship. "What makes those cliffs at Dover so white—bird shit?"

Everywhere I looked at the train station various signs asked, "Is this Trip Necessary?" I was hard put to answer the question honestly because other signs proclaimed, "Pep Up the Morale of Your Fighting Men!" I had decided to do a little pepping up.

For weeks—several months, actually—I had kept the conversation at the bar alive with talk about "Teddy Boy." Early in the fall I had gone to Chicago on the Electroliner to do some shopping and had met "Teddy Boy" on the train. He was a "boy in blue," a "gob," a "white hat," or whatever it is they called sailors. He was on leave from his Norfolk-based destroyer and had been to Milwaukee to see his mother. We had a titillating conversation in the club car. During the course of the conversation I vowed that whenever his ship returned from the high seas, I would come to their port of call and welcome him home. I must, in all truthfulness, add that "Teddy Boy" was only twenty-three years old, but quite mature and well developed for such salad years.

For the following two or three months, we exchanged weekly letters. Knowing that sailors love to read "hot portions" of their letters to their buddies, I practically burned up the stationery with some amorous talk. "Teddy Boy," in return, would answer with similar ardor (so he could read his responses to his buddies prior to mailing the letters). After receiving the first of such letters from him, I read sketches of it to people clustered around the bar. It proved to be so scintillating that customers packed themselves in every evening to hear the latest lovetalk from "Teddy Boy." Fuck letters, we called 'em.

The thing that added spice to the whole business was Martin's puritanical attitude concerning it; he thought it was too disgusting for words, and I did bait him unmercifully about it. After reading aloud a red-hot paragraph I would holler, "Hey, Martin, did you hear that—some scorcher, huh?" Martin would freeze me with an icy look, toss his head disdainfully, and let a blast of sour notes pour forth from his organ. The customers would howl. "Teddy Boy" had no idea what an attraction he had become for the Sun Flower Inn.

One Saturday afternoon in December, during the cocktail hour, the phone rang and it was "Teddy Boy." His destroyer had just pulled into the Brooklyn Navy Yard for repairs and he couldn't get leave to come to Milwaukee. He asked if I could come to New York. I told him not to move from the phone booth and I'd call him right back. Then I shouted to all the customers,

"That was 'Teddy Boy.' He wants me to meet him in New York and marry him!" The crowd went wild and surged around me as I phoned the Pennsylvania Railroad in Chicago for a train reservation.

"Is this trip necessary?" asked the reservations agent.

"It is, indeed," I replied, "I'm going to New York to save a fighting man." I got a compartment on the following afternoon's train. Within twenty-five minutes I called "Teddy Boy" back and told him I'd be there.

Everyone was told that Martin must not hear about this, but they were free to tell anyone else. I sent dozens of telegrams to customers stating that I was on the way to New York to marry "Teddy Boy" and would be back to work on Thursday night. By 8:30 p.m.—the hour that Martin came to work—the customers were jammed in like sardines, all wanting to know if what they had heard was true.

"Yes," I would whisper with my hand over my heart, "I am caught in the torrent of love."

One of my regular customers said, "Helen, you're too old for that boy!"

"Me? Too old? I'm ageless."

"Ageless?" he screamed. "You're so old, I'll bet you were a waitress at the Last Supper!"

"Yeah, well, I'll be around to roast the goose that pisses on your grave!" The crowd went into convulsions of laughter.

My best friend, Marge, had heard about the prospective marriage and scurried over to inquire if I needed help in packing my trousseau.

"Trousseau?" I asked. "My fucking trousseau will be very simple: a beaded dress and a douche bag!" Several customers were actually holding their sides by this time. "Now don't tell Martin!"

Martin never did find out about it that night; there was much whispering around, and more newspaper reporters about than usual, but everyone joined in the game of keeping it from him.

The next morning I left a note for Martin saying: "Martin dear, didn't have the courage to tell you. I am on my way for the 6th marriage, in New York Tuesday p.m. Will return Thursday p.m.Leaving New York Wednesday 4 p.m. Helen."

I packed my "trousseau" (exactly what I had told them) plus twelve bottles of Old Forester and ten cartons of cigarettes, and then I took the Electroliner to Chicago to make my train connection. The club car on the Electroliner was filled with sailors, since Great Lakes Naval Training Station was one of the major stops on the route, and I broke out a couple of bottles of Old Forester as a toast to my "forthcoming marriage" to my own sailor, "Teddy Boy." A rather elderly chief petty officer made the comment that the sailor sure was lucky to be getting a "girl" like me and the club car went into hysterics. We had a fucking ball!

After settling myself in my compartment on the New York-bound train, I took two bottles of Old Forester and a carton of cigarettes and made for the lounge car. My, how popular I was! There was a group of eight or ten young second lieutenants who had just received their Air Corps "wings" and they weren't hesitant in accepting my proposal for "drinks all around." We broke out several more bottles before the evening was over. Even the two hours' delay because of snow was fun—but I had a few hours sleep before arriving in New York.

The line in front of the desk clerk at the Pennsylvania Hotel extended halfway across the lobby. I removed a calling card from my purse, clipped a ten-dollar bill to the back of it and went to the head of the line.

"I have a reservation," I stated, handing the card to the clerk while blocking the view of the people in line.

"Of course you do," said the clerk, fingering the money. "Just sign the register, please."

As the bellboy led the way from the elevator—with the remaining six bottles of Old Forester clanking tremendously in the suitcase—I was alarmed to see that each floor of the hotel had its own female floor clerk seated piously behind a desk in the elevator foyer. This would cause complications with "Teddy Boy"! As soon as I was settled I called for the house detective to come up.

"Merry Christmas!" I exclaimed, handing him a carton of valuable-as-gold Lucky Strikes. "I came from Milwaukee to meet my nephew—a sailor—who has just returned from overseas. I hope he'll be able to visit my room occasionally so we can talk. I wouldn't want a misunderstanding with the floor clerk … "

"Of course not, Madam, I'm sure there will be no misunderstanding," said the house detective as he eyed the stack of Lucky Strike cartons. "I'll just give the clerk a package of my cigarettes—Luckies are her favorite brand—and she'll be sure to remember … about your nephew."

I picked up another carton of cigarettes and handed it to him.

"Maybe this will keep her mind fresh."

"Oh, I'm sure there'll be no misunderstanding now," exclaimed the house detective.

I told the doorman I wanted a cab to go to the Brooklyn Navy Yard and he assured me that no driver would make that long a trip. He suggested the subway. I told him what he could do with the subway and to just blow his little whistle and get me a cab. I had a shopping bag loaded with "goodies."

"Brooklyn Navy Yard, please—Sand Street entrance," I announced to the cab driver.

"Sorry. I can't take you that far," he returned.

I leaned over and dropped a carton of Luckies on the seat beside him. "Still too far?" I asked.

He stared at the cigarettes unbelievingly. "I haven't had anything but a 'roll-your-own' in over two weeks! Are they real?"

"As real as the American Tobacco Company can make 'em. Now get this heap's ass in gear and let's go!"

"This is far as I can go," said the cabbie as we pulled up in front of a big gate with a sign saying STOP! SHOW YOUR PASS. I alighted from the cab and presented my story to a policeman and a naval officer on duty at the gatehouse.

"We can't allow anyone in without an official pass," stated the gate officer.

"Well, I hope you won't mind if I wish you a Merry Christmas anyway," I said, pulling two bottles of Old Forester from my shopping bag. "I did so much want to see my nephew."

"Isn't that nice!" exclaimed the delighted naval officer as the policeman quickly grabbed them and shoved them under a desk. "Why don't we send a messenger to the ship to see if your nephew is aboard?"

"Get going," he said to a bored sailor who was leaning against the wall with a dirty sort of webb belt fastened around his middle. The sailor had heard all the conversation.

"Here, Sonny, present this to the destroyer's captain with my compliments," I said. I handed him a bottle of my pride-and-joy. The sailor clutched the bare bottle and started out the door.

"Wrap it up! Wrap it up!" barked the officer. The sailor rolled a newspaper around it, ran out the door, and jumped into a driver-manned gray jeep.

It wasn't more than ten minutes before the jeep returned and the first one out was a gorgeous hunk of beef—a perfect-looking lieutenant commander.

"I'm the captain of your nephew's destroyer. I want to thank you for your gift."

"Aren't you cute to come and see me personally. Here, have another one." I pulled out another bottle as the skipper jumped for the remaining piece of newspaper stuffed in the trash basket.

"Well, now … eh, that's awfully nice of you," he said. "Your nephew is on a twenty-four-hour pass, I'm sorry to say … but perhaps you can find him at one of the places where many of our men hang out."

The skipper jotted down five or six names of places where my "nephew" might be found and I started the manhunt. In the fifth spot I went—the bar in the Beacon Hotel—I found "Teddy Boy" with a group of his buddies. I took the whole shooting match out on the town; we were all still at it when my train was ready to pull out the next night. It was so much fun—and relatively inexpensive, since it cost only a thousand dollars—to pep up the morale of "our boys in blue." Not once had I returned to my room in the Pennsylvania Hotel, but I wouldn't for the world have let my Milwaukee crowd know that!

I didn't open the bar until Thursday night. Never had so many people been there! Patrons were piled in like Ritz crackers in a box. It was a real "reception." Martin was sullen and refused to play "Here Comes the Bride", no matter how big a tip was offered.

"Did you really marry him, Helen?' I was asked a hundred times.

"What do you think?" I answered over and over. The trip had been good for my morale, too. Not every woman in her eighties today can think of herself as a "V-girl" during World War II!

GRIFF WILLIAMS and His ORCHESTRA

Chapter 28

YOU'VE NEVER SEEN such a party as we had at Dirty Helen's that joyous Wednesday, August 15, 1945. We had all been crowded around the radio but couldn't really believe the good news until someone came running in waving a newspaper with headlines that read "GREAT WAR ENDS: Japanese Will Surrender to General MacArthur." With that, the bar went into a spin that lasted long after the law made all the drinking establishments close up.

After the war my business zoomed directly upwards. Because no matter what the business, if the merchandise sold is the finest of its kind, the owner of the business is bound to be successful. I always took great pride in filling my customers' shot glasses with the finest booze available. Throughout the war years when liquor was so hard to get I had put up with a stupid rule that for every case of Old Forester I got, I had to take a case of piss-poor rum. I wouldn't have thought of charging for the awful rot-gut rum, and I either gave it away or poured it out. I had had it. On January 1, 1946, I switched to the stuff that lights up every bourbon-lover's eyes: Old Fitzgerald.

The OPA[46] had frozen my drink prices during the war: thirty-five cents a drink or three for a dollar (Old Forester bourbon or Martin's scotch yet!). As soon as I was able to get out from under

---

46 The Office of Price Administration (OPA) was established within the Office for Emergency Management of the United States government on August 28, 1941. The functions of the OPA were originally to control money (price controls) and rents after the outbreak of World War II.

that order, I raised the price to fifty cents and that was as high as my prices ever went.

The drink menu at Helen's wasn't hard to remember: Old Fitzgerald bourbon or House of Lords scotch. If they didn't care for the selection, they could get out. One of the big jokes that seemed to never grow old was for a regular customer to bring in a visitor and let the stranger order a martini or a daiquiri! Boy, did the stranger get cursed out for a fare-thee-well. They heard words that are usually only scribbled on restroom walls; if I ran out of words that I knew, I'd make up new ones. Insulting, wow! But I don't recall ever having a customer leave in a fit of pique because of the tongue-lashing.

I'd been on the Old Fitzgerald deal for about six weeks when one Sunday afternoon I had a long-distance phone call. The gentleman on the other end asked to speak to "Miss Helen."

"This is Helen speaking."

"I'm Julian Van Winkle of the Stitzel-Weller Distillery in Louisville, Kentucky," said the gentleman.

"Oh?"

"We make Old Fitzgerald."

"You're telling me!"

"Is it really true that you sell only Old Fitzgerald?" he asked.

I assured him that Old Fitzgerald was the only bourbon I handled, but I also served scotch.

"Well, Miss Helen," he said, "I'm chairman of the board of Stitzel-Weller and we're holding our annual sales meeting at the Brown Hotel in Louisville beginning at ten o'clock in the morning. It just occurred to me that perhaps you'd like to attend the three-day session as our guest of honor. We would handle all your expenses, of course."

"Why sure, Mr. Van Winkle, I'd love to come."

"Excellent, I've checked the airlines and ... "

"Never mind the airlines. I'll get there."

"Your last name is Miss Cromell?"

"Mrs. Cromell, but I've added a 'w' to it to make it easier to pronounce. Mrs. Helen Cromwell."

"I'm looking forward to seeing you, Mrs. Cromwell.'

The customers scattered around the bar couldn't believe that I'd actually go on such short notice. They all asked if I was really serious about going. "Sure, I'm going. Can you think of a better way to get as much Old Fitz to drink as you'd want?" I told them to stick around and see if I didn't go.

The word spread quickly, and it was a busy night. I brought my ironing board into the barroom and between serving drinks I'd press a few dresses. By ten-thirty the place looked like Saturday night instead of Sunday. One of my competitors, who ran a tavern down the street, had heard about it and had locked his door and put out a sign saying he was at Helen's and to come on down! The phone rang continuously and I put customers to work answering it.

At two a.m. I shoved everybody out, threw my things in a suitcase, and called a Yellow Cab. At ten minutes of three I locked the tavern door.

"What's your name?" I asked the cabbie as I piled in the back seat.

"Harold," he said.

"I'm Helen. You and I will be old friends before this ride is over. Take me to the Brown Hotel."

"Where's the Brown Hotel?"

"In Louisville, Kentucky. What the—I thought everybody knew where the fucking Brown Hotel is!"

"Louisville, Kentucky!" he screamed.

"Sure. Now take off. I've got to be there by ten o'clock in the morning."

"Are you tight, lady?" he asked.

"No. I'm not tight. Kick this crate in the ass and take off!"

He claimed he had to go to the garage first and exchange that cab for a different one, so we lost about twenty minutes. Finally we were off and the traffic was practically nil all the way to Indianapolis. Harold was a good driver and kept his foot pushing against the gas pedal. Maybe I should try a plane ride sometime, because I like to go fast in taxi cabs.

It was exactly eight minutes before ten a.m. as I climbed the steps to the lobby of the Brown Hotel and saw a group of men in the outer foyer of the Bluegrass Room.

"Anybody know Julian Van Winkle?" I yelled.

"I'm Julian Van Winkle," said a distinguished-looking gentleman walking toward me, "and you must be Mrs. Cromwell!"

"Sure as hell am," I said with a flourish of my silver foxes. "Call me Helen."

"It's a *real* pleasure to meet you," said Julian Van Winkle.

"Well, I'm here—one hundred and sixty-five bucks, C.O.D. The fucking cabdriver's waiting at the Broadway entrance."

They almost fainted. Then they all started roaring. "Cut out the shit and go pay off Harold," I said, "or he'll think I've skipped out." Well, they were crazy about Harold and insisted he stay, too, as their guest. It was a goddamed ball. I mean a goddamed ball. If you've never had baked country ham, sliced thin, wedged between beaten biscuits and washed down with Old Fitz—honey, you've never lived!

For three days Harold and I were wined and dined all over Louisville like the Duke and Duchess of Windsor. I had never sat on so many green-and-white striped satin settees or patted so many racehorses' asses in my life.

Is it any wonder that Old Fitzgerald and I are such devoted friends? We still get together each evening about five-thirty.

———

"Did someone die?" asked the stranger in a hushed voice as he stepped into the barroom.

"No indeedy, kiddo, it's my birthday," I answered. "Make yourself at home—if you can get in!"

The barroom was filled with wreaths and bouquets of flowers—about a hundred and fifty in all. I had started my birthday parties years before and they had gained in momentum. Originally, I sent out a few invitations to regular customers inviting them to come by on a Saturday night and help me celebrate. What with all the gatecrashers (I must admit I loved them), the party became too large to hold in one evening, so I'd hold open house from Thursday through Sunday. As a time-saving factor, I started sending—by the hundreds—telegrams, cablegrams, and special delivery letters rather than ordinary invitations. Everybody knew when my birthday was, so the messages were worded simply:

"Please come to my birthday party. Helen."

I'd spend days working with Hertha, my maid, getting the food ready. I'd try to have everything all set, but invariably I'd run out of liquor and glasses. Taxicabs would be busy plowing back and forth between my place and Goldman's Liquor Store bringing more scotch and bourbon. Then I'd send customers over to the other bars in the neighborhood—Singer's, the Gashouse or Concertina Harry's—to borrow additional glasses.

What fun we'd have! There'd be guests from Australia, Mexico, South America, Sweden, England, France, and all corners of the United States. These people would make a point of scheduling their business trips to Milwaukee to coincide with my festivities. Scattered among the party-goers would be famous faces, such as, Sammy Kaye[47], Robert Q. Lewis[48], Art Kassel[49], and Bob Considine[50]. There'd be others who were wonderfully interesting, though not always recognizable, such as young Hennessey, the scion of the French brandy-making family. Many times Walter

---

47 Sammy Kaye (born Samuel Zarnocay Jr., March 13, 1910 – June 2, 1987) was an American bandleader and songwriter, whose tag line, "Swing and sway with Sammy Kaye," became one of the most famous of the Big Band Era. His signature tune was "Harbor Lights."

48 Robert Q. Lewis (born Robert Goldberg; April 25, 1920 – December 11, 1991) was an American radio and television personality, game show host, and actor. Lewis added the middle initial "Q" to his name accidentally on the air in 1942, when he responded to a reference to radio comedian F. Chase Taylor's character, Colonel Lemuel Q. Stoopnagle, by saying, "and this is Robert Q. Lewis." He subsequently decided to retain the initial, telling interviewers that it stood for "Quizzical."

49 Art Kassel (January 18, 1896 – February 3, 1965) Kassel formed his first dance band in 1924 for an appearance at the Midway Gardens in Chicago. Led by Kassel himself on saxophone, the orchestra's engagements after their Midway Gardens bow included the Aragon and Trianon Ballrooms in Chicago, with frequent airplay on the sponsored Shell Oil Company Show, Elgin Watch Show and Wildroot Hair Oil Show. They remained based almost exclusively in the Midwest region, with a 15-year engagement at the Bismarck Hotel in Chicago, until Kassel relocated to the West Coast in the late '50s.

50 Bib Considine (November 4, 1906 – September 25, 1975), was an American journalist, author, and commentator. He is best known as the co-author of *Thirty Seconds Over Tokyo* and *The Babe Ruth Story.*

Liberace[51] would be there—people nowadays call him "Lee," but his real name is Walter. And always there would be Griff Williams[52]—one of my dearest friends.

The Griff Williams Orchestra was, and is still, to the Midwest what the Meyer Davis bands are to the East. Griff provided the dance music for all the important society occasions of Mid-America. His orchestra was practically a fixture at the Empire Room of the Palmer House in Chicago and at the Shroeder Hotel in Milwaukee. Whenever Griff was playing in Milwaukee, I knew that when the dancing was over, Griff—and practically his whole band of musicians—would show up at my place and stay until the closing hour.

Griff was a regular customer at the Sun Flower Inn until he left the music field to enter advertising in the early 1950s. At that time he turned over his baton to Bob Kirk[53] who still "fronts" the orchestra. For over twelve years, a framed photograph of Griff, and a separate one of Bob, stood on the chest of drawers behind my bar. As Bob recently told a friend of mine, both he and his bass player, Buzz Michael, became "fans and habitués" of Helen's Place and would bring the rest of the musicians over for big fried chicken dinners on Sundays.

Griff would still come up frequently from his home in Evanston, Illinois, until his health failed in the late 1950s. I was shocked to learn that he died the very day I had received a letter from him. The lovely Mrs. Williams told me later it was the last letter Griff

---

51 Władziu Valentino Liberace (May 16, 1919 – February 4, 1987), known mononymously as Liberace, was an American pianist, singer, and actor. A child prodigy and the son of Polish and Italian immigrants, Liberace enjoyed a career spanning four decades of concerts, recordings, television, motion pictures, and endorsements. At the height of his fame, from the 1950s to the 1970s, Liberace was the highest-paid entertainer in the world, with established concert residencies in Las Vegas, and an international touring schedule. Liberace embraced a lifestyle of flamboyant excess both on and off stage, acquiring the nickname "Mr. Showmanship."

52 Griff Williams (1911 – February, 1959) was an American dance bandleader and pianist.
Williams led a college band at Stanford University in the early 1930s and was a member of the Anson Weeks Orchestra in 1932. Soon after he formed his own group in San Francisco, which included Buddy Moreno as a vocalist, and had its first major engagement at the supper club Edgewater Beach Hotel in October 1933. He toured throughout the United States in the 1930s before relocating to Chicago for another engagement at the Stevens Hotel, where he worked from 1939 through about 1944.

53 Bob Kirk was the vocalist for the Griff Williams Orchestra.

ever wrote. He was a marvelous person and one of the best-liked "local celebrities" in the Chicago-Milwaukee area.

As many of my regular customers came from Chicago as they did from Milwaukee, particularly on the weekends. All types of people would visit the bar and it seemed to be the intermingling of these various groups that gave the place a character all its own.

The Korean War brought almost as great an influx of servicemen customers as I had had during World War II. The Navy people, especially from Great Lakes and Glenview, used to congregate at my place on weekends. One guy, a Navy lieutenant from the air station at Glenview, came into the place cold one night and really got the cussing-out treatment when he asked for a martini or a brandy or something. He seemed so stunned I never thought he'd come back again, but he showed up the very next weekend and we became good friends. In fact, he used to come up during the week when I wasn't terribly busy and I'd fry a chicken and we'd sit back in the kitchen and talk for hours while Martin held down the music and Benny, the bartender, held down the people out front. I think I probably told that guy, Bob Dougherty, as much about my life as I've ever told anybody. After he left Glenview for the Far East I used to hear from him quite frequently, and in recent years he has been living in a far North Shore suburb of Chicago and I see a great deal of him.

Many of my old customers keep in contact with me and I have a great deal of affection for them, but I can't truthfully say that I held great affection for all the people who would frequent my bar! It was rare that I had trouble with rowdiness, but occasionally a fracas would brew up, such as the night with Mr. President ...

The entire evening had been a strain. Apparently, there had been several large parties in the city and suburbs and everyone decided to wind up at my place. The chairman of one of the city's most prominent banks was there with his wife and their charming guest, Gloria Swanson[54]. Mink coats were piled head high in a

54 Gloria Swanson (March 27, 1899 – April 4, 1983) was an American actress and producer best known for her role as *Norma Desmond*, a reclusive silent film star, in the critically acclaimed 1950 film Sunset Boulevard.

Swanson was also a star in the silent film era as both an actress and a fashion icon, especially under the direction of Cecil B. DeMille. Throughout the 1920s, Swanson was Hollywood's top box

corner. The place was really overcrowded, and I was glad when people started thinning out.

Suddenly the front door opened with a great blast of voices and the president of a nationally known brewery entered with scads of his pals. There must have been a stag party earlier because they were all stinking drunk. The place swarmed with people.

"Gimme a bottle of my beer!" yelled Mr. President-of-a-beer-company.

"Go on," I laughed. "You know I don't serve any fucking beer here."

"Then get some! I want one of my beers!" he commanded.

"You're tight, sweetheart," I said. "Scat! Turn around and get your ass out of here."

"Who do you think you are telling me to get out?" He slammed a fist on the bar.

Immediately, Martin dashed over from the organ and said, "Helen asked you to leave. Please go."

The beer man glared at Martin and shouted, "I'll punch you in the nose!"

"Now, now … let's settle down," I soothed. "There's nothing to get excited about." I turned to Martin and gave him the sign which meant get the squad car here quick! While I tried to pacify Mr. President, Martin called the cops.

One of the two policemen who patrolled St. Paul Avenue entered and tried to get Mr. President to leave quietly. Mr. President became even more enraged and grabbed the policeman by the collar of his uniform. "Do you know who I am?" he yelled. With that, he yanked on the policeman's coat, and brass buttons started hitting the floor. For the next few minutes there was much pushing, shoving, and yelling. The officer who was still in the squad car heard what was happening and radioed for the riot squad.

---

office magnet.

Swanson starred in dozens of silent films and was nominated for the first Academy Award in the Best Actress category. She also produced her own films, including Sadie Thompson and The Love of Sunya. In 1929, Swanson transitioned to talkies with The Trespasser. Personal problems and changing tastes saw her popularity wane during the 1930s when she moved into theater, and later television.

When the riot squad arrived, they bundled up Mr. Beer Barrel and tossed him out the door and into the paddy wagon like an old sack of hops, then took off for the local hoosegow. Mr. President's entourage left the place immediately, too.

"Come look at this!" shouted a remaining customer who was standing near a window. We all dashed over and saw the procession heading toward downtown Milwaukee: a paddy wagon closely followed by fifteen—we counted 'em, fifteen—shiny Cadillacs. Some fancy party.

Getting a major league baseball club can be a great tour de force for a city the size of Milwaukee. When the Boston Braves moved to our town to become the Milwaukee Braves the entire population was boiling over with anticipation. For weeks nobody had talked of anything but the Braves. When the move was finally crystallized the local newspapers were filled with the goings-on of the team and I read every printed word. The ballplayers were the toast of the town, and the name players were appearing first one place and then another as the guests of honor. Everyone wanted to entertain Warren Spahn[55], Eddie Mathews[56], and Lew Burdette[57]. There were parties, there were gifts, there was this,

---

55 Warren Spahn (April 23, 1921 – November 24, 2003) was a Major League Baseball left-handed pitcher who played his entire 21-year baseball career in the National League. He won 20 games or more in 13 seasons, including a 23–7 record when he was age 42. Spahn was the 1957 Cy Young Award winner, and was the runner-up three times, all during the period when one award was given, covering both leagues. He was elected to the Baseball Hall of Fame in 1973, with 83% of the total vote.

Spahn won 363 games, more than any other left-handed pitcher in history, and more than any other pitcher who played his entire career in the post-1920 live-ball era. He is acknowledged as one of the best pitchers in Major League Baseball history.

56 Eddie Matthews (October 13, 1931 – February 18, 2001) was an American Major League Baseball (MLB) third baseman. He played 17 seasons for the Boston Braves, Milwaukee Braves, Atlanta Braves, Houston Astros, and Detroit Tigers, from 1952 through 1968. Mathews was inducted into the National Baseball Hall of Fame in 1978.

Mathews is regarded as one of the best third basemen ever to play the game. He was an All-Star for 9 seasons. He won the National League (NL) home run title in 1953 and 1959 and was the NL Most Valuable Player runner-up both of those seasons. He hit 512 home runs during his major league career. Mathews coached for the Atlanta Braves in 1971, and he was the team's manager from 1972 to 1974. Later, he was a scout and coach for the Texas Rangers, Milwaukee Brewers, and Oakland Athletics

57 Lew Burdette (November 22, 1926 – February 6, 2007) was an American right-handed starting pitcher in Major League Baseball who played primarily for the Boston and Milwaukee Braves. The team's top right-hander during its years in Milwaukee, he was the Most Valuable Player of the 1957 World Series, leading the franchise to its first championship in 43 years, and the only title

and there was that. Andy Pafko[58] was appearing here and there; Johnny Logan[59] was being hosted at one place one day, at another place the next day. It was all too fucking exciting.

Every morning and evening I'd read what was being planned for the players. One member of the team, whose name I had noticed in the newspapers, seemed to be missing from the "guest of honor" list. I turned to Benny, the bartender, and asked, "Who's Joe Adcock[60]?"

"He's one of the ballplayers with the Braves. Why?"

"I know he's with the Braves—what I'm asking is who is he?"

"Well he used to be with Cincinnati. First sacker and outfielder. Why?"

Ignoring his question, I pressed on with "What else do you know about him?"

"Nothing. I've heard he's from the South—Louisiana, I believe. He's fairly young ... about twenty-five or twenty-six. Why?"

"Because nobody's having parties for him or giving him presents."

"Oh, for Christ's sake! Who cares?" exclaimed Benny.

"I do. All the Braves seem to be going to parties and getting gifts and things except Joe Adcock."

"Why don't you have a party for him—or give him a gift—if you feel so strongly about it?"

"I think I will."

---

in Milwaukee history.

58 Andy Pafko (February 25, 1921 – October 8, 2013) was an American professional baseball player. He played in Major League Baseball (MLB) for the Chicago Cubs (1943–51), Brooklyn Dodgers (1951–52), and Milwaukee Braves (1953–59). He batted and threw right-handed and played center field.

Pafko was born in Boyceville, Wisconsin. In his 17-year MLB career, he was an All-Star for four seasons and was a .285 hitter with 213 home runs and 976 RBI, in 1852 games.

59 Johnny Logan (March 23, 1926 – August 9, 2013) was a shortstop in Major League Baseball. Logan was signed by the Boston Braves in 1947, having been discovered by Braves scout Dewey Briggs. He was a four-time All-Star and led the National League in doubles in 1955. Logan was the first major league batter Sandy Koufax faced; Logan hit a bloop single.

60 Joe Adcock (October 30, 1927 – May 3, 1999) was a major league baseball player and manager in the Major and Minor Leagues. He was best known as a first baseman and right-handed slugger with the powerful Milwaukee Braves teams of the 1950s, whose career included numerous home run feats. A sure-handed defensive player, he also retired with the third highest career fielding percentage by a first baseman (.994).

"Craziest damn thing I've ever heard of," stated Benny disgustedly.

Unfortunately, there wasn't enough time to have a party before the first home game, so I settled for a gift. I bought the finest ostrich skin wallet I could find, then I took off for the ball park.

Going to the ball park was a new experience for me. I guess any barkeep has to more or less follow the teams, but I'd never known enough about the game to really care about sitting out in a ball park all afternoon. But having a home team like the Braves was a horse of a different color. Overnight, I had become a fan and had acquired—for a small fortune—two season box seats right behind the dugout. My box was next to Lou Perini's[61]; Lou was a contractor-sportsman from New England and he owned the Braves. So, I wasn't in bad company—the Governor of Wisconsin had the box on my other side.

It's not easy to get things sent down to the dugout during a game, so when I arrived at the ball park for the first home game, I went immediately to the box office and asked for Dan Davidson, who was the public relations man for the Braves. When he came I asked, "Would you please see that Mr. Adcock gets this as he goes to the dugout. Tell him Helen sent it. Thanks so much."

Needless to say, Joe Adcock and I became friends and there was many a party for him in later years in the Sun Flower Inn. By the way, did you know that only eight men in the history of baseball have hit four home runs in one game? In 1954 my Joseph Wilbur Adcock did just that and became one of those Hall-of-Fame eight.

Never, never, as long as I draw breath will I forget when the Braves won the World Series in 1957. The games were traded up

---

61 Lou Perini (November 29, 1903 – April 16, 1972) was the principal owner of the Boston / Milwaukee Braves of the National League from 1945 through 1962.

In 1945, he purchased the club from Bob Quinn for $500,000 and the club won the National League pennant in 1948, but lost the World Series in six games. Performance of the club then tailed off, accompanied by poor attendance and revenue. In March 1953, Perini moved the club to Milwaukee, Wisconsin, and the club set the NL attendance record that first season and continued to increase. The Braves won two NL pennants in Milwaukee, in 1957 and 1958, and played the New York Yankees in the World Series twice, winning the first. They also tied for a third straight league title in 1959, but fell in the playoff series to the Los Angeles Dodgers.

even—three to three. That crucial moment arrived in the seventh game when Bill Skowron of the New York Yankees came up to bat. Lew Burdette fed him that nutty screwball and Skowron whammed it on the ground to third; then Eddie Mathews stabbed it and hopped on third for the force, putting that series in the books.

Jesus God, was I proud to be from Milwaukee!

The fine line drawn between a crook and a businessman can be just as frustrating to one party as to the other. I'm sure that the honest-to-God crooks in this country resented having some of the top executives of General Electric, Westinghouse, Cutler-Hammer, Clark Controller, Allen-Bradley, etc., referred to as "crooks" just as most businessmen always resent having known crooks referred to as "businessmen." Much to my chagrin I know practically nothing about the electrical equipment "price fixing" that was touted in the nation's press as having taken place at New York's Hotel Barclay and at my bar. I do, of course, remember the officials of the country's electrical firms who would gather back in a far corner of my place, sit on the floor and swig down their bourbon and scotch just like everyone else.

Did I mention that I didn't have tables and chairs? Well, I didn't. Eventually I put in three barstools—as a concession to some old and dear customers who had stiff joints and couldn't get off the floor once they got down! That's why everybody including governors, senators, movie stars, writers, generals, admirals, corporals, boatswains, and duchesses sat on the floor at Dirty Helen's.

I'll never forget flopping down on the carpeting one night and giving hell to Randolph Churchill[62]; I told him that I knew how Great Britain could get on its feet even if no one else did—turn the whole she-bang into one big Las Vegas! I still think the idea has merit, and I'd like to get the call girl concession if they ever do it.

The years of standing behind the bar for sixteen to eighteen

---

62 Randolph Churchill (May 28, 1911 – June 6, 1968) was a British journalist, writer and a Conservative Member of Parliament (MP) for Preston from 1940 to 1945.

He was the only son of British Prime Minister Sir Winston Churchill and his wife, Clementine Churchill, Baroness Spencer-Churchill. He wrote the first two volumes of the official life of his father, complemented by an extensive archive of materials. His first wife (1939–46) was Pamela Digby; their son, Winston, followed his father into Parliament.

hours a day were showing their effects. My legs were ridged with varicose veins. I tried to stay off my feet, but I couldn't keep the place operating without moving about and circulating among my customers. As the lacerated-veins condition became increasingly aggravated, I finally submitted to surgery.

Once the operations started, they seemed endless. Year after year, I went to the hospital for more surgery. The operations were terribly expensive. My savings were drained, and I needed money desperately. Sure, I had made money. Sure, I had thrown money around. Sure, I had given money to those who needed it. Sure, I had been taken in by many a schemer. Sure, I wore hundred-dollar hats (and still do), but I didn't have the money necessary for a never-ending series of operations.

It was in the middle of that period that I made a grave mistake; I borrowed a large amount of money from a man who was known to charge exorbitant interest, a person known to have loaned other tavern operators money and then foreclosed on the mortgage at the earliest moment when payments got in arrears. I had heard these stories, but I didn't believe them because I knew the man personally. Even my horoscope indicated that I was taking a wrong direction, but I certainly didn't want to allow anything as presumably silly as the hobby of astrology interfering with arrangements for vital operations. So I made the mistake ... I mortgaged the Sun Flower Inn and got the money.

My recovery process from the surgeries was slow. Many times I didn't feel able to open the bar for the evening, but somehow I managed to keep the place going. I had been paying a hundred dollars a week toward retiring my debt, but it became a burden I couldn't keep up. Time was what I needed. I wasn't allowed time. I was told to get out of my Sun Flower Inn.

With the foreclosure came endless hours in attorneys' offices and court rooms, verbal abuses, and threats of eviction. The newspapers covered the whole mess and were most sympathetic to me, but I was evicted—and when I lost my business I lost my home, because I lived in one of the upstairs bedrooms.

One night, after moving to a room in the Juneau Hotel, thoughts of suicide came slinking into my mind; it would solve so many of my problems. I spent the hours between two and six a.m. deciding how I would do it. By the time it was broad daylight I had mentally bumped myself off twelve different ways and was so worn out thinking about it I decided, "Ah, fuck it" and called my hairdresser for an early appointment and went over and had my hair dyed red! The color was really very fetching and looked piss-elegant with black dresses.

During this time of my tribulation I had a visit from two ghosts of my Chicago past. It was in the afternoon and I was sitting alone in the bar at the Plankinton House. The door opened and two men, whom I hadn't seen since 1925, stood facing me.

"Do you remember us, Helen?" asked one of them.

"Of course I remember you," I said and I called them by their names.

"We read about your troubles and we decided to come up here and help you." They had been closely associated with the Chicago syndicate and I had always assumed they were trigger men; now there seemed little doubt of it.

We moved to a table in a deserted corner and they told me that they had been in retirement in one of the country's great southwestern resort cities for almost thirty years. Not once during that time had they utilized their skills, but now they were offering those skills to me. A wire service release in their local newspapers told about my upheavals and the story had named the person who was taking over my Sun Flower Inn. They had flown all the way to Milwaukee to rub him out for me.

The boys assured me their techniques were flawless and that no evidence would ever point to me. I could have an all-day party, sit all day in a hotel lobby, or create some similar spectacular alibi and I could never be touched by the law. They would do the deed, fly back to the sunny Southwest and continue with their retirement—and that would be the end of it. It was my chance for complete and total and absolute revenge.

The prospects of it were absolutely marvelous! I could see myself getting away with it—and it would be so much fun working up a wild alibi! And even if I were caught, wouldn't I be sensational? I could see myself on the witness stand, dressed in something black and terribly smart to do justice to the new red hair color with perhaps just a large pearl brooch as a single accent. What type of hat? Jesus God, no hat—it would cover up too much of the red hair! Bring on the photographers. And if you've got Kodachrome, boys, shoot the hell out of me because this is *LIFE* cover stuff!

Then I remembered that I couldn't do it. I had an appointment with my dressmaker and you can't be fretting over murder alibis when you're trying to get an even hemline. So I thanked the gentlemen from the Southwest graciously for their clever offer, but told them I didn't have time to fuss with it. I could see their disappointment (as I said before, it could have been such fun) so I suggested that they stick around and have a few Old Fitzes while I picked up my new dress, and then we'd have a dinner at Eugene's and do the town before their late-night flight took off—we'd have a ball for old times' sake. They allowed as how that might be pleasant and I allowed as how it might not be too fucking boring after all to be a "lady in retirement."

Epilogue

IT HAD BEEN well over a year since Helen and I started her life story. I lost count of the nightclubs and bars we visited and of the hours spent in that secluded spot on the mezzanine of the Plankinton House. I wound up with a battered old suitcase literally crammed with notes, some written out in Helen's large, generous handwriting, but most of them in my own scrawl. Notes were on crisp stationery, on lined school pads, on cocktail napkins, matchbooks—and some even on toilet paper when we ran out of supplies. We made tapes as Helen reminisced and then I would take them home, play them back, and listen to her vibrant voice, always vital, rich, and twangy. When she told me of her encounter with the trigger-men I decided it was time to assemble the material and complete the book.

Now it was finished. Helen had spent a week approving the final manuscript. I returned home and sent the pages off to our agent in New York. It was a Friday—a wonderful spring day in Chicago—and I thought that ordinarily this would be the day of the week when Helen would call and we'd make plans for where we'd meet during the weekend. Yes, I was going to miss the old gal. I was going to miss the arguments over minor points, even the "coffee breaks" when she'd proclaim that she "couldn't think of one more goddamed thing until we had had an Old Fitz." Then the office phone rang, and the familiar voice asked, "Is that you, Sonny?"

I laughed to myself as I thought that it hadn't ended after all.

"Yeah, Helen, it's me. What's new?"

"Jesus God! Plenty! I mean plenty! Have you sent that manuscript in?" she demanded.

"Yes. Why?"

"Can't tell you on the phone, but I've got to see you," she laughed her famous laugh. "It's important."

"Why don't you come down for the weekend? I'll meet you at the Lake Forest station."

"I haven't been to Chicago for ages and I'm in the mood for the place," she purred. "Can't you meet me in the Loop?"

"Sure. Name the place and time."

"I want to see Miss Abbey at Marshall Field's and check out her new hats. Can you meet me in the French Room hat salon at five o'clock?" I could, and did—at five on the nose.

As I entered the hat salon the most expensive numbers in the place were flying across the room.

"Horrible, tacky!" screamed Helen as she tossed a completely defeated (and mortified) sales clerk a $100 hat. "I don't know what this place is coming to!" She turned and saw me and cried, "Jesus God! You should see this trash they are passing off for hats these days. No pizzazz!" She reached for her own hat and plopped it on her head. It was an absolute hen-house of orange and black feathers—the most gigantic hat I'd ever seen—and it matched the coloring in her orange-figured, shockingly low-cut dress. Slung across her shoulders was a fawn-shaded vicuña coat.

"I see you have a new outfit, Helen," I mused.

"Cocktail clothes, Sonny. Cocktail clothes. So let's get to cocktailing. I've got a piss-pot full of news for you that's going to blow your ass off!"

We proceeded out of the French Room in tremendous style, leaving in our wake a stunned group of highly lacquered sales ladies. Miss Abbey, it seems, had the day off and none of the rest knew anything about good hats. Once in a taxi I demanded to know what was so important in the way of news, and she allowed that she couldn't possibly tell me until we had had an Old Fitz.

Once we alighted from the express elevator that zoomed us up to the penthouse room of the Chicago Press Club there was the usual rush and flurry of hugs, kisses, pats on the back, handshakes. The old-time reporters, even the cubs, dashed to us to pay homage to Dirty Helen. Finally we were alone, in a twenty-second-floor, glassed-wall corner of the lounge that viewed the entire South Side stretches of Chicago. Helen looked at the view longingly. "That's my town out there, Sonny. That's my town." A tear sprang up in the corner of each of her eyes.

I had never seen Helen cry before and it got to me. "I know it, Helen," I said softly.

"When I got off that train from New York—when I came out to meet Bob's folks—the guy who had been mustard-gassed—and that goddamed wind hit me in the face—I knew this was my town." She dabbed at her eyes with a lace-edged handkerchief and then quick as a flash gave me a gleaming smile. "Enough of that horseshit!"

"Now, what was so important that you had to see me immediately?" I asked.

"Didn't I tell you it was too soon to finish that fucking book? Didn't I tell you that things were popping? Well, didn't I?" She was getting terribly het up.

"What in the name of God has happened?" I demanded.

She reared back in a grand attitude, arranged the not-to-be-believed hat, gave me a wicked grin, and said proudly, "I was arrested for hustling."

"What did you say?" I shouted.

"You heard me. Arrested. For hustling." She giggled outright.

"When? Where? Were you hustling?" I couldn't believe it. Or could I?

She ignored the first two questions and answered the last one first. "Of course I wasn't hustling. You know I know how to operate better than that! I've never been caught when I'm really hustling!" She was pouting.

"Go on, go on—get on with the story," I demanded.

"Well, it was Wednesday night. See? I had just gotten a new job! I wanted you to know about the job so when I got off work at two-thirty a.m. I went over to the train depot to write you a note and get it in the mail immediately. So, there I was sitting on a bench writing you a note and when I had finished I found that I had no stamp—so, there was this man, see?—a gray-haired, good-looking son of a bitch, so I meandered over to him and asked him if he had a stamp, see?—and right then and there this rookie cop, new in town, dashes up and arrests me! Can you imagine? Me at 81!"

"Get on with the story, Helen, what happened?"

She started laughing so uproariously I had to wait until she gained control of herself. "The cop called a paddy wagon," she couldn't control her snickers, "dumped me in and took me down to be booked! The first time in my whole fucking life I'd ever been taken to a jail to be booked!" Again she burst out in a scream of laughter. "You should have seen the look on the captain's face when that young rookie herded me in! The captain almost fainted when he heard the charges. He raked that rookie over the coals like a rookie has never been raked over the coals! Oh, it was a goddamed scream! And to think the fucking book is finished—and everybody thinking I've never been arrested!"

"What happened then?"

"I insisted that I be kept in jail overnight, of course! I've never been in jail—and it's good for a person's education. Don't you think?"

I gave a half-hearted nod and she continued. "The captain wouldn't hear of it but I told him we'd been friends for thirty years and he'd just better let me stay there, or I'd let a few cats out of the bag. Then that sweet old bastard said to me, 'Okay, Helen, if you'll let me buy you an Old Fitz tomorrow night.' See, I know the value of promotion and publicity!"

As I let out a long sigh, I asked about this job she had mentioned and she was all excited.

"A guy I know has opened a new bar and he has a special room called 'The Dirty Helen Room.' It has lots of Oriental rugs and a big gold chair where I sit; people come in and buy me drinks and I just sit and talk to them. Isn't that a crock of shit? And I get paid for it to boot. Terrific! But that bastard who owns the place pulled a nasty trick on me. He decided he needed an oil portrait of me, nude of course, so I posed for the face, then he got some eighteen-year-old trick to pose for the body. Awful! Little tits and skinny legs—not me at all!"

The crisis hadn't been as great as she had indicated over the phone. After we talked awhile I suggested we have an early dinner and she allowed as how dinner at the Press Club would be just fine because "such interesting people are here" (all men) and I allowed right back at her that I'd had lunch in the place and didn't want to have dinner there. So we trucked on to another place for our chicken ala king. Following dinner Helen asked me to do her a favor; she said she had never been to a nightclub called Mister Kelly's and she had heard it was the place in Chicago and would I be a fucking love and take her there.

The place was jammed with customers. Phyllis Diller was the star of the show and the only seats available were two stools at the oval bar. The bar was on an elevated platform and only a few feet from the entertainment stage. As soon as we sat down there were calls across the bar and even across the room, "Hi ya, Helen!" People left their seats and crowded around us; as the lights dimmed for the first show it was impossible to get the patrons back to their tables and chairs.

With a blare from the band, Phyllis Diller came on stage to find the customers' interest elsewhere; she could not get them to listen to her repartee—they were much more interested in Helen's repartee ("So I said, don't bump him off, Al!"). Miss Diller had evidently indicated her displeasure and three men elbowed their way to the end of the bar where Helen and I were seated. One of the men, Oscar Marienthal, was an owner of the club and a person I knew. He said to me with agitation, "Good Lord, it's you, Bob! Who's that dame with you? Before I had a chance to answer he shouted, "Dirty Helen!" He leaned close to my ear and whispered, "I'm paying Phyllis Diller a fortune, and she refuses to go on unless Helen is bounced, so you're being bounced!"

Before Helen had a chance to say "Jesus God! What in the fucking, son-of-a-bitching hell is going on?" we were taken individually in arm by giant-size bouncers and led across the room to the foyer, then to the front door, and shoved firmly out into the street.

"Jesus God! Bounced!" screamed Helen. "Why, I've never been bounced out of a place in my life!" Then she threw back her head and laughed her famous laugh as people crowded around us right there on the corner of Rush Street and Bellevue Place in Chicago.

Helen decided we needed to talk (like a hole in the head we needed to talk) and suggested that instead of getting a train for Milwaukee at the main Chicago station, she'd ride out to the North Shore suburbs with me and catch the "400" at Lake Forest. As we drove leisurely up the freeway Helen talked a mile a minute— stories I'd never heard, if you can believe it! Finally she glanced at the car's clock and cried, "Jesus God! I forgot. I'm supposed to go to a big party that starts at one o'clock. Throw this car's ass into gear and let's get to that station!"

As the car screeched to a halt at the station the automatic doors of the train were sliding shut. With a roar the diesel engines started up. Leaving Helen standing on the platform I ran after the engine, hollering "Stop! Stop!"

The engineer in the cabin leaned his head out and looked back down the platform. The big lights of the station fell on Helen. The engineer shouted down to me, "Who is that woman?"

"Dirty Helen!" I yelled.

"That's what I thought!" he shouted back. "Tell Helen to stand still and I'll back the train up!" Slowly the six-car passenger train inched back toward Helen and just as a door was in front of her the train stopped. The door slid open.

"How ya doing, Helen?" shouted the engineer, leaning as far out of the cabin as possible, and waving with both arms. "Fine Louie, fine," screamed Helen. "You getting any?" The conductor came down the train steps, took Helen by the arm, and escorted her up to the platform between cars. Helen turned, gave me a big wink, and blew me a kiss. Then she quickly arranged her orange- and-black feather hat and said to the conductor, "Which way is the bar car?"

The door slid shut.

Sun Flower Inn 1961, after closing.

Afterword

The Sun Flower Inn closed in July of 1960. Helen died in May of 1969. What of her life in those later years? The final story in her book is a raconteur's performance, buffed to perfection, that shows Helen putting on her best hat and bootstrapping her way out of a jam. Yet she was an elderly woman who gained her fame living outside the pale of polite society. What's an aging party girl to do?

The surgeries that led to her losing her business (via a shady lender who foreclosed on the property) and the subsequent recovery pain she mentions at the end of her memoir were very real. The procedure for correcting or at its most necessary, alleviating, varicose veins in the days before lasers was a painfully gruesome process. Patients would spend a few days in the hospital and then instructed to 'stay off their feet' for a month to six weeks for optimal recovery. The surgery wasn't a cure but a stopgap.

She opened another version of the Sun Flower Inn a few blocks down the road from the original location from about fall of 1960 to spring of 1961. In July of 1961, she was hit by a car, resulting in a broken arm and multiple lacerations which put her back in the hospital and again without work. She had been a hostess and 'party-starter' for a couple of Milwaukee nightclubs. Her reputation for fun, even at 78 years old, remained strong but she did not fully recover from this latest physical setback. Her friends and fellow tavern owners hosted some fundraisers to help pay down her bills. It was those friends that encouraged her to write her life story.

From 1962 through 1965 she lived in a quiet studio apartment west of downtown Milwaukee near Marquette University, collecting a Social Security check and spending her days in cafés writing her memoir. The title she gave the work in progress was *Dirty Helen Comes Clean*. She still frequented her favorite bars and nightclubs when she felt in good health. She told anyone who asked about her book. Gossip column writers for the *Milwaukee Journal* and *Milwaukee Sentinel* mention Helen's book with some skepticism that she would finish it. In their view, she was little more than a colorful character who had some local notoriety. Helen was treated with casual sexism—they don't acknowledge her success as a business owner for nearly forty years, only snickering at her 'comedown' in life.

Researching her life uncovers a chasm between truth and facts. What one thinks would be a wild embroidery of events is proven entirely true while the 'lies' or rather omissions mask the pain of a woman's life. She was ahead of her time in that she shared her exploits without succumbing to the modern notion that a woman's truth is in her suffering. The Helen we come to know is savvy and kind-hearted while recognizing her weakness for good-looking men and fine clothing. We suspect that she's an unreliable narrator but personal accounts and press reports readily corroborate her adventures. Her age throughout the book is consistently inflated by about five years. As an older woman who incorporated age as part of her schtick, Helen seemed to use her age as a punchline for those who found her outrageous.

It's true she was a friend to and low-level accomplice of the jewel and payroll thief known as Eddie Mack. John Jerge was the man's real name, and his notorious heists, as well as his devotion to his wife, match well to Helen's timeline. The wild cab ride from Milwaukee to Louisville to celebrate Seitzel Distillery? Also true and verified by both the Van Winkle family and Earl, the cab driver who was behind the wheel. A search through the gossip columns of *Milwaukee Journal* and *Sentinel* confirms Helen's popularity with professional baseball players and the hoi polloi of Milwaukee society. Her success is a testament to her sheer will and determination to haul herself back from any setback and always on her own terms.

Harder to reconcile is the relationship with her sons. In the book, she talks of loving them very much and decides that allowing them to live with their father's family would be in their best interest. Was it a 'Sophie's Choice' that broke her heart or a callous act of a narcissist? According to Helen's great-granddaughter Lori, she regularly traveled to Cincinnati to visit her sons and grandchildren. Phil Jr. and Don tolerated these visits but neither encouraged nor enjoyed them. The men resented not just the forced brotherly estrangement when she took Donnie in her flight from Cincinnati, but later the financial support she gave to various young men attending Marquette University. Beyond her deal with Eddie Mack to pay for Don's boarding school, she never provided them with financial support. Don and Phil didn't attend college but made a good living for their respective families; Don as a jail officer for Hamilton County, Ohio, and Phil as a window treatment fitter for Sears.

It should be noted that anecdotes of Helen's generosity to friends and near-strangers have been told second- and third-hand, but no verifiable proof has been found that she did as legend says—pay the tuition of seven students. Helen tells of her relationship with former Wisconsin Senator Joseph McCarthy but his personal papers and archives that reside at Marquette University are sealed, and every attempt to review the documents of his early life has been rebuffed, though the personalized and autographed photo of McCarthy to Helen should serve as proof of their friendly relationship. Helen talks about the closeness she felt to all the Marquette 'boys' she assisted, and it's not too far of a stretch to think she acted out of misplaced guilt about the neglect of her own sons. Helen's family thinks this may have been the case.

Helen was an extravagant spender. She loved fine clothing, millinery, and jewelry and when she was able, splurged. She once took her then sixteen-year-old granddaughter (Phil Jr.'s only child) on a shopping spree at the most elegant shop in Cincinnati during one of her visits in the early 1960s. As the family story is told, Helen bought her granddaughter an exquisite cameo necklace. The piece is now lost, and Lori speculates that it was possible that Phil Jr. didn't want his daughter to have it.

Both Phil Jr. and Don and their respective families remained friendly with each other, but never close. The years of childhood separation had damaged their fraternal bond. Lori remembers Phil Jr., her grandfather, as fiercely protective of his immediate family. He and his wife moved home to be nearer to their daughter when she married and began her family. They delighted in their grandchildren but rarely, if ever, mentioned Helen—and then only as a cautionary tale, a bad influence best to be avoided.

Lori recalls growing up fascinated by the snippets about the family's legendary matriarch. Helen's favorite phrase was indeed "Live a little," which she said with joy and abandon. Helen called everyone "darling." She remembers hearing that Helen never wore underwear, which was told with a hint of scandal. (Though for a woman born in 1886, Helen would have grown up wearing a chemise or maybe knickers, which were open at the crotch; many women of her day thought modern underwear were inherently filthy.) Lori remembers a story of Don and Phil's outrage of Helen arriving in Cincinnati from Milwaukee via taxi wearing nothing but a fur coat. They promptly put her on a bus back to Milwaukee. Hindsight being what it is, we can mark these years as the beginning of Helen's decline.

Helen was arrested on Christmas Eve 1964 in St. Paul, Minnesota. She traveled to visit her old friend Betty (who, with her husband Howard, is featured in anecdotes about them blowing their inheritance on six months of living the high life) for the holiday season. Helen was picked up by the police and brought before the judge who, intrigued at finding himself faced with an 82-year-old woman standing on a drunk and disorderly charge, quickly found out who she was. The newspaper accounts of the escapade end with her pleading guilty while claiming not to be drunk as Betty picks her up from the jailhouse.

Longtime drinkers build a tolerance to alcohol, and Helen drank hard liquor as an occupational necessity for over sixty years. Was Helen a drunk? An alcoholic? It is impossible to say definitively. We can guess that old habits die hard and without the physical exertion of work, coupled with an aging body and mind, that the booze affected Helen more in the later stages of her life. Based on family history, she may have had progressive dementia as well. She was arrested again in April of 1965 for vagrancy by an eager beat cop patrolling the downtown train station where she sat at the café writing.

Once again, one of her 'Marquette boys' comes to the rescue. The intake judge, Chris T. Seraphim, who himself was a menacing local character noted for his racist views from the bench, had frequented the Sun Flower Inn and so dismissed the charge and released Helen. A *Milwaukee Journal* follow-up interview with Helen a few days later explains her lawyer's argument: as someone who collects a monthly Social Security check of $110 per month, she couldn't be technically indigent. Helen further explains that she had $10.00 in her purse and the law says that to be declared a vagrant you've got to have less than $5.00 to your name. During a breakfast interview with a *Milwaukee Sentinel* reporter at the then excellent Hilton hotel café, Helen shows him a fully typed manuscript of seventeen chapters of her book. It was about to be sold and become a best-seller.

Former bar patron and editor at *Better Homes & Gardens* Magazine, Robert Dougherty, heard of Helen's project and offered to assist her. Dougherty is credited as co-author, yet the Milwaukee press refers to him as a 'ghostwriter.' What is known is that she had high hopes but a pragmatic outlook of whether the book would be seen in print. When publisher Fawcett made an initial offer to buy the book for $5000 in 1965, she was quoted saying, "Oh, hell. That'll be about twenty minutes." Meaning: talk is cheap. The book was eventually sold to Los Angeles-based Sherbourne Press for an advance of $1500 with $500 to be paid upon signing. Helen received $250 that was, in true Helen style, delivered to the bar she frequented.

Upon release in September of 1966, *Dirty Helen* (the name changed sometime during the production) was a hit. The *Milwaukee Journal* reported in November of 1966 that the initial press run of 100,000 copies had sold out. But Helen herself didn't see much financial reward from the book. In early 1967, with her health failing, she moved to a nursing home. A *Milwaukee Journal* report from late 1967 reports that Helen had sued Sherbourne for her portion of royalties, but Sherbourne Press denied that she was legally the author of the book. (The United States copyright records clearly show Helen registered as an author.) It seems that once again, Helen's misplaced faith in men left her destitute.

On Halloween of 1968, Helen was moved to the Muirdale Home, the former Milwaukee County Tubercular home, as the varicose veins that had tormented her for the past twenty years had ulcerated. The records also note that she was suffering from memory loss. She never lost her sense of humor or love of life. Susan Spiegel remembers visiting her very proper grandmother, who happened to be Helen's roommate, at the nursing home. Helen showered the girls with hugs and affection while making them laugh, much to the annoyance of Susan's actual grandmother.

Helen died on May 21, 1969, of blood clot embolism. She was eighty-three years old. Her sons claimed her body and transported to her birthplace, Noblesville, Indiana, twenty miles north of Indianapolis. The service was private and solemn—unlike Helen herself.

MRS. HELEN CROMELL

THANK YOU

Thank you to Helen's great-granddaughter, Lori Ruwe, and her children, who provided photos, sign-in books, and stories. Their family printing company is named in Helen's honor— Dirty Helen Paper Company. (www.dirtyhelenpaper.com)

Thanks to Milwaukee County Historical Society archivist Steve Schaffer and *Milwaukee Journal Sentinel* columnist Jim Stingl for research assistance. And thanks to Chicago gang expert Christian Cippolini, who identified "Eddie Mack" as the legendary John Jerge.

Discussion Questions

This long-lost autobiography of a woman who lived life with no regrets offers a rare look into the colorful criminal underworld from New York to San Francisco and every whorehouse, tavern, and mining camp in between. Dirty Helen, with the self-assurance of a defrocked debutante, takes you through her life and adventures. Demure, sweet, and wild teenage Helen flees from small-town Indiana to Cincinnati with her first of six husbands. She soon realizes that the traditional role of wife and mother isn't for her. She meets cunning millionaires, bank robbers, detectives, and gangsters as she hustles her way through life. Her friends were everyone else's enemies—Al Capone, Big Jim Colosimo, and Johnny Torrio all spend time with Helen as she bounces from adventure to adventure. It's the true-life story of a woman who never said "No" and carved out an independent life that transgressed every societal boundary.

1. A recent theme in magazines and news features is breaking the narrative mold of how a woman 'should' behave. Would Helen be considered transgressive in today's society?

2. For a girl growing up in the 1890s, sexual desire is rarely discussed in mainstream stories, yet in telling her own story, Helen is never afraid of her sexual feelings. Is Helen an outlier in her talking about her desires or a rare truth-teller? Why have women's coming-of-age stories been repressed from popular books until the past few decades? How would Helen's life be different if she was allowed to discuss and explore her sexual feelings safely?

3. Patriarchal laws severely limited the choices for a single mother in the early 1900s. Women could not vote, open a bank account, or take out a mortgage, had limited employment opportunities and were paid less for the work, and in many states were prevented from keeping custody of her children. Many of the decisions Helen made for herself were within the narrow confines of what was available to her; the most lucrative jobs were the ones that were most looked down upon by society—sex work, saloon-keeping, performance. Imagining yourself in Helen's shoes, would you have made similar choices?

4. Helen's career as a call girl, kept woman, madam, and speakeasy operator was firmly outside the laws of the time, but was she a criminal? Is sex work, though illegal according to statutes, wrong when the woman is choosing to do it? What about when her life circumstances don't allow for any other opportunities?

5. American culture tends to romanticize the Prohibition era. Does Helen's story fit into that narrative? Did our grandparents (or great-grandparents) step out to the nightclubs and speakeasies in their town or city? Does the prohibition of alcohol and the resulting speakeasy culture correspond in any way to the current movement to legalize marijuana?

6. Motherhood is a complex relationship fraught with expectations from society, extended family, not to mention the needs of children. Women were then and still are today judged about their reproductive choices. Helen separates her two sons, leaving one behind with his father and taking the other with her as she exits the failed relationship. Was Helen making a heart-wrenching "Sophie's Choice," to save at least one son from both a terrible father as well as herself (by putting him in boarding school), or was she just punishing her husband and wanting to keep at least one son nearby for her own benefit? Can we reconcile the pain she caused her sons with the generosity and kindness she showed others?

7. In Helen's later life, she transitioned to being a legitimate business owner, yet when health issues forced her to seek medical treatment she faced insurmountable financial challenges that resulted in her losing the business she built and ran for over 40 years. Would a man with a decades-old business face the same financial issues? What are the challenges a single woman business-owner faces even in today's culture and economy?

Exterior of the Sun Flower Inn.